COMPLIMENTS OF:
    Learning Institute
    1111 Bethlehem Pike
    Springhouse, PA 19477
    1-800-843-3459

Allen N. Mendler
Richard L. Curwin

Taking Charge in the Classroom

A Practical Guide to Effective Discipline

ST. JOSEPH'S UNIVERSITY

3 9353 00240 7565

LB
3011
.M44
1983

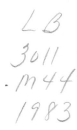

RESTON PUBLISHING COMPANY, INC.
A Prentice-Hall Company
Reston, Virginia

Library of Congress Cataloging in Publication Data
Mendler, Allen N.
    Taking charge in the classroom.

    Bibliography: p.
    1. School discipline.   2. Classroom management.
I. Curwin, Richard L.,   II. Title.
LB3011.M44   371.1′024   82–7626
ISBN 0–8359–7537–1   AACR2

Editorial/production supervision and
interior design by Camelia Townsend

© 1983 by Reston Publishing Company, Inc.
A Prentice-Hall Company
Reston, Virginia 22090

All rights reserved. No part of this book may be
reproduced in any way or by any means without
permission in writing from the publisher.

10 9 8 7 6 5 4 3

PRINTED IN THE UNITED STATES OF AMERICA

To my wife Barbara for her love and acceptance and to my sons Jason and Brian for being the little, alive people they are.

Allen Mendler

For Ann; for a lifetime of support and love; and for Liza for our time of enchantment.

Rick Curwin

Contents

Preface

When we finished writing the DISCIPLINE BOOK (Reston Publishing Company, 1980), we subtitled it, A COMPLETE GUIDE TO SCHOOL AND CLASSROOM MANAGEMENT. This subtitle seemed appropriate because we thought we included everything a teacher or administrator needs to know to set up school and classroom environments where discipline problems would be prevented; to take appropriate action when a problem occurs; and to deal with those students who never follow the rules.

We called our approach Three Dimensional Discipline and provided the reader with many strategies that were designed to help teachers learn how to become more aware of themselves and their students; how to effectively and safely express feelings generated by disruptive students; how to match a strategy and technique to one's own educational philosophy; and how to use the students' participation in the development of classroom rules and consequences. We referred to these procedures as the Prevention Dimension. The Action Dimension included verbal and non-verbal behaviors that we observed as necessary to stop misbehavior when it occurred in the classroom. The Resolution Dimension defined strategies for resolving conflict with students who frequently misbehave.

It was our belief that if readers followed our guidelines in a way which was consistent with their own educational philosophy, they would have the necessary tools for dealing with most discipline problems.

Soon after the publication of the book, we were besieged with questions about discipline which were not addressed in the COMPLETE GUIDE. We answered many discipline questions in our monthly column, "Readers Ask," in INSTRUCTOR MAGAZINE. We answered others in our inservice training programs and we answered some in a number of articles we wrote on discipline. Some of the most commonly asked questions included:

- How can I deal with stress related to discipline?
- How does the way I teach subject matter affect discipline in my class?
- How can I set up an effective program with special students who have been mainstreamed into my class?
- How can I develop effective consequences?
- What makes an Effective Consequence?
- How can I avoid power struggles? What's the best way to handle a power struggle once I find myself in one?
- What are some ways to deal with chronically disruptive students when the resolution dimension strategies are not successful and I must keep the child in my room?
- What are some variations of the social contract? How can I modify it to fit my unique situation and personality?

When we looked at all these questions we realized that it would be helpful to organize our responses into a single source so that you can be in charge and stay in charge of your classroom. TAKING CHARGE IN THE CLASSROOM is the result of that effort. We have organized information from a number of articles, experiences presented in workshops and seminars, and questions and answers from our monthly column into ten chapters: Taking Charge, Three Dimensional Discipline, Stress and Discipline, The Social Contract, Consequences, Taking Action, Creative Discipline For Out-of-Control Students, Special Problems, Discipline and the Process of Teaching, and Twenty Questions.

For administrators who are concerned with helping teachers in the classroom, we have included a section titled "For the Administrator" at the end of each chapter, which outlines specific steps that the administrator can take to improve discipline.

We have learned that it is naive to label anything related to discipline as complete. In our workshops we are often reminded by teachers that dealing with discipline is a never ending process. If you follow all aspects of Three Dimensional Discipline, you will not eliminate the need to deal with discipline problems. As long as you are teaching a group of students with a variety of needs and personalities, discipline will be an important and constant part of your daily life in the classroom. This reality might be scary enough to frighten many teachers out of the profession. However, if you choose to view discipline as an opportunity to communicate with your students and as a challenge which will help you and your students grow, then the fearsome becomes exciting. When you take charge, your teaching becomes a dynamic, exciting, constant source for learning.

For their help in preparing this book, for generating new ideas and for sharing with us, we wish to thank the following individuals: Barry Culhane, Barbara Fuhrmann, Norm Martin, Mary Dalheim, Debbie Martorelli, Pat Demarte, Stu Horton, Jeanne McGlynn, Rocco Feravolo, Teachers of School 27 in Rochester, New York, Laurie Mandel, Bruce Johnson, Barbara Coloroso. We also thank the many teachers, administrators and special education personnel from our courses and workshops whose feedback inspired us to write this book.

Allen Mendler
Rick Curwin
Rochester, New York, 1982

ONE

Taking Charge

*I*t is time to *take charge of your classroom*. For too long, teachers, administrators, and other school personnel have given up their control in school by either taking a laissez-faire position or by trying to turn school into a tightly controlled boot camp. Taking charge means facing up to the problems related to discipline. Effective classroom and school management occurs in a systematic, yet flexible, manner that allows and encourages both student and teacher growth through communication and understanding. It means working cooperatively to set up an atmosphere of trust, based on clear guidelines and expectations that are consistently implemented. Teachers who take charge do not need to flex their muscles by proving they are the boss. They do not need to give up control to their students. They do not have to try to make their students like them although most are well liked by their students. They are equipped with a multitude of options and strategies that help them to prevent discipline problems before they start, to actively stop misbehavior when it does occur, and to resolve problems with those students who chronically misbehave.

This book is about discipline and what to do about it. We do not and cannot offer you a cure for every problem because discipline is not a disease. You will discover in these pages many valuable strategies and techniques that thousands of teachers have found to be effective in reducing discipline problems and the personal distress that accompanies those problems.

When you are in charge of your class, you have students who come to class on time; they are prepared for the day; they are motivated to learn; they can settle disputes through talking rather than fighting; they respect each other's belongings; and they respect you!

You will learn techniques and strategies that put you in charge by:

- preventing most discipline problems from occurring
- stopping misbehavior when it does occur
- resolving problems with students who chronically disrupt the learning process
- reducing student stress as well as your own
- using special guidelines for rules and consequences that work

Few would argue that maintaining good discipline is a necessary precondition to establishing a school or classroom climate that is conducive to learning. James Coleman, the controversial University of Chicago sociologist, recently studied the effects of private versus public school education. He concluded, after surveying 58,728 sophomores and seniors in 1016 high schools, that private schools do a better job of educating than do public schools.[1] Coleman pointed to the ability of private schools to maintain better discipline and provide more challenging academic demands. He found that public school sophomores appear twice as likely to disobey, fight, or commit acts of vandalism than do their private school counterparts.

While one may question Coleman's credibility in light of his 1966 study which found that schools make little difference in educating students, it is unlikely that contemporary educators will argue against the notion that discipline problems in schools throughout America are on the rise in scope and intensity.

Despite a plethora of classroom approaches to discipline that espouse differing and overlapping philosophies, disruptive student behavior has become a severe problem. The 1978 Safe School Study, which investigated the incidence of violence in the public schools, found that 15% of schools in large cities and 8% of all schools had serious discipline problems.[2] Heisner (1981), describing an extreme example, wrote about Karl, an urban elementary teacher, who said:

I teach fifth and sixth graders. And on any given day I'd guess that about a quarter of them have guns in their pockets. One kid has a virtual cannon—an old .45-caliber automatic his father or some relative brought back from World War II. And these kids are ready to use those guns, too. Man, we (teachers) are no more than a bunch of guards at a prison. Except in our case, the inmates have weapons and the guards have nothing . . . these kids are mainlining heroin; popping all sorts of pills and smoking grass. That's almost as common as air around school! And they are doing all that right in the building. And booze too. Some of those kids are already alcoholics. Rotgut wine and gin; that's what they're into. And cheap whiskey.[3]

Karl's comments do not describe the environment of most teachers, but the 1978 Safe School Study indicated that 27% of all junior high school teachers and 29% of senior high school teachers who were interviewed said that they hesitated to confront misbehaving students out of concern for their own safety. A recent study conducted by the Tacoma Association of Classroom Teachers showed that 13% of its teachers reported threats of physical injury by students and 40% reported themselves to be targets of verbal abuse by students.[4] The Senate Subcommittee on Juvenile Delinquency conducted an 18-month study of 757 school districts in America. They reported that between 1970–1973, the cost to the taxpayer for school vandalism was the same as the cost for textbooks ($500,000,000 a year).[5]

Some of the other findings of the Senate Subcommittee showed that assaults on teachers increased 77%, assaults on students increased 85%, robberies were up 36.7%, rapes and attempted rapes were up 40.1%, homicides increased 18%, and weapons confiscated were up 54.4%. The National Education Association estimates that more than 110,000 teachers were physically attacked by students during the 1978–79 school year. The same survey indicated that one out of every three teachers would select another career if he or she could begin college again.

In 1978, Alfred Bloch, a psychiatrist, reported the results of interviews that he had conducted with 253 inner-city teachers in the Los Angeles area over a five-year period. These teachers had been referred for psychiatric evaluation because of varying degrees of psychological stress or the threat of assault in inner-city schools. He coined the label "battered teacher" to describe a syndrome that was equivalent to combat neurosis and common to the experiences of many teachers. Symptoms included insomnia, high blood pressure, anxiety, depression, headaches, irritability, and sometimes psychotic collapse.[6]

Discipline problems are certainly not specific to the inner-city teacher. The New York State United Teachers, in a survey that included 5000 respondents, found that every group of teachers (urban, suburban, and rural) were reporting the same thing: discipline or "managing disruptive students" is the leading cause of teacher stress.[7] Cichon and Kloff (1978) found the same result with Chicago teachers,[8] and Kyriacou and Sutcliffe (1978) noted the same finding among teachers in Great Britain.[9]

What are the many causes of problems in schools? The causes of disruptive student behavior are many but can generally be categorized as *out-of-school* and *in-school* causes. Dillon, in discussing today's student, notes:

> Teachers today are working with a different kind of student . . . parents more and more frequently admit that they cannot control their children. Many even abandon them. Many students act as free agents. They do not live at home and are responsible to no one. They have few personal restraints . . . the number of students placed on permanent suspension from school for misbehavior or maladjustment is increasing. The age of those being suspended is decreasing. Growing numbers of elementary students are out of school because they are disruptive to the teaching-learning process. The growing clarity of student rights and due process has taken away traditional discipline strategies in which many teachers found security; and many teachers are without skills to replace them.[10]

What causes discipline problems? What can be done about them? Much of this book addresses itself to the latter question, but it is first necessary to consider those factors responsible for the alienation experienced by too many youths in schools. The causes of discipline problems will be discussed *briefly* because it is our belief that far too much time and energy is typically wasted by schools in an effort to understand why students misbehave rather than how to change their pattern of misbehavior.

A common scenario that exists in schools which "care" is for a disruptive student to be referred to guidance, mental health, and administrative resources for an evaluation. Following the evaluation by all of the specialists, a conference is called, which informs the teacher about the student's background, home situation, test results, and other descriptive information. An hour or more is spent telling the teacher much of what he already knows, and most school people are left with a consensus about those factors responsible for the misbehavior. But converting this descriptive information to concrete and specific action is rare. The teacher, while filled with empathy, often feels incapable of responding differently because he views these recommendations as not feasible for a regular class setting. But he does not want to appear rigid and uncaring, so he simply nods his head in agreement with the recommendations and proceeds to do the best he can.

Psychologists or social workers, well-trained in counseling, are often unavailable for needed intervention because of their limited time and excessive caseloads in most schools. Instead they meet with the child's parents, suggest the need for individual or family counseling at the local child guidance clinic, write their reports; perhaps nine times out of ten, no further action ensues. The administrator, wanting to be supportive of the teacher, makes himself available for crises, which occur with frequency, and often elicits a series of temporary promises from the student to try harder and behave better. The overall effects of this process: a lot of understanding and very little change!

Schools do not exist as isolated institutions untouched by the social events surrounding them. Schools are both a mirror image of what transpires in the communities that surround them and a force that attempts to convey and shape the values, beliefs, and attitudes of students. Being both a mirror image and a dynamic force makes it essential that we understand how factors that occur both within and outside the boundaries of schools interact to create discipline problems. Once the context is understood, teachers can learn how to act upon those factors that are within their control and learn how to live with those that are not.

Let us first examine factors that influence children outside of school.

Out-of-School Causes of Discipline Problems

Violence in Society

Without belaboring the social ills of our world, the fact is that we live in a violent society in which the resolution of problems through shootings, knifings, fist fights, extortion, and threats of injury is all too commonplace. Every day we pick up the newspaper and learn of another violent death. People's inhumanity to one another is news. Our children are constantly exposed to violence and have become rather insensitive to its horrendous effects. Shortly after the assassination attempt on President Reagan, we interviewed schoolage children to learn of their reaction. We were astounded by the near absence of emotion to such a shocking event. But the *absence* of shock waves is perhaps a sad commentary on the state of the human condition. The real horror of violence is how easily we seem to adjust to it and accept it as a natural way of life.

Effects of the Media

Television has often been cited as responsible for the increase in violence among children, and with justification. We recently watched a well-known and daily broadcast cartoon show. We noted at least fifty acts of violence during one half-hour broadcast. Try observing children's television and notice how children digest more violence than breakfast food on Saturday mornings. The most popularly watched television shows glamorize and glorify anti-authority protagonists as they blow up buildings, or behave irresponsibly.

A recent study that reviewed a decade of research concerning television and youth concluded that children will have viewed approximately 18,000 acts of television violence by the time that they enter adolescence.[11] Although it is impossible to know the full extent of the influence of standard programming, we believe that television and other media have a potentially damaging effect on children. Commercials also make a negative effect. In his two books *Media Sexploitation* (1976) and *Subliminal Seduction*, (1973), Wilson Bryan Key points out how violent and sexual messages are implicitly and explicitly built into television and print advertisements. His studies show that people become agitated and nervous when confronted with these messages, which are really selling sex, death, and violence.

"Me" Generation

The absence of emotional nourishment for many of our children, in a society still reeling from the values permeated by what Christopher Lasch so aptly calls the "me generation," is another external cause of school discipline problems. We have become a throw-away society that includes discarding husbands, wives, and children as well as things. Rightly or wrongly, many people seek refuge from unhappiness and depression by altering their life styles and leaving little time and commitment for their children. Recent statistics have suggested that between 35% and 50% of all school-age children will experience significant shifts in their family constellation before they complete school.[12] It is no secret that many students come to school hungry, preoccupied, and more concerned for their basic security needs than for learning their times tables. The loss of reliance upon parent(s) for basic security needs has created a large body of children who are desperate for help in assuring healthy emotional development. Many students have adopted the me-generation attitude of "Meet my needs first. I do not intend to wait. I come first."

Lack of a Secure Family Environment

Perhaps the largest single influence on children is the quality of their home life. Our society, throughout the last century, has undergone major shifts in values and traditions. The extended family of the past has been replaced by smaller nuclear units, which are comprised of a multitude of possible configurations. Single parent families, two working parent families, one and two child families are all common. The divorce rate has steadily risen in America so that some states have more divorces than marriages. All those changes, while neither good nor bad in themselves, have made it increasingly difficult to raise children in the traditional ways. And because we have not been as successful in developing family systems that match these shifting life styles, many parents have no new options for providing a secure family structure. The home is the place where self-concepts are first developed and most strongly influenced. Parents need to learn more skills for helping children to develop strong self-concepts in the face of constantly shifting family patterns.

In-School Causes of Discipline Problems

Student Boredom

Teachers have spent many years accumulating a body of knowledge that they value, and the excitement that they derive from their work is the spark and enthusiasm that they feel from their students when they are turned-on to what their teachers have to offer. Nobody wants to have students in class who appear disinterested, will not participate, do not do their assignments, and generally appear bored by what they have to offer. Some bored students do not present themselves as problematic (in terms of discipline) because they have developed good classroom etiquette. In other words, they can sit up straight, appear attentive by making eye contact, and nod their heads up and down every so often. They present themselves as being interested and somewhat involved even when they are downright bored. But there are some students who either have not or will not develop these survival skills. Instead they choose to participate in various acting-out behaviors as a way of satisfying their needs. They have no desire to hide their boredom, and they appear unconcerned with the consequences of poor grades, a trip to the principal's office, or a phone call home. Most teachers feel fed-up and angry with such students. They view them as a waste of their time, and they probably return home at night praying that they are absent the next day. These students derive pleasure in making the teacher angry, and their teachers derive a measure of satisfaction in catching them being ''bad.'' When this interactive spiral continues (bored student, angry teacher), conflict ensues. The teacher will often resort, consciously or not, to negatively labeling the student, who will then accuse the teacher of picking on him unjustly. A discipline problem has occurred, and both are responsible!

Powerlessness

Powerlessness is another factor in the etiology of school and classroom discipline problems. Some students rebel as a way of voicing their dissatisfaction with the lack of power that they really have. In most schools, for six hours every day students are told where to go, what time to be there, how long to take for even basic biological necessities, which learning is relevant, what to learn, and how their learning will be evaluated. These decisions are often determined by the local school board or by the school administration in consultation with members of the school community. Student participation in decision making is often excluded. The result is that one group develops rules and procedures that define behavioral standards for another group, which has had little or no input in the decision-making process. More than one revolution among Third World nations has been precipitated by a similar division of power. Schools that exclude students from school or classroom policy-making committees run a major risk of widespread student dissatisfaction against rules that are perceived as arbitrary and unfair. In the classroom, students show their dissatisfaction by acting out when they perceive themselves as having no say in how the classroom is to be run. Powerless students have more power than many school personnel give them credit for, and many students are more than willing to show just how much power they really have.

Unclear Limits

At the very least, teachers and administrators must clearly and specifically inform students what the standards of acceptable behavior are, *before they are violated,* and what will happen when these standards are violated. At best, students are often presented with unclear or fuzzy rules and less clear consequences. And in most schools, students are unwittingly encouraged to break rules because they are not informed of them in advance. When limits are unclear, students will test the system to find out what they are. The following case illustrates the necessity for clarity of rules and consequences.

A junior high school for which we recently provided consultation was having a widespread problem of student fighting. Upon investigation, we discovered that a "No Fighting" rule did exist in the student handbook, but no mention of consequences was made. An interview with the principal revealed that the actual unwritten consequences ranged from teachers not even referring the student, to a talk with the student, to a one-day suspension when such students were referred. Because fighting had become a serious problem in this school, we suggested an immediate, short-term solution to the problem—a solution that reveals one of our biases. We met with the faculty who reached a consensus which stated that from that time on, any student who fought on school grounds would be suspended from one to five days depending upon the severity of the infraction. The student would not be allowed to return to school until he had developed a written plan for how he would behave if such a circumstance again presented itself. In addition, a parent conference was mandatory prior to a return to school.

The principal was initially uncomfortable with the recommendation because it was his belief that suspension was an ineffective option for student misbehavior. He believed that it would not be helpful to the offender because it would give him a sanctioned vacation. Our belief was that if all teachers agreed on the procedure it was worth trying. Furthermore, we felt that all students (and teachers) have a right to attend school without concern for their own safety and that if people live in fear then their ability to learn (and to teach) is adversely affected. If a student chooses to fight, then he is violating the safety rights of others and is choosing to be temporarily excluded from school.

Feeling desperate, the principal reluctantly agreed to try the plan. He next met with every faculty team, and they presented the plan to the students. In short, he specified the rule, solicited support from his staff, and told students *in advance* what would happen if fighting occurred. During the first few days after the plan was implemented, there was an increase in fighting. After one week, the incidence of fighting dropped to near zero. Students needed to test the rule, and when they found out that violations would be strictly enforced, they stopped!

Lack of Acceptable Outlets for Feelings

Along with the concept of unclear limits being a source of discipline problems is the lack of acceptable outlets for expressing feelings. Don't run. . . . Don't fight. . . . No throwing food. . . . Most teachers have such rules. So students know what *not* to do. But rarely do we teach students what to do instead. We assume that they know how to behave properly. We forget that it requires skill and training to learn what else to do instead of fighting, in the same way that drivers need more than intellectual knowledge of how a car operates before they can drive safely. Students need more than only knowledge of what they should not do. They need emotional, behavioral, and intellectual skills for following rules. Books have been written that purport to teach people how to "fight fair." Other books have been written to help people learn how to identify the feelings they have and how to communicate these feelings to others assertively. We have found in our training with hundreds of schools that those schools that provide substitute outlets for the feelings that motivate misbehavior have less misbehavior. This theme will be discussed further in Chapter 6.

Negative Self-Concept

Finally and most significantly, most students who have chronic problems with behavior believe that they cannot and will not be successful in school. Such students often appear to give up before they have even tried. They do not believe that they can receive the attention and recognition they need through school achievement. They see themselves as losers and have ceased trying to gain acceptance in the mainstream. Their self-message is, "Since I can't be recognized as anything other than a failure, I'll protect myself from feeling hurt. To do nothing is better than to try and fail. And to be recognized as a troublemaker is better than being seen as stupid.''

Schools Do Make a Difference

While there is little question that family instability, violence in society, garbage on the boob tube, confused values, lack of positive self-concepts, powerlessness, boredom, and unclear limits are significant contributing factors to discipline problems in the school, the fact is that schools as institutions show wide variance in their ability to maintain and promote effective systems of discipline.

Rutter and associates conducted a longitudinal study of secondary schools in Great Britain and concluded that the school a child attends does make a difference in behavior and achievement even when factors such as socioeconomic status, location of the school, and family background are controlled. He studied mixed comprehensive schools, the English equivalent of American public schools.[13]

Many of the findings of that study have important implications for teachers and administrators in regard to discipline because the focus of the research was to identify specific factors that promote a positive or negative climate within the school. While an exhaustive review of the study is beyond the scope of this book (the interested reader is referred to *Fifteen Thousand Hours*, by Rutter, *et al.*), some of the findings that appear to relate directly to effective or ineffective discipline are as follows:

1. High levels of corporal punishment and frequent disciplinary interventions led to worse behavior on the part of the students.

2. Praise for work in the classroom and frequent public praise for good work or behavior through general assemblies or other meetings were associated with better behavior. (The use of praise will be discussed in more depth throughout this book.)

3. Schools and classrooms that were well decorated with plants, posters, and pictures were associated with better student behavior.

4. The willingness to see children about problems at any time was associated with better student behavior.

5. Better behavior was noted in those schools in which a high proportion of students had opportunities to hold some position of responsibility.

6. An interesting and perhaps unexpected finding was that schools that had the least continuity among staff (staff turnover was the highest) tended to have the best behavior among students.

7. Schools with good outcomes had most decisions made at a senior level (administration) when staff felt that their views were clearly represented in the decisions.

8. Rules and approaches to discipline were less important than the existence of some generally recognized and accepted set of standards. In other words, an agreed upon set of standards, consistently maintained, appeared more important in maintaining effective discipline than specific rules or a certain type of teaching approach.

9. Frequent homework and a check on staff regarding administering homework was associated with better student achievement and behavior.

10. Very little class time (2–13% of the class time) spent in setting up equipment and materials was associated with better student behavior.

11. Starting the class on time, pacing throughout the lesson, and not ending early was associated with better student behavior.

12. A high proportion of topic time per lesson (65–85%) spent in interaction with the whole class rather than with individuals (when using a formal class-based teaching approach) was positively related to good student behavior.

Rutter's findings are cause for optimism in contrast to prior research by Coleman, Jenks, and Plowden. He is clearly suggesting that despite all of the aforementioned causes of discipline problems, schools can and do make a difference in affecting student behavior and achievement.

Three Dimensional Discipline

While Rutter and his associates provide optimism, there is still difficulty in translating principles of successful schooling into tangible and realistic procedures that can be implemented in the classroom. After all, discipline problems have existed for as long as schools have. Any time a group of twenty-five to thirty people are in close proximity to each other for six hours every day, ten months of the year, a variety of interpersonal conflicts occur. Three Dimensional Discipline offers many ways to help you take charge of your classroom. It will help you to prevent problems from occurring by acknowledging that they will occur and by providing many behavioral skills, interpersonal skills, and anxiety-management skills that will reduce the impact of misbehaving students upon the teaching-learning process.

If we allow ourselves to become helpless in the face of the overwhelming causes of misbehavior we described earlier, it becomes impossible to teach. Three Dimensional Discipline is designed to help the teacher work effectively with children despite these numerous problems. We have identified thirteen processes that form the foundation of implementing an effective program of discipline. A brief description of each follows.

Processes of Three Dimensional Discipline

Take charge by . . .

1. *Letting students know what you need.* In order to run the classroom, you must establish clear and specific guidelines that define rules and consequences for both you and your students (Chapters 3 and 4).

2. *Providing instruction at levels in which success is reachable.* If a student is acting out, assume that this is his defense against feeling like a failure because he cannot or believes he cannot handle the material. You may want to conduct some brief tests to determine academic level or have the child referred to educational specialists in your building for an assessment. If you are unable or unwilling to adapt your teaching style to lower or higher academic levels based upon the student's needs, then you are offering the student a valid excuse for acting out.

3. *Listening to what students are thinking and feeling.* There is probably no skill more important than active listening * to defuse potentially troublesome situations when they emerge. Students misbehave when they are feeling anxious, fearful, or angry. Those teachers who learn how to identify with students who have negative feelings and who can convey understanding and empathy through reflective or active listening are usually able to short-circuit the cycle that leads to disruption.

---

* See Thomas Gordon, *Teacher Effectiveness Training.*

4. *Using humor.* You are not paid to be a comedian nor should you be expected to come to class prepared with an arsenal of jokes. But many frustrating situations can be lightened by learning how to poke fun at yourself and by avoiding defensiveness.

Make sure not to make students the butt of your jokes. Lou, a seventh grade student, obviously intent upon hooking Mr. James into a power struggle, announced one day in class as he looked squarely at his teacher, "You smell like horseshit!" Mr. James responded by promptly lifting up each of his armpits, smelling them, and with a puzzled look saying, "That's strange. I took a shower this morning, put on dry deodorant and a fresh shirt, and came to school. I think I smell rather good!" The class laughed and a tense moment had abated.

Mrs. Klein, a sixth grade teacher met Janet, one of her former students, at the local supermarket. Janet said, "I just want you to know that you were the best teacher I ever had!" To which Mrs. Klein, feeling wonderfully refreshed (how often do you ever get appreciations from students), asked, "Why?" Janet noted, "I'll bet you didn't know that most teachers do not laugh! We had fun in your class—you were human—you laughed!" Moscowitz and Hayman found that students who rated their teachers as "best" mentioned the following teacher characteristics: they listened well; they were able to focus upon the current interests of students; they avoided yelling when disciplining; and they used humor.[14]

5. *Varying your style of presentation.* Research has shown that older children have a maximum attention span of fifteen minutes and younger children ten minutes for any style of presentation. If you lecture for fifteen minutes, it helps to have a discussion for the next interval. If you have a large group discussion, switch to small groups. Continually using the same approach will create inattentiveness and restlessness, which may lead to disruption.

6. *Offering choices.* Students should always be offered a choice and must be helped to see that the consequences are a result of their choices. For example, "You can do your assignment now or during recess." "You can borrow a pencil, buy one from me, or provide collateral." "You chose to fight and so you've chosen to go home for the remainder of the day." Coloroso* suggests that the teacher offer the student "good luck" with his decision, recog-

---

* We wish to thank Barbara Coloroso from whom we learned this timely strategy.

nizing that decisions are not easy to make, but that the student is responsible for the decision after the choices are offered.

7. *Having high expectations.* You must expect appropriate behavior from your students. We are reminded of Sam, a student identified as emotionally disturbed, who was acting crazy. When asked why he behaved as such, Sam responded, ''Because I'm emotionally disturbed.'' To which his special education teacher replied, ''In this class, everybody is emotionally disturbed, so acting crazy is no excuse here!'' Sam started to act a lot less crazy.

8. *Refusing to accept excuses.* Once there are sensible rules and consequences established in the classroom, all misbehavior is greeted with a specific consequence. If there is a fight, it makes no difference who started it. If a student is unprepared for class, it makes no difference that his homework was destroyed by the washing machine. In short, when you allow students to explain away their misbehavior, you place yourself in the uncomfortable position of being judge and jury. If there are legitimate excuses in your class, they should be included as part of the rules and stated clearly *before* an incident occurs. Students with good excuses learn that a good excuse will avoid trouble. Students with bad excuses learn that they need some practice in improving their excuse-making. Either way, accepting excuses teaches students how to be irresponsible!

9. *Legitimizing misbehavior that you cannot stop.* If you have done everything humanly possible to stop a certain behavior and it still continues, think of creative ways to legitimize it. If there are daily paper airplane flights buzzing past your ear, consider spending five minutes a day having a paper airplane contest. If abusive language persists, ask the student to publicly define the word to ensure understanding. If your students like to complain chronically about one thing or another, have a ''gripe'' session that is limited in time and announced in advance, or a ''gripe'' box in which students are encouraged to deposit their written complaints. If your school has chronic disruptions in its study halls, then offer a game-filled non-academic study hall in addition to one that is quiet for those who really want to study. When certain types of misbehavior are legitimized, the fun of acting out fizzles! And if the behavior continues, then it will be easier on your nerves because you will no longer have to stop it.

10. *Using hugs and touching in communicating with kids* (even junior high and high school kids). A pat on the back, touch on the

shoulder, or handshake can go a long way towards establishing bonds with kids. One of the biggest educational fallacies is the prohibition against using touch with older students because of sexual misunderstanding. Hogwash! If you are intentionally attempting to seduce a student then don't touch! If you want to use touch only to communicate anger and to force compliance, don't touch! If you know of a student who has been physically abused, then exercise caution. If you want to communicate with human warmth, caring, and concern, words will take you only so far. Supplement your words with non-verbal displays of caring and concern.

11. *Being responsible for yourself and allowing kids to take responsibility for themselves.* You are responsible to come to class on time, present your subject in as interesting a fashion as you can, return papers with meaningful comments in a reasonable period of time, provide help for students having difficulty, and end class on time. You are *not* responsible to come prepared for the student, to judge the excuses a student gives, or to do his work for him.

12. *Realizing and accepting that you will not reach every kid.* Some students, after all is said and done, must be allowed to choose failure because they are consistently telling you that they need more than you can give.

13. *Starting fresh every day.* What happened yesterday is finished! Today is a new day. Act accordingly.

These concepts provide the framework by which you can, should, and will take charge in your classroom. We will neither preach nor proselytize in the succeeding chapters. We will offer you numerous activities, strategies, and experiments. Some will work for you while others will not. We encourage you to consider each carefully and to be the judge of which to implement and which to discard. Three Dimensional Discipline has as its foundation the belief that teachers need to match strategy, activity, and action to their specific educational philosophy. As such, not all activities will feel right for you, and because you are the leading authority about yourself, we believe that you are in the best position to decide what will work and what will not. We do encourage you to experiment with each idea before you judge its utility.

The remainder of this book will help you to take charge by

1. understanding the three dimensional approach

2. implementing a personalized program of Three Dimensional Discipline

3. establishing a social contract with your class(es)

4. developing consequences that work

5. understanding the relationship between discipline and stress and learning how to alleviate the tension that you feel when students misbehave

6. stopping misbehavior when it occurs

7. shaping your subject matter to help you prevent discipline problems from occurring

8. resolving problems through negotiations with disruptive students

9. creating unusual approaches and developing your creativity in working with "out-of-control" students

10. considering ways of dealing with special problems such as drug use, handicapped students, and the inner-city

We do not offer instant cures or a panacea. We offer a multitude of ways for you to be in charge of yourself and your class(es). It is time to take charge now! Good Luck.

For the Administrator

The Safe School Study (1978) clearly indicated that the schools with the fewest discipline problems had the strongest administrative people, especially the principal. We suggest that the first step you, the administrator, can take to improve discipline in your school is to set up an atmosphere that encourages faculty to discuss their problems freely and openly without fear of censure. Teachers are often fearful that they will be considered weak or incompetent if they admit to problems with student behavior. When we do in-service training for a school faculty, we always ask the teachers who have discipline problems to raise their hands. Usually only one or two hands go up. But when we ask, "How many of you know another teacher in the school who has discipline problems?" every hand is raised. Once you have an open atmosphere, positive things can begin to happen.

We find that most school faculties represent a wide range of feelings, beliefs, and attitudes when it comes to discipline. Some are for a great many rules, strictly enforced, with the administration being tough in every case with student violators. Other teachers feel that it is best to have few rules and that the students themselves should solve their own problems. One of your first tasks will be to generate open discussion among your faculty, both in formal settings, such as department and faculty meetings, and in informal settings so that at least each teacher knows where they stand in relation to other teachers. An attitude of acceptance of different points of view should be strived for, along with clarity on what agreement also exists. Build unification from the points of agreement while allowing for individual differences. Developing this kind of open communication will go a long way in helping your faculty feel supported and ready to make specific changes in the way they discipline students.

To help focus your discussions, you can begin with the list of in-school causes of misbehavior listed on pages 7–11. Set up working groups or task forces on each of the following causes: student boredom, powerlessness, unclear limits, lack of acceptable outlets for expressing feelings, and failure of positive self-image. Each group should include a variety of school people including teachers, administrators, parents, and students. Each group can work to develop a specific plan for your school to minimize their chosen specific cause of misbehavior. Notice the following example.

A group in a suburban middle school tackled the issue of giving students a greater sense of power in their school. Their recommendations included

1. a student council of ''poor achievers'' and ''in trouble students'' (different labels were used) to help set school policy and to help modify rules and consequences

2. students who served detention were given the job of commenting on how school climate could be improved

3. students took the job of running the school for a day once a year with the teachers and administrators taking student roles, and

4. each class was required to have at least two student rules for teacher

Whether you like these suggestions or not, they are a clear example of what one school did to give its students a feeling of more power in the school.

Task forces such as the ones suggested above will be more beneficial if they have full administrative support (this does not mean you must agree with every recommendation) especially if their goal is to develop a plan for action. Committees that study school problems and make general recommendations are usually ineffective and are viewed by the faculty as having little worth. The plan should state what will be done, who will do it, when it will be done, and how it will be evaluated. Each member of the school community (teachers, parents, administrators, students, librarians, nurses, bus drivers) should know clearly and specifically what their responsibilities will be for the success of the plan. There should be at least 75% agreement by the community on any aspect of the plan before it is implemented.

Another suggestion we offer to help improve discipline in your school is to use the guidelines on page 13, titled, "Processes of Three Dimensional Discipline" as a checklist for classroom observations. The items on this list are the following:

1. Let your students know what you need to run your classroom.
2. Provide instruction at levels in which success is reachable.
3. Listen to what students are thinking and feeling.
4. Use humor.
5. Vary your style of presentation.
6. Offer choices.
7. Have high expectations.
8. Refuse to accept excuses.
9. Legitimize misbehavior that you cannot change.
10. Use hugs and touching when communicating with students.
11. Be responsible for yourself and allow kids to be responsible for themselves.
12. Realize and accept that you cannot reach every student.
13. Start fresh each day.

This list can become the focus of classroom observations and discussions between faculty and administration. Before actually using the list in actual observations, it is important to discuss all the items in detail with each teacher and reach agreement on which items the teacher believes are worth having in the classroom. Do not force any item down the teacher's throat; limit your observations only to those items the teacher believes are right for him. Then meet after the observation and discuss your data. Remember that the most useful and acceptable data are those that are descriptive and free from judgment and assumptions. Tell the teacher what you saw in relation to the agreed upon items, not what you interpreted. Notice the difference in the following statements taken from classroom observations.

One: Your class was boring and dull. You never changed your pace and it was obvious that your students were turned off.

Two: You lectured (presented information) for twenty minutes. You discussed the topics (asked questions of the students about the lecture) for six minutes. You used small group discussion for five minutes and seven minutes were used for noninstructional time (giving directions, answering questions unrelated to task, writing a bathroom pass).

By establishing an open communication atmosphere in your school, by creating task forces which work, and by gearing your classroom observations on discipline to those items most directly related to improved discipline, you will be on your way to using the structure and processes of Three Dimensional Discipline to improve discipline in your school as a whole and in each individual classroom.

References

1. "Can Public Learn From Private," *Time, 117,* April 20, 1981, p. 50.

2. United States Department of Health, Education and Welfare, "Violent Schools–Safe Schools. The Safe School Study Report to the Congress, 1978," (Eric Document Reproduction Service No. Ed 149 464).

3. Heisner, J., "The Ugly Side of the Urban Coin," *Instructor, 90(10),* 1981, p. 20.

4. "Report of Stress Conditions within the Tacoma Public Schools," Tacoma Association of Classroom Teachers (Prepared by Irene Mazer), May 1979, pp. 3–4.

5. "Our Nations' Schools, A Report Card," Report of the Subcommittee to Investigate Juvenile Delinquency to the Committee on the Judiciary of the U.S. Senate, Washington, D.C.: U.S. Government Printing Office, 1975.

6. Bloch, A. M., "Combat Neurosis in Inner-City Schools," *American Journal of Psychiatry, 135(10),* 1978, 1189–1192.

7. "New York State United Teachers Stress Survey Information Bulletin," New York State United Teachers Research and Educational Services, 1979.

8. Cichon, D. J., and Kloff, R. H., *"The Teaching Events Stress Inventory."* Paper presented at the meeting of the American Educational Research Association Conference, Toronto, Ontario, March 1978, (Eric Document Reproduction Service, No. 160 662).

9. Kyriacou, C., and Sutcliffe, J., "Teacher Stress: Prevalence, Sources and

Symptoms," *British Journal of Educational Psychology, 48(2)*, 1978, pp. 159–167.

10. Dillon, E. A., "Did We All Let Barry Die?" *Journal of Teacher Education, 29(5)*, 1978, p. 30.

11. Reported in *Behavior Today, 12(43)*, November 9, 1981, p. 4.

12. Reported by Joseph Corsica in an unpublished doctoral dissertation.

13. Rutter, M.; Maughan, B.; Mortimore, P.; Ouston, J.; with Smith, A., *Fifteen Thousand Hours*, Cambridge, Mass.: Harvard University Press, 1979.

14. Moscowitz, E., and Hayman, J. L., "Interaction Patterns of First Year, Typical and 'Best' Teachers in Inner-City Schools", *Journal of Educational Research, 67(5)*, 1974, pp. 224–230.

TWO

Three Dimensional Discipline

George Nelson is a new teacher who, like most teachers, has never had a course in discipline. The topic of classroom management was covered during two class sessions in his general secondary methods course. Now he is continually finding himself making threats to his students that he cannot or will not implement. The thought of keeping the entire class after school for two months does not appeal to him one bit. Yet he finds that he resorts to ever escalating threats to try to get the class to follow his rules.

Sally Aldredge states very clear rules and tells her students what will happen when rules are violated. But Miss Aldredge carries out her consequences only when she is in a bad mood and usually only with the students she dislikes. When her favorite students break the rules, she reminds them if they "do that again they will have to. . . ."

Joan Stevenson took a course in behavior modification and learned how to set up a contingency program in her class. Her principal supported the concept and even brought in a consultant who worked with five teachers to set up model programs. Unfortunately Mrs. Stevenson's plan failed. No one bothered to tell her that because her value system was opposed to the philosophy of behavior modification, the plan would not work for her. One must believe in what one does in order for any approach or technique to "work." Joan felt like a failure when she was told by the consultant that behavior modification was a "proven method" that worked if correctly applied.

Tom Wilson has few problems with most of his students, but he has two students who continually drive him crazy. He has noticed an increase in the number and intensity of headaches he has when he goes home and has taken to carrying his Excedrin bottle with him throughout the day. None of the traditional approaches have worked with these two students, and because the school will not suspend them, Tom must face them almost daily. Unfortunately for Tom, these students are rarely absent. They enjoy driving their teachers crazy too much to stay at home.

These teachers and thousands like them all suffer from one basic problem. They do not have an established plan or system for implementing a discipline policy that is consistent with their needs and with the needs of their students. They need to take charge of their classrooms. Three Dimensional Discipline is a systematic, yet flexible approach to discipline. It is designed to help teachers meet their needs and the needs of their students so teachers can spend more time teaching and less time policing.

Because the three dimensional approach is eclectic, encompassing a variety of theories and approaches, it is not always an easy process for teachers to implement. We have found in extensive work with teachers that improving discipline requires hard work that involves examining and expressing feelings, gaining awareness, and establishing a structured process. It takes an integration of many ideas and methodologies to make a meaningful difference in the area of classroom or school-wide discipline. We see value in mobilizing all that we are rather than picking and choosing limited parts of ourselves. The three dimensions are:

1. *The Prevention Dimension:* what the teacher can do to actively prevent discipline problems from occurring, and how to deal with the stress associated with classroom disruptions.

2. *The Action Dimension:* what actions the teacher can take when, in spite of all the steps taken to prevent discipline problems, they still occur. Included are ways to keep simple records, and how to avoid escalating minor problems into major ones.

3. *The Resolution Dimension:* what the teacher can do to resolve problems with the chronic rule breaker and the more extreme, "out-of-control" student.[1]

FIGURE ONE   **Three Dimensional Discipline Overview**

Prevention dimension   *Action dimension*

What Can Be Done to   What to Do When
   Prevent Discipline Problems: Discipline Problems Occur:

1. Be aware of self (Teacher)   1. Choose best alternative
2. Be aware of students   consequence
3. Express genuine feelings   2. Implement consequence
4. Become knowledgeable   3. Collect data
   of alternative theories   4. Avoid power struggles
5. Establish social contracts
6. Implement social
   contracts
7. Reduce stress

Resolution dimension

Resetting Contracts Negotiation
with Individual Student

1. Find what is needed to
   prevent another problem
2. Develop mutually agreeable plan
3. Implement plan
4. Monitor plan/revise if
   necessary
5. Use creative approaches
   when necessary

The Prevention Dimension

The first goal of the three dimensional approach is to set up an environment in which discipline problems are prevented. The prevention dimension is designed to minimize or prevent classroom problems from occurring. We think of the prevention dimension as similar
to a subject curriculum. The purpose of a curriculum is to provide the
teachers and students with a well-thought out plan to guide the learn-

ings of a particular lesson or course. The best curricula are flexible enough to allow day-to-day changes as new needs arise and to incorporate evaluations as to how well the plan is working. The prevention dimension is a plan designed to provide you a structure and a direction, yet is flexible enough to accommodate both day-to-day changes and long-term developmental changes as you and your students develop new needs and new awareness. Like content curriculum, our prevention dimension includes cognitive, behavioral, and affective components, blended together so that awareness leads to understanding, which leads to action, which leads to awareness.

Stages of Prevention

The seven stages of prevention, are discussed below.

1. INCREASING SELF-AWARENESS

The first stage of the prevention dimension is increasing awareness of self (teacher). We have discovered that those teachers who are the most effective at classroom management also have a high degree of congruence between their real and ideal teaching selves. They do what they say, and their words match their actions.

> The ideal self is comprised of values, feelings, attitudes, past experiences, influence from significant others, and self-perceptions. This ideal is not a fantasy, like childhood dreams of superhuman feats, but rather has its basis in real people as they really are. Given who people are, with all their assets and limitations, it's what they can be at their best. It is potentially within them, and is obtainable. Before they can attain it, though, each individual must personally discover and identify his/her own unique ideal self. Each individual also has a real self, which is comprised of his/her feelings, attitudes, and behaviors right now. The real self is not static; it changes from moment to moment; and is always available for inspection by both the individual and others.[2]

There is little difference in effective classroom management between teachers who are democratic, authoritarian, or moderate. What does make a difference is knowing who you are, allowing yourself to be what you are, and permitting your students to see you as you are. Many classroom discipline problems occur because of double messages (a symptom of lack of congruence) that the teacher gives the students. For example, Mrs. Jones, a fourth grade teacher, wants to be liked by her students. She has trouble understanding why her kids are so rowdy and rarely listen to her. Unfortunately, she is unaware of her very soft tone of voice and non-assertive body posture when she tells the class to line up, to open up their books, etc. She is afraid that they will think she is mean if she raises her voice. Mrs. Jones, without being aware of it, is constantly sending double messages. Her verbal message states anger while her non-verbal message always expresses her wish for the students to like her. When incongruence exists, most students will respond to the non-verbal, for this is the music behind the words.

Mixed signals often lead to agitation and anxiety in students, particularly those who for other reasons are already sensitive to mixed messages. They often culminate in conflict, confusion, and classroom management problems. Mrs. Jones would be better off by becoming more aware of what she wants to be as a classroom manager.

Becoming aware of ourselves is no easy process because it requires a commitment to on-going self-reflection. Most of us simply do not take the time from our busy schedules to indulge in such self-reflection during an era in which accountability and management by objectives have seeped into our daily lives. Yet this process need not be either exhausting or particularly time-consuming. We invite you to try the following experiment as an example of what we mean by teacher self-awareness. It should take you approximately five or ten minutes to complete.

R–M–L Scale (Self-Awareness)

Read the following statements and decide which you do the right amount of, which you want to do more of, and which you want to do less of. Circle the appropriate key letter.

Right Amount	More Of	Less Of	
R	M	L	I encourage students to speak spontaneously, without necessarily raising their hands.
R	M	L	I expect my students to ask permission to leave the room.
R	M	L	I often threaten punishment of one kind or another for misbehavior.
R	M	L	I encourage students to work independently in self-directed activities.

(cont.)

Right Amount	More Of	Less Of	
R	M	L	I allow my students to make decisions about classroom management.
R	M	L	I allow my students to openly disagree with me.
R	M	L	I ignore student misbehavior.
R	M	L	I laugh a lot in class.
R	M	L	I probably let students take advantage of me.
R	M	L	I frequently touch students.
R	M	L	I sometimes use sarcasm to win a point with a student.
R	M	L	I take time to tell my students what they do that I like, and to ask them to tell me what they like about others and myself.

Now take one statement you want to do more of and list three specific steps you can take to do more of it.

EXAMPLE

I want to touch more frequently.

- I will touch Susie on her shoulder when she sits in her seat for 10 minutes.
- I will hold Johnny when he starts to fight.
- I will greet my students with a handshake at least two mornings a week.

1. I will _____

2. I will _____

3. I will _____

Do the same process for one statement you want to do less of.

1. I will _____

2. I will _____

_____

3. I will _____

_____

Keep a record of how often you do your list of six "wills" for one week. See if you have changed enough to satisfy yourself. Write what changes occurred as a result of your experiences:

Change you expected:

Positive   Negative

Change unexpected:

Positive   Negative

2. INCREASING AWARENESS OF STUDENTS

The second stage of the prevention dimension is developing an increased awareness of your students on your part. The three dimensional approach is an interactive one that takes into account your students as real people who are living with you in a classroom, which is a microcosm of society. Their needs and desires play a major role in developing a preventive environment. The more aware you are of your students, the more effective you will be in working with them.

Kathy Myers was a first-year twelfth grade Spanish teacher who loved foreign languages. Before teaching her first class, she prepared all her lesson plans for her first quarter, based on her favorite college classes in Spanish. She found that all her lesson plans were useless because few of her students liked Spanish enough to commit themselves to the rigorous study Kathy thought of as fun. Soon her students were acting out to show their dissatisfaction with the class.

Bruce Johnson taught for five years in a junior high school. He spent most of his time working with the three most disruptive students in his class. After teaching for three months he noticed an improvement in the three students, but he also noticed some of his better students acting out. When he asked why, they told him that the only way to get attention was to be bad. When Bruce denied this accusation, one bright student asked Bruce what his (the student's) favorite school activity was. Bruce showed surprise when he couldn't think of it, and his accuser correctly said, "But you know Bill's, Fred's, and Tom's."

There are many activities that you can use to become more aware of your students that take little time and serve to promote a positive classroom climate. Canfield and Wells, Glasser, and

Palomares[3] offer many strategies that serve both functions. We advise you to familiarize yourself with all of your students through a cursory glance at their school records. When you discover which students have had an unhappy or unsuccessful prior school experience, it becomes necessary for you to find out more about that student's interests or hobbies so that you become able to connect with him in a way that promotes positive feelings. If, for example, you know that Jimmy has been unsuccessful and disruptive in the last several math classes and you teach math, and if you discover that he enjoys baseball, you might greet him with a discussion of yesterday's baseball scores. The following activity is designed to illuminate the importance of knowing who your students are.

Student Awareness Inventory

Write the name of one of your favorite students on the top of column one and the name of one of your least favorite students on the top of column two. Answer the related questions about each student as best you can.

Most Favorite Student   *Least Favorite Student*

favorite in-school activity:

favorite out-of-school activity:

favorite hobby

favorite television show

best friend (name)

one thing this student likes about your class:

one thing this student dislikes about class:

one short-range goal

one long-range goal

one skill he is most proud of:

Questions

Which student did you know more about?

Which student do you spend more time with?

What would happen if you spent more time talking with the student whom you knew least about?

What specific steps can you take to know all your students regardless of whether they are your favorites or least favorites?

3. Expressing Feelings

The third stage of the prevention dimension is the expression of genuine feelings. Although this process is one of the most important steps in preventing discipline problems, it is traditionally ignored in most, if not all, teacher preparation programs, both in-service and preservice. In this stage you will learn how to genuinely express your feelings and how to use these expressions to help yourself manage your classroom more effectively.

We find that most teachers have trouble expressing feelings. Our Western culture, with its emphasis on task, outcomes, and problem solving often regards genuine expression of feelings as immature, useless, silly, or a waste of time. We are reminded of Jack Washington, a senior high teacher who always appeared uptight. When asked to speak to an empty chair to express his feelings about his most troublesome class, he laughed saying that "that 'shrink' stuff wouldn't work with him." After some moderate encouragement, including telling him that this practice was used to help major league ballplayers improve their performance, Jack tried the technique. Soon he was crying, sharing a long-standing feeling of inadequacy. After three sessions like this, Jack learned some alternative methods of expressing his feelings. Eventually he was better able to deal with his feelings of helplessness which were in direct conflict with his macho self-image. A month later he reported that he enjoyed teaching more than at any other time in his life.

Expression of feelings, especially negative feelings, is very difficult for most of us because of all the injunctions we have learned against such expressions early in our lives. And while most teacher education programs pay considerable attention to curriculum, methods, and other cognitive "how to's," it is rare that any attention is given to the feelings of the teacher. Many in our school society have become numb to their own feelings and go mechanically about their business day-to-day as if feelings were not a part of teaching. It indeed can become frightening when disruptive students challenge our sense of equilibrium and refuse to follow our rules and guidelines. It is these

difficult students who often get us in touch with feelings that we have
learned through the years to value as "bad." As part of an effective
program of classroom or individual student management, it is important that the teacher take care of himself by both recognizing and
learning to express feelings.

To help you see the connection between expressing feelings and
successful classroom teaching, try keeping a simple journal for one
week. The following sample questions and answers can serve as a
model for this experiment. Take two or three minutes each morning
before your first class, just before lunch, and immediately after your
last class to answer those questions.

Monday:

Morning: Right now I feel (fill in any four words).

1) _____   2) _____   3) _____   4) _____

Circle the strongest feeling.
Write one sentence about the strongest feeling.
    Noon: (Repeat format)
    End of Day: (Repeat format)

Tuesday:

                    (Repeat format)

Friday:

Once you have completed your format for one week, answer the
following questions.

1. How many feelings words would you classify as positive? How
   many as negative?

2. How many of your circled words would you classify as positive?
   How many as negative?

3. Were your feelings more positive in the morning, afternoon, or
   at the end of the day?

4. Do you see any pattern in your feelings?

5. What methods do you use to express, acknowledge, or deal with
   your positive feelings about your teaching? Be specific.

6. What methods do you use to express, acknowledge, or deal with
   your negative feelings about your teaching? Be specific.

7. Are you satisfied with your pattern of feelings?

8. If not, what can you do to change it to one you prefer?

4. DISCOVERING AND RECOGNIZING ALTERNATIVES

The fourth stage of the prevention dimension is discovering and recognizing many different alternatives or models of behavior, theories of discipline, and some of the research into psychology and education as they apply to discipline. This knowledge alone will not make you a better classroom manager, but along with the other preventive stages, knowledge can generate viable alternatives that you can borrow from, adapt, or use as they are. Once you have personal awareness, you can use the work of others in your own way. It is most important to remember that the only approaches that will work for you are the ones that are congruent with your values, attitudes, and experiences as they relate to your professional and personal self.

5. ESTABLISHING SOCIAL CONTRACTS

The fifth stage of the prevention dimension involves establishing social contracts with your class. A social contract is a list of rules and consequences governing behavior, either in class or on a school-wide basis: rules agreed upon by you and your class. You will make a list of rules and consequences for your class and then ask your students to develop a list of rules and consequences for you. Students also develop rules and consequences for each other. Some teachers resist the use of the word "rule" because they see it as conceptualizing a rigid classroom structure that constricts the development of humanistic teacher-student relationships. To us the word "rule" means an agreed upon standard of behavior intended to facilitate an understanding of the limits that are necessary to meet individual needs and those of the group.

The lists are discussed and evaluated by the total class, and when agreement has been reached, the list of rules and consequences becomes the classroom social contract. Thus, your class will be involved in a process of setting rules and consequences and will feel that the contract is theirs. It is not only you, the teacher, who will decide the rules, but rather the class as a whole will assess needs and come to decisions about rules that will govern behavior. This process will be explained more fully in Chapter 4.

6. IMPLEMENTING SOCIAL CONTRACTS

The sixth stage of the prevention dimension involves a transition into the action dimension. By implementing the social contract you will set up a classroom environment that is governed by the rules, and when misbehavior occurs, a consequence is implemented or acted upon.

7. DEALING WITH STRESS ASSOCIATED WITH DISRUPTIVE STUDENTS

Stress management could fit into the Three Dimensional Discipline model in the action dimension (the discussion of which follows this section) because teachers feel stressed when students break rules. Our bias, however, is to teach stress management strategies as part of prevention. We feel that by practicing stress reduction activities before you encounter problems, the greater your results will be in effectively dealing with your problems.

Stress reduction involves two components: The first involves strategies for solving problems so that stress is experienced minimally. The prevention dimension is mostly based on a problem-solving orientation (with the exception of expressing feelings). However, there are also many activities, both structured and unstructured, designed to reduce and/or prevent stress that is produced by the following conditions: problems that cannot be solved, the time needed to solve problems is not available, or the process of solving the problems does not reduce stress immediately. Stress reduction will offer activities and strategies for both components.

The Action Dimension

Despite all your efforts (and those of your students) to prevent discipline problems from happening, conflicts will inevitably occur in any setting in which twenty to thirty people are expected to be together over an extended period of time. The purpose of the action dimension is twofold. When a discipline problem occurs, somebody (usually the teacher) needs to do something to stop the problem as quickly as possible. This requires action. The first step is to implement the consequence associated with a rule violation, as stated in the social contract. However, there is more to implementing consequences than saying, ''Nancy, there is no gum chewing in this class and because you are chewing gum, you must stay after school and clean all the desks. Don't argue! You agreed with this rule and consequences last September.'' The method of implementation is at least as important as the consequence itself. One's tone of voice, physical distance from the student, body posture, use of eye contact, and other non-verbal gestures determine the effectiveness of a consequence as much or more than the actual content of the consequence itself.

However, merely implementing consequences as rules are

broken can become mechanical and dehumanize the whole three dimensional approach. For simple violations of rules, consequences can be implemented quickly and without a great deal of fuss. Nevertheless, rule violations provide the teacher and students a chance to interact in positive ways. By terminating the conflict using the consequences and positive interaction, your class can realize its full energy and aliveness.

The second purpose of the action dimension involves the monitoring of the effectiveness of your class' social contract. The social contract is not to be seen as a series of fixed, inflexible sequences, but rather as rules and consequences that govern classroom or school behavior at any given time. This means that contract modification and rewriting can and should occur if the current social contract is not effective. Your needs and that of your students may change during the course of a school year. For example, if you notice that one of the rules is being violated with considerable frequency by a number of students, then we suggest that you consult with your class and possibly rewrite this part of the social contract. The prevention and action dimensions take care of most classroom discipline problems. Only the more troublesome and chronic problems will occur once the first two dimensions are implemented.

The Resolution Dimension

The resolution dimension is designed to help the teacher resolve conflicts with those students who chronically misbehave and who are "out-of-control." The first step in the process is to develop a mutually agreeable plan in which the needs of the student, the needs of the teacher, and the needs of the class are taken into account. This process, called positive student confrontation, helps both teacher and student, with the help of a coach,* to share both positive and negative feelings, make demands, and find a workable solution. If the plan fails, as it occasionally will, the documentation can be helpful in obtaining special services for these children.

The following positive student confrontation contracts were developed with Louis Morton, a 14-year-old eighth grader who was

---

* A coach is a third person who was agreed to by both teacher and student and whose responsibility it is to keep the process of positive student confrontation moving. It is not the role of the coach to solve problems but rather to facilitate a solution between the aggrieved parties to the conflict.

being chronically disruptive in all of his classes. His guidance counselor served as a "coach" in a meeting with Louis, his four academic teachers, and the study hall monitor. Notable behavioral improvements were reported by his teachers and study hall monitor following this meeting, which was succeeded by a series of biweekly conferences between Louis and his teachers to monitor and revise the contract as needed.

Contract with Louis M.

Social Studies Class

Date: 1/30/81

1. Louis will be on time for class.
2. Louis will not visit guidance during class unless called there by Mr. Smith (guidance counselor).
3. Louis will have books, paper, pen or pencil when he comes to class.
4. Louis will not leave his seat except to sharpen his pencil and then he must not visit with other students on the way to or from the sharpener.
5. Louis will not grunt, squeal, or make other such unnecessary noises in class.
6. Louis will not make comments about other persons or events which do not concern him.
7. When group work is assigned, Louis will work only with persons assigned.
8. One warning will be given for any infraction. Warning will be given in writing and signed by both teacher and Louis. Second infraction of any of these rules during any class means removal for the remainder of class period.

Signed: _____

_____

Revised

Feb. 2, 1981

I, Louis M., agree to improve my behavior in English by

1. being on time to class
2. bringing pen/pencil and paper every day

3. being quiet and completing my work

4. reading correctly when called upon to read aloud in class

5. not disturbing other students especially Lois L

6. not eating food or candy in class

Signed: _____

_____

Louis M.

Math Classroom Rules

1. Arrive at class on time and seat yourself immediately.

2. Be prepared to work—bring pencil, pen, paper, and homework with textbook.

3. Raise your hand to volunteer answers. Remain seated. Also, raise your hand to ask questions. Be patient and respect the same rights of other students.

4. No talking during quizzes or tests.

5. Remain in the classroom the whole class time. Lavatory or locker passes are not issued unless there is an emergency.

6. No eating of any foods in the classroom at any time.

7. When leaving the classroom, clean the area around your desk of any waste and dispose of it in the waste basket.

Thank You.

_____

Louis M.

Science Classroom Rules

1. Be to class on time.

2. Be prepared: a. pen or pencil
                   b. science notebook or folder
                   c. textbook

3. No food or drink in the classroom.

4. No sitting on the counter tops or tables.

5. Shoes must be worn in the classroom at all times.

6. Students will not open and close windows or blinds unless instructed to do so by the teacher.

7. Gum chewing is permitted as long as the teacher doesn't see or hear it.

8. No radios or tape players will be used in the classroom.

9. Do not wear coats or bring extra books to class.

10. All students should be quiet and in their seats before dismissal.

11. Don't stand in the doorway.

TO: Louis M.
FROM: Mrs. R.
RE: Behavior Contract/Study Hall
DATE: Feb. 21, 1981

Behavior Contract for Louis M.

1. Louis will come to class on time. If he is late he will have a pass.

2. He will take his assigned seat and begin his work.

3. If Louis has no studying or homework, he may draw.

4. Louis will control his temper and think before he lashes out with his remarks to fellow students and myself.

5. Louis will not get involved with other students' problems or contradict me when I am disciplining another student.

6. He will conduct himself in an appropriate manner and follow the study hall rules as outlined in the student handbook.

The consequences for not following these rules will be that Louis will receive 2 warnings and then a referral will be given to him, and he will be sent to his administrator.

I agree with the rules set down for my study hall.

_____ date _____

Louis M's Rules for Guidance

Student Appointments:

1. Two modules a week
   a. Either consecutively or separately
   b. Must be during study hall time
   c. Louis is to come alone

Counselor Appointments:

1. At counselor's discretion
   a. During study hall time

Behavior:

1. Will be on time
2. Pass will be signed by teacher
3. Will not request any deviations from agreement or rules
4. Will conduct himself in an orderly manner
5. Will leave without any argument when session is finished
   a. Counselor will make decision when session is finished
6. Louis will go directly to class when he leaves guidance area

Consequence:

1. Loss of appointment privilege
2. Referral to building principal

The resolution dimension also focuses on more creative and nontraditional approaches for dealing with the out-of-control student. Chapter 7 will give many examples of strategies that are both creative and unusual.

The process of Three Dimensional Discipline will help most teachers by providing a framework for the prevention of most discipline problems, by offering a strategy for taking appropriate action when problems do occur, and by providing creative solutions to the problems of students who chronically misbehave.

For the Administrator

Three Dimensional Discipline is a broad based program flexible enough to fit any teacher's individual, unique style of teaching. As the administrator in your building, it is important for you to accept that your faculty is diverse, has a variety of values, and uses a multitude of strategies when managing student behavior. In the same way you might suggest to a teacher to begin working with student strengths, you can begin helping your teachers by identifying their unique strengths in relation to discipline. Improvement in classroom management can be built upon these strengths.

To ensure that your teachers are receiving the support they want from you, ask each teacher to discuss their plans with you for preventing discipline problems from occurring. Suggest that they provide you with details of their rules and consequences early in the school year so that both you and they are clear about what each teacher expects from you!

To facilitate the process of teachers seeing the benefits of self and student awareness you can present the R-M-L scale (page 2 7) and the Student Awareness Activity (page 30) at one of your faculty meetings. A discussion of awareness and how it can be used in relation to discipline can follow the activities.

You can also establish support groups of interested teachers so that there is a regular, sanctioned meeting time for your faculty to express their feelings and receive colleagial support for issues related to discipline. These groups can be incorporated into the regular school day or can meet after school on a weekly or biweekly basis. This time should be seen as a regular part of the job, the equivalent of a committee or other school event, and should not simply be an "added on" responsibility.

A discussion group of teachers who have had experiences with one discipline approach or another can be established. The group can first read about an approach and then discuss it with the teacher(s) who have experienced it in the classroom. The groups should focus on adapting each strategy in a practical way. While theoretical discussions can be fun, they rarely lead to an improvement of discipline.

To help with positive student confrontation, the administrator can practice the role of coach and be available to teachers who want to use this method. You can also help by training others in the school to act as coaches, so that teachers and students have a wide array of choices when they need the services of a coach.

References

1. For more information see Curwin, R. L. and Mendler, A. N., *The Discipline Book: A Complete Guide to School and Classroom Management*, Reston, Va.: Reston Publishing Co., 1980.

2. Curwin, R., and Fuhrman, B., "Mirror, Mirror on the Wall: Developing Teacher Congruency," *Humanist Education*, September 1978, p. 34.

3. Bessell, H. and Palomares, U. *Methods in Human Development*, El Cajon: Human Development Press, 1972.

THREE

Stress and Discipline

*T*aking charge in the classroom means learning how to be in control of school factors that may burn you out! Dealing with disruptive students is a major source of stress confronted by teachers. Effective classroom management that enables you to be in charge requires you to remain confident, secure, and cool in the face of unruly behavior. In order to do this, you must have available a variety of strategies that you can use to reduce the tension created by disruptive student behavior. Throughout this book we will remind you to take good emotional care of yourself. Several options are offered in this chapter to help you express your feelings, release tension, and experience a new level of inner peace.

During the last few years, the issue of teacher stress and burnout has received increasing attention. As Hendrickson points out,[1] a burned-out teacher is losing, or has lost, the energy and enthusiasm needed to teach children. Little if any joy remains in the teaching process. Coming to work becomes an unpleasant chore, and excitement focuses around how many days, hours, and minutes are left until Friday or the next vacation. Its symptoms include physical, social, and emotional maladies, such as headaches, exhaustion, sleeplessness, ulcers, frequent colds, chronic back pain, loss of appetite, depression, frustration, irritability, low morale, feelings of inadequacy, absenteeism, boredom, outbursts of anger, apathy, anxiety, and lack of concern for self and others, as well as a loss of pride in the job.

While there are many factors that drain the energy reserves of the contemporary classroom teacher, we believe that there is no doubt that the leading cause of teacher burnout is the tiring and exhausting effects of disruptive student behavior upon the teacher. The National Education Association (NEA) cites a number of reasons for teacher burnout, but the big one is the pervasive sense that teachers have lost effective control of their classroom. Many teachers are faced with the daily reality of going to work and being uncertain of their own safety. The problems of the inner city have received much attention as evidenced by the ever-increasing number of violent student assaults upon teachers. Many of these teachers are satisfied to avoid physical harm and thereby yield to the numerous minor disruptive events, which have a cumulative effect of leading to stress, tension, and ultimately burnout. Teachers in suburban and rural schools also find more and more of their time and energy devoted to dealing with disruptive students, who come to school unmotivated to learn and with poor self-concepts. These students only know how to connect with school through displays of power, which often leave the teacher engaged in endless power struggles. To illustrate the symbiotic relationship of stress and discipline, we invite you to imagine a classroom situation in which every student was interested in the lesson, was prepared for class, did not make derogatory remarks, had no weapons, resolved disputes through talkng (rather than fighting), followed the rules, and accepted the consequences when rules were broken. We maintain that were such a situation the norm, rather than the exception, there would be few instances of teacher burnout occurring throughout our schools, despite the myriad of other causes.

We recently conducted a study that was comprised of a series of interviews with several teachers who represented a broad spectrum of teaching experience, types of school, and grade level taught. We asked them to describe the stressors they viewed in their work settings and what physical symptoms or emotional difficulties they attributed to teaching. In addition, we wanted to know what elements teachers would describe as the most difficult classroom problems that they deal with on a recurring basis.[2]

What Do Teachers Say about Stress?

Our first question was:

> Discuss any physical symptoms of illness or emotional difficulties that you or others that you know experience as teacher job-related, and what you believe the primary source(s) of these difficulties are.

Teachers in our study indicated a variety of physical and emotional reactions to stress that they believed to be job-related. Among these are headaches, backaches, tension in the neck and shoulders, loss of emotional control, ulcers, emotional withdrawal, heart conditions, alcoholism, lockjaw, and suicide. The scope of perceived job-related illnesses would seem to confirm the notion of Bloch's "combat fatigue" and indicates teaching to be a "high-risk" profession.

Some unedited comments of subjects follow. These are useful aids for the reader to understand what teachers are experiencing as the causes of stress and how they manifest various symptoms. The comments are verbatim except for names and locations.

An elementary school teacher in describing two of her colleagues says:

CASE ONE Sally was a teacher of what was called a junior first grade. The children in her class were extremely immature. They had been through kindergarten but were not considered to be ready for first grade, and so this new group was formed—a limbo, as someone labeled it. Sally was a young, relatively inexperienced teacher who was put in charge of this class. To say that these children were difficult to handle is an extreme understatement.

Soon the effects of this experience began to take its toll. Sally was sometimes found outside her classroom, crying. One day during an in-service course I observed her slumped over in her chair, seemingly unaware of what was happening around her. A school nurse was called but found no physical signs of illness. Others who worked closely with her stated that this was not the first time she had "shut out the world." Since class was almost over, we decided to leave her alone. At the end of class we again called her name and said that it was time to leave. She "came to" with no trouble and walked to her car and drove herself home.

Shortly thereafter Sally was asked to take a psychiatric examination. She refused and resigned. The primary source of Sally's difficulties was most likely her own emotional makeup with the secondary cause being the nature of her class. She had received support from the administration and other teachers at first, but it became apparent very soon that the pressures put upon her had been too much. At that point the welfare of the children, who needed a very strong teacher, took top priority.

CASE TWO Joan, on the other hand, is an experienced, extremely well-organized teacher with an excellent reputation among administrators and students. She herself is a perfectionist and is very demanding of her students. She relates well to slow groups and top students as well.

There have been occasions, however, in which Joan has exhibited behavior that in a young child would be called temper tantrums. When greatly upset for one reason or another, such as trouble with a parent, a change in schedule, or disappointment in students' achievement, she has been seen crying, shouting, even cursing. These outbursts have taken place in the office, her classroom, and the teacher's room.

Another teacher describes her experience with a difficult class:

CASE
THREE
I used to dread this class so much that as soon as I entered the classroom I would get a severe case of lockjaw. My whole jaw and neck would tighten up and there was nothing I could do to loosen up. I used to try to chew and exercise my jaw in hopes that I could lessen the tension, but this was done to no avail. After this class I would get a migraine headache every day. The curious thing was that I never got the headache in the classroom, but as soon as I stepped out of the classroom into the hall to go home, it would hit me like a Mack truck. Luckily I had a long drive home and was able to unwind somewhat during this time period.

The manifestations of stress most often mentioned by the teachers in our study were: headache, stomach upset, drinking, fatigue, ulcers, lockjaw, spastic colon, hiatus hernia, colds and flu-like sickness, elevated blood pressure, temper flare-ups, and less patience for family.

Disruptive Students and Stress

The most frequently reported source of teacher stress among the subjects was student provocation. One teacher's comments serve as a summary of what many others said.

CASE
FOUR
Ultimately, however, the greatest stress for a teacher probably revolves around student behaviors and classroom management. Students who lie, cheat, swear, steal, cut classes, fight, vandalize, never turn in homework, are rude and disruptive or unmotivated are sources of extreme stress for teachers. Coping with difficult students within the classroom framework produces the ultimate in stress because to some degree and in one way or another, the above situations can manifest themselves almost daily. Coping effectively with these students means the difference between a successful teaching-learning

situation on the one hand, and a stressful, unproductive experience on the other.

Effectively coping with such students is probably the most difficult task that faces the contemporary teacher. Disruptive student behavior is difficult for many teachers to cope with because the teacher must often walk a tightrope between being firm and yet unoffensive to the student, his parent(s), or the administration.

The next case illustrates how the teacher's sense of humanism, caring, and concern faces its sternest challenge with antagonistic students.

CASE FIVE
Larry Smith was a seventh grade Social Studies teacher who had endured crazy Carl and nasty Ned for nine months and one week. On Monday, crazy Carl brought a "cherry bomb" into the class. The teacher took it and Carl to the office. Ned went also because he was interfering by his verbal defense of Carl.

The principal moved both boys to another class against the teacher's advice. He then wrote a note stating that Mr. Smith (teacher) didn't directly cause the move, but then again. . . . Mr. Smith spent a miserable three weeks nervous and upset.

With the exception of Thoresen, *et al.* (1973),[3] most research on stressors related to disruptive students have concluded with vague generalities. While it is useful to know that every Gallup poll in the last decade has rated "discipline" the #1 public concern regarding its schools and that teachers in New York State rate "managing disruptive students" to be their leading stressor, investigators have typically failed to pinpoint what the exact meaning of "discipline" is to teachers. One goal of our study was to collect data from teachers that would help to shed light on the important issue of specificity regarding discipline. To this end, subjects were asked to list and explain the three most difficult recurring events they face in the classroom.

A cumulative list of events follows. Although some items were mentioned more than once, this list represents items that were viewed as distinct enough from others to warrant a separate listing.

1. belligerent and disruptive behavior regarding class failure
2. excuses and "song and dance" routines about teacher unfairness
3. lack of motivation on the part of students with a history of failure
4. lack of interest in the class (including apathy about learning; doing homework; coming to class unprepared)

5. vandalism (writing on desks most often mentioned)

6. stealing

7. expressions of bigotry in the classroom

8. cheating

9. teacher harassment (verbal abuse directed at teacher)

10. frequent and persistent talking out-of-turn

11. put-down or rejection of one student by another or by a group of students

12. high noise level

13. chronic class cutting

14. not paying attention

15. leaving seat without permission

16. lateness to class

17. temper outbursts in class

Five items were mentioned by 50% or more of all teachers. These were:

1. excuses and charges of unfairness

2. lack of interest in the class (unpreparedness, apathy about learning, not doing homework)

3. frequent and persistent talking out-of-turn

4. put-down or rejection of one student by another or by a group of students

5. belligerent and disruptive behavior in class

Let's take a closer look by examining a sample of comments solicited from teachers in our study. A high school teacher so aptly describes a key issue involved in the management of disruptive student behavior: ego deflation or "loss of face!" The tendency to personalize rule violations as expressions of student disobedience to the teacher often leads to a power struggle in which nobody can emerge the winner (least of all the teacher).

CASE SIX The three most difficult events I face in my everyday classroom management are: recurring unexcused lateness to class on the part of a few students, coming to class unprepared (i.e., no textbook, notebook, pen, etc.), and unauthorized speaking out in class. Although it is a very small minority of students who cause these problems, I find them stressful because, as I now realize, I see these violations of the rules as a loss of face for me. MY rules have been broken!

Bardo, a researcher who conducted her own study in 1979, concurs with the comments of the teacher in our study. Bardo says:

> What I encountered in recent years was much more disturbing, even frightening. In increasing numbers, teenagers have begun using their ultimate weapon against the school and themselves. They are simply refusing to do the work that leads to learning.[4]

Forgetting books, pens, pencils, showing no interest in the assigned work, appearing bored, and refusing to do homework are manifestations of Bardo's statement. Several teachers in our study (including some elementary teachers) experienced one or more of these concerns and felt stressed as evidenced by the following comments:

CASE
SEVEN

One of the most difficult recurring events faced in my classroom is dealing with the child who is unmotivated. A few of my students, even when working on an individual basis, are reluctant to do the tasks assigned in the resource room. This causes me great concern and sometimes unmanifested anger.

CASE
EIGHT

Lack of interest in my course is a general problem which leads to a whole host of secondary difficulties. Although I try to make my course as stimulating as possible, there will be, either because of my lack of creativity or because some students are almost impossible to stimulate, a certain percentage of a classroom full of young people who will not respond favorably to what is taking place in the course. While some students remain quietly bored, others act out by distracting others and by misbehaving in other ways. During lectures and discussions, some students may not pay attention and either talk or fool around with others. Other bored individuals may not involve others, but instead doodle, write letters, do homework, or in other ways tune out what is going on. Boredom also leads to complaining by some of the more vocal students. Some chronic complainers can be nasty. Nasty or not, the verbalization of their attitude can contribute to a general negative atmosphere in the classroom.

CASE
NINE

Over the years, I've had two or three students who absolutely refused to become part of the class in any but a most negative way. This is the student who wouldn't do homework, who shouted out in class, who wouldn't stay seated, who harassed other students and the teacher, etc. That student would consistently arrive late to class, enter the room causing some minor disruption and continue from one acting-out activity to another until he could no longer be ignored. A comment in any form from me generally resulted in a defensive harangue on the inequities and unfairness of my attitude toward him.

CASE
TEN
One difficult recurring event that is very typical in my classroom is when a student or students do not do their homework assignments and therefore cannot participate or benefit from that work when I review it with the class. When the class is engaged in learning a new concept in grammar, most often homework is given every night in order to reinforce the day's lesson; some independent study and work must be done by the student in order for him to fully grasp a new grammar concept. Naturally, when doing homework, the student will also discover how well or how little he understands the new work. If he comes to class unprepared, he will not only not have reinforced the previous day's lesson, but he will not be able to participate in a good portion of that day's work reviewing the new concept.

Put-downs and/or the rejection of one student by another student or a group of students, or the put-down by a student of the teacher was frequently mentioned as requiring some disciplinary action. It should also be noted that in our experience of working with thousands of students, the use of put-downs by teachers of their students is often accorded a high ranking in concerns expressed by *students*.

A junior high school teacher describes the problem:

CASE
ELEVEN
The cruelty of one student or group of students toward a classmate is especially disturbing. At this grade level, (senior high) being "in" is very important to many children, or, at least being accepted is a necessity to almost everyone. It seems that every year there are at least a few boys or girls who find themselves ostracized by the group. Many of these students have been dealing with this problem for years, whereas others who were popular in the lower grades suddenly, and for no reason (in their opinion), find themselves to be the object of ridicule and scorn.

The following two cases illustrate the problem and different, yet effective, methods of intervention.

CASE
TWELVE
It is very difficult to hear cruelties and not respond cruelly. Since neither physically nor emotionally can I be nasty or cruel, I have chosen different approaches to students in my class who find pleasure in making others uncomfortable. Since I am dealing with 14-year-old students, I have found "humor" the best reversal. In linking the "distainer" with the "distained" romantically the overt stage of the "put-down" is stopped. When the torment starts, I simply say, "This must be love." Also, I'll act out in pantomine being injured. If the remark is

serious, a public apology is required and most often requested not only by the teacher but the offending student's peers.

CASE
THIRTEEN
Every year there is at least one child in the class who is disliked and harassed or rejected by the others. In my experience, the obese child has had some of the most trying times. "Nobody likes a fat kid!"

A fat kid with acne is worse. Mary fits into this category. On top of it she came to us in December. By that time of the year everyone had already made their friends (and enemies). Also, sixth graders are entering puberty, and personal hygiene requires more care. Mary had very poor personal hygiene. I had the school nurse discuss this with her in private. I found it necessary to talk to the class in her absence to enlist their support in making her feel more comfortable. I knew that it would be difficult for most, if not all, to really accept her as a friend because physically she was most unappealing. I found ways of enlisting her help in and out of the classroom. I worked with her individually to improve her skills in math and reading. Upon entering the class she was reading on a second grade level. At the end of the year she was on grade level. She looked better, seemed to like herself more, and did develop a friend or two in class.

Talking-out-of-turn, (off-task talking, interrupting) was one of the leading sources of classroom stress identified by teachers. Notice the following report by a teacher from our study.

CASE
FOURTEEN
Without question, my number one gripe about the kids is their endless devotion to talking out-of-turn. Every year in every class, there is always that element of at least five kids who simply have too much to say to too many people to be able to stop their mouths from yakking during my class. No matter what is going on in class, be it a movie, lecture, filmstrip, demonstration, or the explanation of some directions, these students will yell out to a friend something that is sure to shatter any semblance of order and concentration. No amount of discussion with the kids or disciplinary action can stop these stout-hearted talkers from the completion of their sacred duty (blabbing at the wrong time), and thus I simply must grin and bear it. It is just part of the job.

Excuse making and complaints about teacher unfairness, particularly when done in the view of other students, can be a source of considerable frustration among teachers. Power struggles are difficult to resolve because both parties feel a need to save face: the student does not want to appear weak to his peers and the teacher fears losing control of the class if he does not show who is boss. A tenth grade inner-city teacher explains:

CASE
FIFTEEN

A difficult situation that often recurs is that a student who has failed the course, becomes belligerent and disruptive in class. At first, it is directed at other students, and then at me, the teacher. The disruptive student has much face to save, since he is now repeating the course and is not doing so well. When I try to calm him down, a tirade is directed at me: "You don't like me. You're not doing a good job of teaching. You're getting even. . . ." The more I try to settle the student down, the worse it gets. The other students are either shocked, taking sides, or upset because they're being disturbed.

Finally, a high school teacher succinctly describes the cycle involving the unmotivted student, teacher warnings, no-improvements, and cries of unfairness. (See page 57 for more detail).

CASE
SIXTEEN

My second most difficult event would have to be students complaining about low grades after spending an entire term goofing off and getting numerous warning notices about it. These kids seem to be in a fog when it comes to responsibility and just haven't learned yet about deadlines. They assume that if they ask for all past due assignments the day before grades come out, they can sit up late that evening and crank out enough garbage to make up for their ten weeks of "vacationing." And when you try to tell them they failed as you stand there with your computer sheet in hand and they with their scrawled out "junk" pile of term assignments and extra credit, they are simply aghast to hear of their demise. After a 10-minute debate on the validity of their excuses and the inequity of your policies, they go off to their seats mumbling an avalanche of complaints, obscenities, and parental threats. It is really quite frustrating.

Stress can be caused by acts of vandalism, and the following teacher's report describes how she felt about vandalism.

CASE
SEVENTEEN

Vandalism and theft are occasional, but constant, problems especially in science classes. Anonymous damage, breakage, stealing, and graffiti are difficult to cope with. While most people will tell you not to personalize the action, since in most cases it is not the teacher whom the student has in mind when committing the petty crime, it is the teacher who ultimately bears the burden. If I do not catch the graffiti artist, it is usually I who cleans it up. If something is damaged intentionally or is stolen, it is I who must reorder the item and, in some cases, locate a substitute item just to teach a particular lesson. All of this unnecessarily takes away from the total amount of time available to me. It affects my professional time and personal time outside of school as well. I find it difficult not to personalize this behavior. In fact, on several occasions, personal items which I have brought to share with my students have been damaged or stolen. I do not find it easy to cope with this type of inconsideration and the resultant stress. Since this behavior cuts into my time, I have tried sacrificing other professional responsibilities, which I must fulfill, if I have to make up for someone's mischief. This method is rarely successful since most things that I do have to be done. The best method that I have come up with so far is prevention. I have learned from experience to lock drawers, to watch certain items carefully, to check desks regularly for scribbling, and to not pass around items in a class where damage has occurred. Certain irreplaceable items are never passed around the room. To that end, I have had to program myself to try to accept the occasional vandalism and theft that will occur. It is unfortunately part of the game and staying as calm as possible, or kicking an occasional table leg, seems to be my only solution.

One of the most acutely stressful classroom situations for teachers is the presence of one or more ''out-of-control'' youngsters who seek attention, power, and control through emotional outbursts. Jennifer (third grade) is described by her teacher along with what her teacher did in efforts to resolve the problem.

CASE
EIGHTEEN
She was a bright, able, very verbal, and obnoxious child. When her name was mentioned in the faculty room, everyone would moan. She often showed impatience with peers, criticized her teachers and other staff members and was very impatient with everyone.

I spoke with Jennifer alone, after one of her critical outbursts in class and learned that she was not aware of behaving unacceptably. She was the oldest child in her family and her parents permitted such behavior.

We discussed why she should not scream and scold whenever she felt a person was not doing something in exactly the way Jennifer wanted. I shared my feelings and thoughts of indignation and anger when I heard her spontaneous outbursts. At the same time, I commended her on her excellent scholastic ability and told her that I thought she was capable of controlling her actions. We talked of tolerance and I shared an old and favorite saying with her:

You don't have to blow out my candle to make yours burn brighter.

Jennifer appeared to be willing to try and I felt that her behavior was impulsive and not truly naughty. The following week, Jennifer returned from the library trying very hard, but unsuccessfully, to curb her anger with the teacher across the hall whose class was permitted to run and misbehave in the halls. She was very critical and told me she was going to have her mother call up the principal. I explained to Jennifer that it was best to overlook the situation because everyone approaches tasks differently. We should accept others as they are and although I appreciated her indignation, I was sure the principal would take care of all unacceptable behavior in the halls. She seemed unwilling to accept this. I concentrated on encouraging her to be a "little girl" with a more carefree outlook. Throughout the year, Jennifer and I had many "chats" and I felt that her quick, sensitive, astute mind hindered her progress of just being a happy eight-year-old "child." Moreover, her parents had fostered her trait of speaking her mind and acting outrageously when she was not happy with a situation. I respected her as a person and felt no antagonism toward her after I knew her better but I did feel a degree of frustration when I attempted to help her curb her temper. At one point, I suggested that she write down her feelings instead of voicing them. At the end of the school year, Jennifer was more controlled but I feel that she will always be a bit critical of others.

A sixth grade teacher describes her encounters with "out-of-control" students and what she did to take care of the resulting stress.

CASE
NINETEEN

Over the past few years there have been about eight students with such serious emotional problems that abusive, unacceptable behavior and language were for them commonplace. Each appeared to have at least one goal in common: to have each teacher so irate as to be irrational in front of the class. For these students I especially chose to remain outwardly calm, to hold all conversations on their behavior privately, never in front of the class. Initially, the administration wished to play "savior" to each of these self-destruct students at the expense of the teachers and the classes. Realizing their inertia, I gathered information on the way other districts handled such students. I worked for as broad a base of support as I could find (specialist-teachers with a three to four student load, home-bound instruction, if necessary expulsion from the district). I kept feeding such information to the administration (gently). In my class these students were made to realize that they "worked or walked" to the office. I completely documented the facts on their behavior each time they were ejected from class. While the students may not have been removed from my class, an eighth grade Social Studies class in a junior high school, special help was sought for some of them in the ninth grade. I believe that my documented file eventually brought help to them.

Once I devised consistency in my own plan and my reaction to their harassment, I was released from a great deal of the stress I had initially experienced. In half of the cases their behavior modified for the better.

Summary

Our study asked teachers to focus on job-related effects that have been defined as *stress*. It offers us a glimpse into the emotionally stressful lives of teachers and what they are attempting to do to cope with their stress. As you can see, many teachers are experiencing what they believe are job-related symptoms of stress that can be summarized as being caused by one or more of these problems: (1) inappropriate student behavior, (2) job inflexibility, limited professional opportunities, (3) lack of administrative support related to disruptive students, and (4) social irresponsibility. More specifically these problems were:

1. no freedom or opportunity to vent one's emotions
2. very difficult to pace oneself
3. no opportunity to take a day off when one needs it without feeling irresponsible
4. no flexibility to change jobs and learn a new one (I'm not sure if I could survive at this time out in the business world.)
5. non-support from administrators for needed changes that would make it possible to do one's job.
6. receiving contradictory demands from various administrators that make it almost impossible for you to do your job (Instead of putting in oil to make the machine run efficiently, "they seem to enjoy putting in sand.")
7. not being at all clear about what is expected in regard to enforcing school policies (*Some teachers do*—the bad guys, *some teachers don't*—the good guys.)
8. concerns about who will get elected on the school board, and what drastic changes will they instigate
9. dealing with rude students
10. the constant stealing, lying, cheating, class cutting, and vandalism
11. as a teacher I'm not respected for my knowledge or teaching skill, but feared for my authority (students' view point)
12. concern with the state evaluating teachers with indivdual achievement scores for his or her students (Pay raises will be withheld or possible firings if individual scores are not satisfactory.)
13. supervisors treating fellow teachers as if they were children

14. lack of morale (The realization that no matter how good a record you may have, your supervisors may not back you at a time of trouble.)

15. the lack of respect for authority by students (whether you are a policeman, principal, judge, or teacher)

The feelings of frustration and resentment have become deep seated among some teachers who increasingly find themselves overwhelmed by the demands of the job with little appreciation coming from administrators, students, the school board, parents, or each other. A junior high teacher's poignant comments help to epitomize circumstances confronting today's teacher.

CASE TWENTY

Today's youths appear to be confused and drifting away from the basic values set down from previous generations. The total lack of discipline and the constant lying, cheating, vandalism, vulgarity, create stress to the teacher in charge. This stress can make many trained professionals learn to hate their job and sometimes make them physically sick.

Within the past five years I have known of fellow coworkers who have died from strokes which were clearly job-related. I know of one conscientious teacher this year who was put under great stress by a father and mother. His principal did not support him whatsoever, and he was driven to suicide. He left a wife and two children. On the day of his suicide he presented his lesson plans for the substitute teacher. The entire staff gave a vote of no confidence to the local school board; they in turn elected to give that principal his tenure.

Teachers with High Burnout Potential

Why is it that two teachers with the same number of years of teaching experience, who graduated from the same college, have taken the same in-service courses, who have worked in the same school, and whose out-of-school lives are comparable can have such different experiences as teachers? Why is it that one teacher (let's refer to him as teacher A) can maintain his energy and enthusiasm in the classroom while another teacher (teacher B) feels drained and overwhelmed?

As evidenced by the numerous comments in the preceding section, all teachers face considerable stress in their lives as educators. But as Hans Selye, perhaps the best renowned authority on the subject points out, stress can be felt as distress, which ultimately leads to burnout, or it can be used positively, leading to energy and enthusiasm.[5] The real difference resides not in the stressor, but in the teacher's perception of it. For example, suppose Johnny calls you a "son-of-a-bitch." His remark creates stress. You have two choices in responding to your stress. You can feel personally attacked by his comment and view him as an insulting, disrespectful brat (a majority view) in which case you will probably retaliate in some way, or . . . you can view this as a challenge for contact that Johnny has just made and an opportunity to connect with him on his level. Teacher B would view Johnny as threatening, and should his response to the threat not stop Johnny's misbehavior, then "distress" would result. Teacher A sees Johnny as a challenge and the challenge generates energy and excitement for contact.

A fitting analogy to this discussion is a baseball scene. It is the bottom of the ninth inning of the last game of the World Series. Your team is behind by one run, there are two outs, the bases are loaded, and it's your turn to bat. You are under great pressure: stress! The "burnout" views the pressure as an opportunity to fail and most often will! He defines the situation as distressing. By contrast, his counterpart sees the pressure as an opportunity to do well. For him it is a challenge that creates positive energy. While the outcome will not always turn out favorably, his positive energy increases the odds for success.

Teachers with high burnout probability generally fall into one of the following four categories:

Please Like Me

These teachers are dependent upon student approval and are often willing to ignore misbehavior in order to continue to feel liked. They apologetically set limits and rarely follow through with consequences when rules are broken. Such teachers prefer to give themselves headaches, back pains, and other forms of physical tension rather than feel guilty for acting "mean" to their students. Disruptive students see these teachers as weak and ineffective and take control of the classroom because the teachers are at their mercy.

Muscle Flexer

Muscle flexers adopt the attitude, "I don't care if they like me or not, but they'd better do as I want or else." They often resort to power based methods, including open confrontation, which invite resistance, retaliation, and rebellion in response. These teachers are quick to write referrals and inevitably feel that the administration is too soft. Unless these teachers have a warm and caring support system outside of school, they are likely to receive so few positive strokes on the job that loss of enthusiasm and early burnout result.

Guilt Giver

The attitude of the guilt giver is, "Can't you see how miserable I feel when you misbehave—I *wish* you would stop," or "Look at all I'm doing for you, and look at how ungrateful you are!" These teachers lack self-confidence and resort to whining and complaining with hopes that students will come to their senses. Such teachers are personally hurt and angry when students misbehave, but they are unable to express this anger. And so limits are set through an appeal to the guilt of students, which is thoroughly ineffective with students who feel no guilt. These teachers are often seen with clenched jaws and fists accompanied by a soft, submissive tone of voice. The students hear the message that they have the power to make the teacher angry, and the worst consequence will be complaining and whining. Such teachers are likely to have numerous interpersonal difficulties because of blocked feelings, which lead to very high levels of stress and burnout.

Marine Sargeant

This is the tough and fair approach. "Everybody gets treated the same way in here, and there are no exceptions to the rule," is the prevailing attitude. While this position is more effective than the others because of its "fairness," it works but mostly with those students who want to be marines. Because of the rigidity inherent in this approach, pride often gets in the teacher's way of dealing with tough-to-reach students who read rigidity as an invitation to act out. These teachers are likely to be victims of fear and anxiety when disruptive students succeed at threatening their control.

Summary

It is our contention that the above mentioned teacher types represent the most likely candidates for early burnout. They respond to misbehavior ineffectively, and their responses lead to continuation or regression of the student's behavior. Faced with not knowing what to do, the teacher feels tense and either holds in the tension, or yields to explosive outbursts. If this pattern continues, teacher burnout (leaving teaching, or waiting until Friday) occurs.

FIGURE ONE | **Discipline and Burnout Cycle**

1. Student misbehavior
2. Ineffective teacher response
   a. blaming
   b. rationalizing
   c. provoking
   d. denying
   e. revenge (I must be in control, I'll get even)
3. No student improvement, or worsening
4. Teacher feels tension and frustration
5. Withdrawal or explosive outbursts by the teacher
6. Increased misbehavior by students
7. Burnout

The above paradigm illustrates the "Discipline-Burnout" cycle. It begins when a student acts in a way that interferes with the teaching-learning process. The teacher ineffectively responds by *denying* (pretending not to see or hear misbehavior), *rationalizing* ("I can't expect her to behave herself because of her home situation, history of school failure," etc.), *blaming* ("I saw you do it, it's your fault"), or *provoking* ("I will test your limits as much or more than you test mine"). Each of the aforementioned "teacher types" resort to one or more of these ineffective methods (in some cases the cycle continues even when the teacher responds effectively as with the out-of-control, incorrigible student). When the teacher's corrective response meets with a continuation or worsening of behavior, tension and feelings of frustration occur. When these feelings are allowed to accumulate and no relief is in sight, then the teacher responds either through withdrawal ("I don't want anything to do with you") or explosive outbursts ("You say that again, and I will break your neck"). If the cycle becomes repetitive, then burnout is fast approaching.

What Does Stress Look Like

Generally speaking, burnout victims suffer from either mental, muscular, or visceral symptoms. Mental symptoms include fatigue, irritability, exhaustion, lacking motivation to go to work, and dwelling on negative thoughts. Musculature symptoms include tension headaches, backaches, tension in shoulders, and tightness in limbs. Visceral symptoms include cardiovascular problems, gastrointestinal problems, high blood pressure, ulcers, and colitis.

Strategies for Reducing Stress

Strategies for reducing stress can broadly be conceptualized in two basic categories. Lazarus speaks of these as *problem solving* and *emotion focused.*[6] *Problem-solving methods* attempt to change the situations or events that are viewed as stressful. Most of the strategies contained in this book have such an emphasis. Establishing social contracts, becoming aware of yourself and your students, and familiarizing yourself with various discipline theories aim at eliminating factors in the teaching environment that contribute to disruptive student behavior. Having effective consequences that are implemented with a firm tone of voice, in close proximity to the acting-out student with good eye contact is designed to stop misbehavior when it does occur, providing you practice it consistently. Learning how to effectively resolve differences with "hard to reach" students through negotiation, understanding the art of paradoxical behavior, and utilizing other strategies described in Chapter 7 (Creative Discipline) are designed to problem solve difficulties with particularly disruptive students.

Unfortunately, not all people or situations lend themselves to change. The fact is that in some circumstances, and with some students, no matter what you do or how effectively or consistently you do it, no improvement occurs. The stress that you feel either continues or worsens. It does not simply go away.

Emotion-focused methods provide opportunities for you to release tension and induce relaxation within yourself. Various techniques such as meditation, yoga, biofeedback, guided visualization, and neurolinguistic programming have been useful to many people in providing rather rapid relief to the debilitating effects of stress. Many teachers use psychotherapy and/or groups of teachers who face similar problems for support.

The following activities are stress-management techniques that are quick, effective ways of teaching yourself to relax both before problems arise and when students do not respond favorably to your efforts to stop their misbehavior. They provide a non-destructive relief from tension that may be felt as frustration, anger, or sadness when the teacher's corrective response is met with no behavioral improvement. There are several self-help books that describe in greater detail various relaxation methodologies that you may want to investigate. The activities in the next section provide a sampling of strategies and should not be construed as all-inclusive, although we trust that they will provide needed relief from stress.

We want to point out that these activities are not meant as substitutes for exercise or nutrition, which have been identified as important to low-stress living. They are intended to provide quick relief during a five-minute break between classes and can be done in your room, the bathroom, or any other location that is relatively distraction free.

Private Retreat[7]

This activity is done by yourself, requires approximately five to ten minutes, and is most effective when done in anticipation of a stressful situation. For example, before your cafeteria assignment, study hall, arrival of a particularly difficult class, the end of recess, and other predictably tense times during the day that are easy to anticipate. The "private retreat" is designed to help you to remove yourself mentally from these realities so that when you return, you feel refreshed, alert, energized, and capable of dealing with the difficult situation.

Approximate time: five to ten minutes

Directions: Read all steps before you do the activity

1. Be in a place that is relatively free of distraction for the duration of the activity, for example, the library, an empty classroom, a free guidance counselor's office.
2. Find a comfortable position either seated or reclining.
3. Focus on your breathing . . . inhale . . . and as you exhale, quietly say "one." Repeat this five or six times. Close your eyes.
4. Remember a quiet, calm, serene setting that you have visited at least once. Most people return to the seashore, the mountains, the woods, or their own backyard. If you cannot recall such a time, then let yourself imagine what such a place would be like and where it would exist—let yourself be creative.
5. Now step into your picture and see all the colors and the sights . . . listen to the quiet, soothing sounds . . . notice all of the smells and aromas, and feel the texture of your surround-

ings . . . notice how you smoothly allow yourself to flow in this wonderfully peaceful place.

6. Stay for a few moments and realize how your mind and body are being renewed and refreshed.

7. After five to ten minutes, let yourself slowly come back to where you are right now, taking with you the calm and peacefulness from your ideal place. In a few moments, some situations that can cause stress will be here again, but you will retain this feeling of relaxed alertness for as long as you like. You have the realization that you may instantly return to your private retreat whenever you wish.

8. Slowly open your eyes and stretch your body.

Replacing Tension with Strength[8]

When students misbehave, there are many suggested strategies such as ignoring, reinforcing incompatible behavior, punishing, using ''I messages,'' behavioral contracting, and a host of others that have been developed to elicit positive change in the student's behavior. Despite all of these educational strategies, many teachers will often resort to blaming, provoking, rationalizing, or denying when confronted with a student who makes life miserable. When people feel tense, they often resort to old behavior patterns in an attempt to reduce their tension even if accompanied by a self-defeating outcome. Even when a teacher knows what ''should'' be done, in the face of a tense moment an ineffective, self-defeating response to misbehavior is common. It is very difficult to think clearly when confronted with a stressful situation. This activity is designed to teach you how to feel calm, relaxed, and confident even with those students you would like to strangle.

Approximate time: ten to fifteen minutes

1. Go back to a situation that you have recently had with a student that left you with negative feelings. Concentrate only until you can relive these feelings . . . when you have these negative feelings, touch yourself lightly on the right knee.

2. Return to the present.

3. Touch yourself on the right knee (most people report upon doing this that they again experience the negative feelings).

4. Return to the present.

5. Now close your eyes and think of a resource that you have inside of you that gives you strength. Your resource should be something you do now or have done in the past that made you feel secure and confident. Step into your picture and relive this experience . . . when you have contacted this resource, lightly touch your left knee.

6. Return to the present.

7. Now close your eyes, and once again see and/or hear this resource of yours (left knee) . . . and now take this resource with you back to the situation (right knee) with the student that left you with negative feelings. Experience dealing with this student using your resource.

8. Many teachers report a lessening of tension and a return to feelings of strength and confidence. If this has happened for you, proceed to the next step. If not, skip steps 9 and 10, and read step 11.

9. Now just to make sure that your resource will work effectively, close your eyes and touch your right knee. If you feel your strength when you do this, then you have succeeded in creating a new way of reducing tension.

10. Now realize that the next time a situation like the one that generated negative feelings occurs, you have this new resource available to effectively deal with your feelings.

11. Some people do not experience any positive change with their resources, while others simply cannot think of a resource that makes them feel strong and confident. If you have a resource that does not work, then close your eyes and think of another. If this still doesn't work, continue to think of others, which when paired together will have the effect of creating the desired change. If you cannot think of a resource, then visualize somebody else who you imagine has the strength and resources to deal with difficult situations. It may be a colleague, a former teacher, your spouse, or a friend. After you have recalled such a person, let yourself momentarily become that person, and feel what it is like to experience this strength . . . imagine how this other person would deal with the difficult situation. If this still doesn't work for you, then let yourself become a fantasy character. For example, become Superman, and as Superman, ask, "What strengths and resources do I have available to me?" If after all of this, you still feel tense and ill at ease, then this strategy is probably not going to work for you right now. There are lots of ways

to relax yourself, so do not despair if one or more are not compatible for you.

Quick Release Exercises

Imagine having read every book on discipline, being thoroughly familiar with every approach, and being aware of what the experts say will effectively change a student's behavior. Such a teacher will clearly have more strategies and techniques available and, theoretically, will deal better with disruptive students. However, even our theoretically ideal teacher will no doubt encounter at least one or two students every year that defy even the most advanced strategies, and who persist in their anti-authority behavior at all costs. Such students can be punished, praised, verbally shamed, confronted, have all privileges removed; and it just does not make any difference. Although the teacher is ultimately powerless to effect change, it is critically important that he recognize and safely express the tension generated by such a student.

Directions: Both of the below "quick release" activities are best done in the privacy of your home, office, car, or other place in which you will not think of or worry about other people's judgments.

PILLOW RELEASE

(Time 5 minutes) Take a pillow and place it in front of you. Imagine that the pillow is really the "out-of-control" student. Now tell this student what you resent (Sammy, I resent_____). See if your body wants to say or do anything to Sammy. If you'd like to crack Sammy over the skull, then let him have it! (Don't hold back: Remember he's not really there.) Let yourself yell, scream, punch, or squeeze until you feel a lessening of tension.

TOWEL TWISTING AND BITING

(Time 2–3 minutes) Because we believe that we have to walk on eggshells around the "out-of-control" student, we often keep our mouths shut to avoid escalating a power struggle. While this is sometimes the best direct method to use, repeated use causes tension to develop in the face (particularly the jaw) and upper torso. As a way of releasing this tension, take a towel and let the towel represent the student. Twist the towel (student) until it is taut, and keep twisting. Notice how your jaw and face become even more tense as you do this. Now take the twisted towel (student) and bite down, giving the towel all the tension that this student usually gives you . . . repeat a few times. Notice how a relaxed, tingling sensation replaces the tension that you felt just moments ago.

Tension Awareness

Many teachers feel the effects of tension through the psychological and physical symptoms described earlier in this chapter, but have little idea of what causes the tension, how often during the day they are in stressful situations, and what events are most likely to create stress. Likewise, many teachers are unaware of the many activities that can relieve stress and give them positive energy.

The first step of this activity is to plan four specific times during the day to "log" your feelings and your activities. One should be just before the beginning of a class or activity, one just after the completion of a class or activity, another prior to a time when you know you will be involved with one or more difficult students, and the last one at the close of school. Take a few minutes at these times to answer the following questions:

Date _____ Time _____
Activity prior to log writing _____
Activity coming up (in the next few minutes) _____
_____
My two most positive (energy) feelings are_____
_____
My two most negative (energy) feelings are_____
_____

Keep the log for at least two weeks, preferably three weeks, and then review it by answering the following questions:

1. List all of the positive feelings listing each one even if it was a repeat.

2. Look at the activities that gave you these feelings. Are there any activities that always lead to them? Were there any activities that often lead to these feelings?

3. Look at the situations that usually create tension. Did you experience any positive feelings during these times? What hap-

pened to generate these feelings? How can you recreate these feelings in other stressful situations?

Group Problem Solving and Support

Although teacher burnout is common to most schools, teachers generally have the feeling that they must face their tension alone. Stress, especially related to discipline, is seen as a sign of weakness or failure by teachers and administrators. Unfortunately, many teachers feel that they will be perceived as failures, or as being weak, if they admit to their feelings. Thus group problem solving and group support, two of the more effective strategies for coping with stress, are not available to most teachers. This strategy is designed to help reduce the obstacles by using a group to combat stress.

1. Invite teachers in your school who are interested in looking at stress in a group setting to participate. A good group size for this activity is between six and fifteen (more participants indicate a need for a second or third group).

2. Once the group is convened, each participant is to write anonymously on a piece of paper one problem that creates tension or stress in him on a regular basis.

3. All the papers are then collected. The group facilitator or a volunteer then reads each paper as if he were the person who wrote it.

4. Each group member then writes a short paragraph, which first states whether or not they have faced a similar situation, and if they had similar feelings. Then they write as many helpful suggestions as they can think of to solve the problem.

5. The leader then lets each participant read their response and, by asking questions, clarifies the answers, so that everyone in the group understands them.

6. Finally, all of the paragraphs are collected and titled. Once everyone has had their problem discussed, each teacher can collect his packet for experimenting in class. If there is not enough of them for everyone to finish, then plan several meetings, perhaps once a week, to give everyone an opportunity. Follow this activity up with another meeting in which teachers are only allowed to report which suggestions helped. Repeat as often as necessary, perhaps by scheduling a regular meeting each week or biweekly for the entire school year.

Psychodrama and Tension Release *

The technique of psychodrama is a good way for teachers to see new ways to eliminate or reduce tension. With a group of trusted colleagues or friends, establish a role play similar to a school situation that creates tension for you on a regular basis. Explain each of the roles and list the events that occurred at the time each upset you. Choose someone to represent yourself. Once everyone understands what the plot is, direct the drama as if you were a "director" and try to recreate accurately the events that led to your tension. Watch carefully, as an outsider, what the situation looks like.

Now redo the drama assuming your own role, and change the sequence so that you don't feel tension. Maybe you throw Johnny out on his ear, or perhaps you yell at the top of your lungs at Sue. Do whatever you want, without hurting anyone, relieving your tension at the time the event is being acted out.

Once these two steps have been completed, sit with the group and brainstorm as many new ways to behave in this or a similar situation to positively resolve the problem and to release your feelings in a positive, non-destructive way. Go back to the drama, and role play one or two of the ideas you feel are best for you. The next time this or a similar situation occurs, try your new behavior, and see how it works for you.

Guided Visualization (Blackboard Fantasy)[9]

1. Read all steps FIRST!
2. Close your eyes and take a few deep breaths. After you inhale, hold your breath for a moment before exhaling. Feel your body rise as you inhale and sink as you exhale. Continue doing this until you begin to feel some relaxation.
3. Picture yourself in front of a large blackboard with a piece of chalk in hand. Slowly write the number "10" in the upper left-hand corner.
4. Next to the number 10, slowly write the word "relax."
5. Now write the number 9, and slowly write the word "quiet."
6. Write the number 8, and slowly write the word "peaceful."

---

* Because this activity is likely to generate a range of strong feelings, it is recommended that you have a facilitator/leader who has some background and familiarity with group process (particularly psychodramatic techniques).

7. Write the number 7, and slowly write the word "tranquil."

8. Write the number 6, and slowly write the word "calm."

9. Write the number 5, and slowly write the word "serene."

10. Write the number 4, and slowly write the word "sleepy."

11. Write the number 3, and slowly write the word "very peaceful."

12. Write the number 2, and slowly write the words "very calm."

13. Write the number 1, and the slowly write the words "very relaxed."

14. Keep your eyes closed for another moment and silently count to 5 telling yourself that when you reach the number 5, you will open your eyes feeling relaxed, refreshed, and alert.

Guided Visualization (Troubles Balloon Fantasy)

1. Do the same as steps 1 and 2 in the Blackboard Fantasy.

2. Picture a large helium balloon in front of you. It is a large balloon with a big basket attached at the bottom just like the one flown in "Around the World in 80 Days." The balloon can be any color you choose. Slowly walk toward the balloon and notice how much room there is inside the basket.

   Slowly begin to deposit all of your troubles in that basket. Place all of your disruptive students, annoying administrators, and all other hassles in that basket. Now slowly walk away from the balloon and seat yourself under a beautiful shady tree. Notice the balloon begin to rise slowly into the air. Keep watching it and all of your troubles getting higher and higher, further and further away from you. It is now so high that it looks no larger than a small dot in the sky . . . and now you can't see it at all anymore. You may realize that you can have these troubles back whenever you want, but for now just enjoy the calm and peacefulness that exists in you. Smell the freshly cut grass, hear the chirping sounds of birds, and watch the quietness of your peaceful surroundings.

3. When you feel ready, count to 5, telling yourself to open your eyes when you reach 5 feeling relaxed, refreshed, and alert.

Breathing

When we are tense, our breathing often becomes shallow and irregular. Irregular breathing may constrict our blood vessels leading to insufficient blood flow and various visceral problems. Frustration, sadness, and worry that contribute to visceral problems can often be alleviated through proper breathing.

1. Inhale slowly to the count of 5, feeling your rib cage and lungs fully expand with air (notice your whole body moving upward).
2. Hold your breath to the count of 5.
3. Slowly exhale to the count of 5 (notice your whole body sinking downward).
4. Count to five before inhaling again.
5. Repeat this sequence several times.

Tightening and Releasing the Muscles

Mental tension is often accompanied by a tightness in one or more of the muscle groups that manifests itself as tension headache, neck pains, shoulder tightness, lower back pain, or aching legs and feet. Releasing this muscular tension often leads to feelings of relaxation.

1. Do a body inventory by checking out each of your body parts to spot tension (some people find biofeedback to be an excellent aid in helping them to discover where they are manifesting tension).
2. Now tightly squeeze each body part that contains tension (if it is in the shoulders, then push the shoulders up towards your head and release; if in the neck, slowly roll your head back and forth and to each side; if in the head, squeeze your face and clench your teeth, then relax; if in the legs or feet, squeeze each leg and as you are doing this make about five clockwise circles with each leg (foot), followed by five counterclockwise circles.
3. Now imagine yourself to be a tight, stiff, mechanized robot. Tighten your whole body and walk around for a few moments as this stiff robot.
4. Now imagine yourself to be a loose bouncing rag doll, or puppet on a string. Let your whole body sink towards the ground (don't fall down) and walk around for a few moments as this rag doll letting each body part flail about.
5. Take a few relaxing breaths (see previous activity).

Hot Tub Fantasy

The California hot tub craze provides a wonderful context for teachers all over the country to reduce their tension. Imagine yourself on a visit to a beautiful part of California (if you have not been to California, another surrounding that emanates beauty and that you have visited will do just fine) where a relaxing hot tub experience is waiting for you.

You may try this fantasy lying on your bed, or in a hot bath, or in any comfortable setting. Close your eyes and imagine the following:

You are alone in a hot tub lying supine, watching the stars on a perfectly clear night. The water temperature is about 105°, and the water is bubbling under you at a fairly rapid rate. The bubbles relax every muscle in your body—feel your muscles relax.

Now imagine your biggest stressor in your class. Maybe it's a troubling student, or a situation you are having trouble resolving. Feel the bubbles generate from the bottom of the tub and make contact with your body. Watch the stressor be swallowed up by a big bubble, feel it leave your body, and then watch it slowly lift into the sky, getting higher and higher until it reaches the stars.

Repeat this procedure for that stressor until you can feel it fly away and until your body feels lighter and freer without it.

Repeat this procedure again for all other stressors that are distressing to you until you feel free of all the tension associated with them.

Try to memorize and implant the relaxed feeling you are now experiencing in your mind and in the muscles of your body. Focus on this relaxed state so you can recall it when you need it in your classroom.

For the Administrator

Stress, like discipline, is an instrinsic part of the teacher's everyday school experience; and like discipline, many teachers are reluctant to admit their feelings of stress because they do not want to be considered weak or ineffective. You can help your faculty by making it perfectly clear that you understand that job-related stress is not only acceptable, but it is also a natural part of the teaching profession. Studies indicate very precisely that all professionals in the helping professions experience stress.

Your main concern related to teacher stress is to accept it, provide strategies for dealing with it, and to help remove from your school as many creators of stress as possible.

On page 45 we list the combined stressors reported by teachers in our study. This list is a good starting point for examining your school for causes of teacher stress. However, every school has its unique sources of stress. We recommend that you do your own survey of school and classroom stressors. Ask your teachers to list (anonymously) the main causes of stress in their typical day, or use any of the standard stress surveys listed in the chapter. If you find that there is a common agreement on causes of stress, you can use faculty meetings or task forces to create ways to either eliminate or minimize the causes. You may find logistical or organizational ways of solving some of your stress problems with a minimum expenditure of resources.

For example, one school reduced stress by teaching its students how to use the open campus effectively. The instruction was enough to cut down on students interrupting classes by yelling and running through the halls during instructional time.

Another way you can help deal with the issue of teacher stress is to be particularly sensitive to teachers who are potential burnout victims. Use the descriptions in this chapter of potential victims as a guide and pay attention to the way your teachers walk, talk, and behave in school. If you identify teachers who are highly stressed or burning out, take the time to offer guidance and comfort. Be supportive of them and see if there are ways you can help as an administrator. If the main cause of burnout for a particular teacher is discipline, as it is in so many cases, offer suggestions for improving discipline using the suggestions in this book. These burnout teachers might benefit from a reduction in responsibilities until they turn the corner and should be first on the list for some of the ''better'' assignments of classes and other responsibilities. Worry less about assigning classes on seniority and more about meeting the real needs of your teaching faculty. When working with potential burnouts, encourage them to talk with you or with others about their problems and help them feel cared for by the school.

Another way you can help reduce distress is to provide a time and a place for your teachers to practice stress reduction activities. Stress reduction activities such as meditation, fantasy, breathing correctly, improving body posture, and others should be considered healthy, not faddish, and you should do all you can to recognize publicly their legitimacy. Offer training and support groups for practicing such things as yoga, meditation, dance, breathing, and all of the activities suggested in this chapter.

Another way to deal with stress is through physical activity. Provide outlets for stress by opening the gymnasium and other facilities for faculty use. Help organize both formal and informal exercise groups, dance groups, basketball and volleyball games, jogging, frisbee, and other competitive and cooperative games. One school we know had monthly run-ins with all teachers earning a tee shirt for finishing the race regardless of the time it took to complete the race. When setting up a program of physical stress reduction, emphasize enjoyment not competition. You might want to include your physical education staff to help develop a program similar to the one described here.

Finally, one important goal for all administrators is to take care of your own stress. Administrators have the difficult responsibility of being a buffer zone between teachers and the upper administration and policies of the school system, between students and teachers, and between parents and teachers. They must deal with parents and students in a myriad of ways that are often stressful. Be a role model for your entire faculty by dealing openly and effectively with your own stress.

References

1. Hendrickson, B., "Teacher Burnout: How to Recognize It, What To Do About It," *Learning*, 7(5), 1979, pp. 36–38.

2. Mendler, A., "The Effects of a Combined Behavior Skills/Anxiety Management Program upon Teacher Stress and Disruptive Student Behavior," Union's Graduate School, Unpublished doctoral dissertation, 1981.

3. Thoresen, C. E.; Alper, T.; Hannum, J. W.; Barrick, J.; and Jacks, R. N., "Effects of Systematic Desensitization and Behavior Training with Elementary Teachers," Unpublished paper, Stanford University, 1973.

4. Bardo, F. The pain of teacher burnout: a case history *Phi Delta Kappan*, 1979, *90*, 252

5. Selye, H., *Stress Without Distress*, New York: The New American Library Inc., 1974.

6. Lazarus, R. S., *Patterns of Adjustment*, New York: McGraw-Hill, 1976.

7. Adapted from Carey Howard in Brown, B., *Stress and the Act of Biofeedback*, New York: Bantam Books, 1977.

8. Adapted from a training workshop with Dr. Sam Graceffo, a proponent of neuro-linguistic programming at the Institute for Change Unlimited. Syracuse, N.Y.

9. This activity was introduced to us at a workshop with Edith Saiki sponsored by the Drug and Alcohol Council in Rochester, New York.

FOUR

The Social Contract

*O*ne of the most effective ways of taking charge in the classroom and still giving a voice to the needs of your students, is to develop a social contract. The contract is effective because it clearly defines acceptable and unacceptable behavior in the classroom or school *before* the students misbehave. Without a contract, many good rules and resulting consequences that teachers purport to have in their classrooms are only fully understood by students after they break them. Obviously, more problems are created for the teacher when the only way students can discover the limits is to go beyond them. Another reason the contract is effective is that it gives the students a sense of ownership in what happens in the classroom. It has been our experience that the more the students feel that they own a share of the responsibility for the classroom rules, the more likely they are to follow them.

The process is based upon democratic decision making. White and Lippitt's studies (1960) of ten- and eleven-year-old children showed that an authoritarian teacher approach led to high work output by children but was accompanied by aggression directed at the teacher. Children in democratic groups that were guided by the teacher, but also clearly involved in decision making, had nearly as high a work output, got on "best" with the teacher, and worked slightly better than the authoritarian group when the teacher was out of the room. Children with laissez-faire teachers did worst on all criteria.[1]

Another important reason for using social contracts is that it spells out an exact procedure for both the students and teacher to follow when rules are broken. Thus, the key ingredients that make the social contract work are

1. clarity of rules and consequences
2. a student voice in the decision making of the rules and consequences
3. joint responsibility between teacher and students for behaving in an appropriate way

The purpose of this chapter is to review briefly the social contract process, to suggest various modifications of the process to match your educational philosophy with the needs of your students, and to provide you with several examples of social contracts that have been developed by different teachers at different grade levels and with a wide range of student populations.*

Steps of the Social Contract

In establishing a social contract with your class the following steps are suggested:

1. Teacher states his ''flag'' rules to students. These are rules that he believes must exist in order to maintain minimal control of the classroom. (e.g., people are not for hitting.) They are non-negotiable.
2. Teacher proposes other rules that he thinks are important for effective classroom management. Ideally, rules must be clear and specific—there is no doubt when a rule has been broken or followed. Your rules should not violate school rules, local or federal laws; they should say what behaviors are acceptable as well as which ones are not; and finally they may relate to behavior or study habits (including homework), but not to academic achievement.

---

* The interested reader is referred to our last publication *(The Discipline Book[2])* for an in-depth treatment of the social contract.

3. Teacher develops consequences for each rule. Consequences should be clear and specific; they should have a range of alternatives so that the teacher can always implement a consequence and still pay attention to individual needs; they should be designed not to punish, but to help students learn "cause and effect" in relation to rule violations; the consequences should relate as directly to the rules as possible and state "positives" (such and such will happen if the rule is followed, as well as "negatives." Chapter 5 will deal with consequences in more detail).

4. Students work in small groups to develop rules for the teacher's behavior. (The guidelines for rule development as stated above are shared with the class.)

5. Students develop consequences in case the teacher breaks or follows a rule.

6. Students in small groups develop rules regarding each other's behavior in class.

7. Students develop consequences that define what happens when any of these rules are broken or followed.

8. All of the rules and consequences are reviewed by the class to ensure proper understanding of what they mean. Role play is often a useful strategy to illustrate the exact meaning of a rule or consequence. For example, some students want the teacher *not* to yell. It is important for the teacher to speak louder and louder until agreement is reached as to what constitutes yelling.

9. Decision making occurs in which the class and teacher decide which of the proposed rules and consequences will become the contract. The decision-making process is as follows:

   a. *Unanimous Consensus* Each rule and consequence is read aloud and the teacher says "Raise your hand if you do *not* want this to be a rule (consequence)." If nobody raises their hands, then all agree this rule is wanted. Unanimous consensus has been reached. The teacher should vote as a member of the group at this time. If all flag rules have been shared prior to the decision making, this process should not cause conflict for the teacher. Remember that the teacher can "flag" student rules for teachers or for each other by including any rules that the teacher must have, or by eliminating any rule that is not acceptable.

   b. *Consensus* If anyone raises his hand, then go on to the next rule. Later on (after a check for unanimous consensus of all remaining rules and consequences has occurred), return to those for which unanimous consensus was not possible and ask those students who do not want the rule to again raise their hands. Ask each, ''Can you reword this rule in such a way that you would be able to accept it.'' This may ultimately lead to unanimous consensus. If there are one or two students who continue to reject the rule or consequence, ask them if they would be willing to live with the rule for a few weeks to see if it will be as bad as they imagine. If they say ''yes,'' then consensus (it's not everybody's first choice, but everybody agrees to live with it) has been reached.

c. *Vote*   On all remaining rules take a vote. But by contrast to the American way in which 50.1% of the vote can dictate for the remaining 49.9%, it is recommended that no rule be accepted unless at least 2/3 and preferably 3/4 of the class vote for it (as in Congressional voting for presidential impeachment, or voting on a constitutional amendment). Remember, the purpose of the social contract is not to have a contest but rather to maximize the chances that rules will be followed.

10. *Test for comprehension:* Each student takes an exam that tests his knowledge of the social contract. A perfect score is required for passing. (See page 75 for an example of a test.)

To solve the problem of students who try not to pass the test and to help promote responsibility among your students, we believe that all classroom privileges should be earned, not given. Privileges can be earned by passing the social contract test with a 100% score. This process helps your children appreciate the privileges because they are earned and motivates them to pass the test.

Some examples of privileges are:

1. going on field trips
2. being a hall monitor
3. passing out materials
4. going to the office with a note for principal
5. earning free time
6. getting choice of assignments
7. being a line leader
8. washing chalkboard
9. working in library
10. being a playground monitor

To summarize, here are the specific steps in the process of establishing Social Contracts:

Establishing Social Contracts

1. Teacher develops flag rules for students.
   a. Rules must be clear and specific.
2. Teacher develops negotiable rules for students.
3. Teacher develops a range of consequences.
   a. Each consequence must be clear, enforceable, and realistic.
   b. It is not designed to punish, although some students might perceive it that way. Each consequence should relate to the rule as directly as possible.
4. Students develop rules for teacher.
5. Students develop consequences for these rules.
6. Students develop rules for each other (and consequences).
7. Class uses decision-making process to form social contract.
8. Class is tested for comprehension.
9. Social contract is posted in the classroom.

EXAMPLE OF SOCIAL CONTRACT TEST*

NAME _____

Health 301

1. Besides a notebook or folder and clean, lined paper, what else do you have to bring to health class every day?
2. What do you have to bring to health class every Friday?
3. What time does your health class begin?
4. If you hand in your homework only one day late, what happens to your grade?
5. You cannot use the lav pass for the first _____ minutes of class.
6. What is the time limit on the lav pass?
7. When can you write or draw in a health book?
8. It's OK to write or draw on a desk in health.   T   F

---

* We wish to thank Judy White from the Rush-Henrietta School District, Rochester, New York, for this material.

9. If you wear a hat to health, what must you do with it?

10. It is possible to get an assigned seat in health for the rest of the year.   T   F

11. When is physical fighting OK in health?

12. For ''horsing around'' in health, you may eventually be put on class pass restriction.   T   F

13. In health, students must not destroy or harm the property of others.   T   F

14. When may students play a quiet game in health?

15. The free time on Wednesday is for games and talking. T   F

16. Mrs. White can change a rule when?

17. When can't Mrs. White give homework?

18. How much notice must be given for tests and quizzes?

19. When can Mrs. White give homework for punishment?

20. If two students have a problem in health, Mrs. White only has to listen to one side of the story.   T   F

21. Mrs. White can give homework on test and quiz days.   T   F

22. When can Mrs. White be late for class?

23. Mrs. White can give homework _____ times a week.

24. Tests and quizzes must be returned by Mrs. White within _____ days.

25. When a few students are bad, Mrs. White can punish whom?

26. It's OK for Mrs. White to read students' notes to herself. T   F

27. Mrs. White can read students' grades in front of the whole class. T   F

28. You need _____ plusses in a row for a free day coupon.

29. If you have 6 plusses in a row and then get a minus, you start counting plusses all over again.   T   F

Why a Social Contract?

The concept of a social contract is comparable to the process used in negotiating agreements between teachers and boards of education. We may easily forget that rules, when presented to students in an autocratic manner, can leave them feeling powerless and resentful. We wonder how teachers might have felt about the following list of rules that were commonplace in the last century. We trust that you will agree that the existence of such arbitrary policies led to the growth of unionism among teachers:

Rules for Teachers[3]

1872

1. Teachers each day will fill lamps, clean chimneys.
2. Each teacher will bring a bucket of water and a scuttle of coal for the day's session.
3. Make your pens carefully. You may whittle nibs to the individual taste of the pupils.
4. Men teachers may take one evening each week for courting purposes, or two evenings a week if they go to church regularly.
5. After ten hours in school, the teacher may spend the remaining time reading the Bible or other good books.
6. Women teachers who marry or engage in unseemly conduct will be dismissed.
7. Every teacher should lay aside from each pay a goodly sum of his earnings for his benefit during his declining years so that he will not become a burden on society.
8. Any teacher who smokes, uses liquor in any form, frequents pool or public halls, or gets shaved in a barber shop will give good reason to suspect his worth, intention, integrity and honesty.

Note: The teacher who performs his labour faithfully and without fault for five years will be given an increase of twenty-five cents per week in his pay, providing the Board of Education approves.

The Social Contract and Your Educational Philosophy

Every time we have taught a course or presented a workshop to teachers on discipline, there are some who for philosophical reasons have trouble accepting one or more of the steps of the social contract. Some educators find it appalling to allow students to have rules for the teacher, while others think it folly to make classroom privileges contingent upon passing the test for comprehension. Teachers of young children sometimes see the process as too dependent upon language skills that their children have yet to refine, while high school teachers sometimes view the process as too elementary.

It is not our intent in either a workshop setting or through the written word to dictate the doctrine of social contracts. We are believers in the process because those teachers (K-12) who have used it completely have been excited with the results they have obtained. We have also found that teachers with differing philosophies can use those parts of the social contract process that are consistent with their beliefs, while omitting those that just do not make good sense for them. There are several entry and exit points within the social contract that make this possible. Some of these are discussed in the following section.

Check Points for the Social Contract

1. CLEAR AND SPECIFIC RULES

Simply check the rules you currently have to make sure that they are clear and specific. Can you always tell whether or not a rule was broken? Can your students tell? Does your rule state what behaviors are acceptable as well as those that are not? If not, then simply making your rules clear and specific will improve discipline in your classroom.

2. SET SPECIFIC CONSEQUENCES IN ADVANCE

Most teachers do something when students break rules, even if that something is ignoring. But in many classes, consequences are not specified in advance so that when rules are broken, the teacher often appears arbitrary and unfair to the students. This perception can be minimized by letting students know what will happen before it happens, and by consistently implementing the consequence when misbehavior occurs. Check your consequences. Ask yourself, ''If I were a student in this classroom, how well would I know what might happen to me if I chose to break a rule?'' Does this teacher (you) mean business by following through, or does he just make idle threats that carry no weight? Do good things happen for students who follow rules or are students expected to behave only to avoid bad things happening to them? Are your consequences primarily designed to *teach* students how to behave more appropriately or to *punish* them for inappropriate

FIGURE ONE   *Here is an example of a rule that is not specific enough. How would you feel if you were caught breaking this rule? Your rules should not be this general. (Concept by Dr. Barry Culhane.)*

behavior? Are your consequences natural and logical where applicable? Teachers who have clear rules and specific consequences, even without student involvement, are less likely than their wishy-washy counterparts to have serious discipline problems in their classrooms.

3. LIMITED STUDENT DECISION MAKING

Teachers who are opposed to allowing students to generate rules and/or consequences for the teacher's behavior, but who value student involvement in decision making, can have students generate rules and consequences that they want for each other. They can then use the suggested decision-making paradigm to decide which of these rules and consequences will be implemented in the classroom.

4. STUDENTS MAKING RULES FOR TEACHERS

Teachers who like the idea of students developing rules and/or consequences for the teacher, but who fear a breakdown in their authority if they allowed students this freedom, can make student rule-making for teacher contingent upon the demonstration of the ability to follow the teacher's rules. The teacher can tell his students, "I am thinking of allowing you to make some rules and consequences for me. And I have decided that if, during the next fifteen days (for example), you are able to follow these rules (no more than X violations), then I will give you a chance to make some rules for me. You might want to start thinking about what rules you would like me to follow in our classroom."

5. YOUNG CHILDREN

For young children and others with limited language skills, more structure is often useful. The language you use to present your rules and consequences must naturally fit the ability of the children to understand. When it is their turn to create rules and consequences for you, teaching the process through the use of examples is suggested. For example, you might say, "I want to give you (students) a chance to have some rules and consequences for me, your teacher, and for each other. Now that might sound silly to some of you because usually children aren't allowed to tell grown-ups how to act. But I remember that when I was in first grade, I wished that my teacher would say hello to me in the morning, not yell at me when I made a mistake, let me choose which of my papers to hang in the room, and even though I was scared, to call my parents when I hit someone or to call someone else's parents when they hit me. So, what I want you to do is to think about (in small groups preferably) rules that you want me to follow or rules that you want each other to follow."

6. DETERMINING REWARDS AND PRIVILEGES

Occasionally, a teacher will have trouble thinking of privileges that exist in the classroom. Because they know of no privileges, they have difficulty pairing the passing of the "test for comprehension" with classroom privileges. If you cannot think of privileges in your classroom, then either they don't exist, which in itself can be a cause of discipline problems, or they do exist, but you are not aware of them. We have found that students are generally very adept at pointing out privileges. When groups of students are asked, "What privileges or good consequences exist in your classroom?" they often generate long lists. If they do not, then one way of discovering age appropriate privileges is to say, ''If rewards and privileges could exist in this classroom and you could determine what they will be, then what privileges would you choose?'' Hold a brainstorming session, and choose those privileges that were generated by your students that make you feel comfortable.

7. TIME INVESTMENT

Some teachers, especially those at the junior and senior high school levels, view the social contract process as too time-consuming. ''After all,'' they argue, ''I have five classes a day of 150 students and a lot of material to cover. I don't have time to do social contracts.'' Our response is that the full social contract is a time-consuming process that takes an average of three class periods per class to complete. In order for you to feel that your time is well spent, you need to ask yourself, ''If I counted the minutes and hours that I now spend in managing disruptive behavior during the course of an entire semester or trimester, would this come to at least the equivalent of three class periods?'' Our experience in observing many teachers working in various schools confirms that most teachers spend far more than three days dealing with discipline. In many junior and senior high classes, five to ten minutes of class time is wasted at the beginning of class trying to focus the attention of the students. At least another five to ten minutes is directed toward off-task behavior (students not paying attention, using put downs, arguing, etc.) during class time. This amounts to minimally ten to twenty minutes of a forty-five- to fifty-minute class period doing things other than what you are paid to do and want to do: teach!! If your school has a ten-week grading period and you are teaching in an average situation, then you are probably spending between ten and twenty class periods per ten-week interval reminding students to pay attention; being interrupted in the middle of a lesson; or reprimanding them for coming late to class, for fighting, for talking out of turn, and so on.

Naturally, you must be willing to believe that the three class periods used to develop the social contract will ultimately save you a lot of instructional time, and the only way to believe it, is to do it!

If you are still skeptical, that's fine! But we suggest you try an experiment. Choose your worst class, or the one that at the beginning of the semester you anticipate will be your worst, and try developing a social contract with them. We suggest this because if you begin with your worst class, then you have nothing to lose. The worst that can happen is that they stay as bad as they are. Perhaps your experience will parallel that of one high school English teacher who, after learning the social contract process, took our advice and implemented it with her worst class. Two months later, she said, "They've been terrific. It's my good kids that are driving me crazy!"

Although developing a social contract requires a commitment of time and involvement with your students, it is usually far less difficult to do (with all classes at a secondary level) than you might initially think. The idea of having five separate contracts (one for each class) is sometimes sufficiently scary to your sense of organization to make you avoid the process. However, when you consider each of the steps separately, you will find that your flag rules will be the same for all classes. Your other rules and consequences are also likely to be the same for all your classes. So, steps one through three require no more effort from you for all classes than for one. We have also found that student rules closely parallel each other (e.g., teacher should neither yell nor use put-downs with us; students aren't for hitting each other; teacher is not allowed to search our belongings without our permission; we want our papers returned to us within a reasonable time; teacher is expected in class on time).

Once the contract is developed for each class, it is no more difficult for you to implement than it is for you to have two to four different lesson plans. Actually, it is less difficult because there is no preparation time needed. In the same way that you shift gears for each class, even when you have the same level and the same course (assuming you do not teach each class in exactly the same way), you can shift your social contracts for each period. Most teachers simply have a large sheet of newsprint that contains the contract, and they attach the new contract on the wall each time the bell rings. Others give a handout to each student for them to attach to their class notebook.

Monitor System with Social Contract

Ms. McGlynn,* an intermediate level art teacher, used a social contract along with a creative system of behavior management to improve student behavior in the art room. She reports:

---

* We wish to thank Jeanne McGlynn of Sussex, New Jersey, for sharing her ideas.

The following information will illustrate how I used the social contract to improve a system I employed in my classroom. The "Monitor System" was developed to structure my overcrowded art room. I wanted to cut down on movement, talking while working, and bickering over materials. The idea is based on the children's natural inclination to choose a leader. I use this system with grades five, six, and seven at Lounsberry Hollow Middle School in Vernon, N.J. Each grade level attends art classes every day for a 13-week cycle. The class periods are approximately 40 minutes long for grades five and six, and 35 minutes for grade seven. The art room is set up with 6 tables which seat 5 students.

Social Contract

1. Each table group will have a monitor who is in charge of getting materials, distributing them, supervising behavior according to the classroom rules, collecting materials, and cleaning up.
2. The monitor is voted on by the members of the group based on his leadership qualities, dependability, or whatever other qualities the group feels constitutes a good leader.
3. All members of the group must cooperate with the monitor.
4. The monitor must fulfill the duties and responsibilities of his position.
5. No one else in the group may leave his seat, unless instructed by the monitor or the teacher.

The above social contract has been set up by the teacher in this situation as flag rules. I feel that they are necessary for effective management of the monitor system.

INCENTIVE

The incentive I used to encourage successful cooperation in the group is the merit/demerit system. Each table is given a table number. These numbers are used for identification and reference only. The groups are referred to as Table #1, Table #2, Table #3, Table #4, Table#5, and Table #6, instead of Bobby's table, Jane's table, etc. At the end of every class period the table that most successfully worked as a team gets a merit. This is indicated by a plus sign in a column in my record book. The column lists the table number and the individual members of the group. When a table receives a merit, every individual in that group receives an extra credit to be calculated into his grade at the end of the cycle. This is particularly attractive to the student who does not feel he can achieve success by his art work alone.

A demerit is received by a group that has broken the contract in any way. Demerits are not given out daily. They are given out as the last in the sequence of consequences. They are for the purpose of deterring uncooperative behavior within the group. The demerit stage is seldom reached. Problems are usually settled before the group gets to this point.

Consequences for Failure to Comply with Monitor System Contract

1. The monitor verbally reinforces to the group that he is the person in charge.

2. The group reminds the monitor that he is the person who accepted the responsibility of being the monitor.

3. The group has a consultation with the teacher present to find out what the problem is and how to solve it. The teacher will act as arbitrator, or coach.

4. Failure to resolve problems through an agreeable compromise results in a group demerit.

5. If the problems continue, the group may choose to vote for a new monitor.

An Example of a Problem and Resolution

Table 4, Grade 7
Members of the group: Don, Debbie, Billy, Lori
Monitor: Jay

Lori:	Jay! I need a ruler, get me one now!
Jay:	Tough, get it yourself, I'm busy right now.
Lorie:	You know I can't get it myself. If I get up we won't get the extra credit.
Debbie:	Yeah stupid! Table #2 got the merit twice this week, and I really need the extra credit.
Billy:	Jay, you promised us you'd be a good monitor, get Lori's ruler.
Jay:	O.K., get off my back.

(Jay gets the ruler, gives it to Lori, and gets involved in his project again.)

Don:	Oh no! I spilled my waterjar on the table. Jay get me a sponge quick!

Jay: In a minute, wait 'till I finish this.

Don: Now! My picture is getting all wet!

(Jay ignores Don's dilemma for a few minutes, then slowly gets up for the sponge.)

Don: Mrs. McGlynn, Jay is a lousy monitor. We want a new one. I can do the job better than him anyday.

Mrs. McGlynn: Let's meet after class for a consultation.

(It has been established through the dialogue that consequence 1 and 2 have failed to effect a change. Therefore the teacher suggests consequence 3.)

During the consultation the group airs the following problems with Jay.

1. He is too slow in getting equipment.
2. He doesn't remember what to get for the group.
3. He doesn't act fast in emergencies.

Jay felt the following problems with the group.

1. The group treated him like a slave.
2. The group wasn't helping keep the table area clean.
3. Their "emergencies" kept him away from his art project.

These recommendations were agreed upon as compromises that would have to be made by each individual member of the group.

1. The group would be nicer to Jay when asking for equipment.
2. The group would anticipate what they would need for the period at the beginning so as not to disturb Jay too frequently.
3. The group would write down on a sheet of scrap paper their list of materials for the period to help Jay remember what to bring back.
4. Jay would assign an alternate monitor to help during emergencies when he was not readily available.
5. Jay would delegate authority in the group to facilitate more efficient clean up.

All members of the group signed the agreement and shook hands. Each class period that the solutions are not put into effect because of lack of cooperation, a demerit will be given to Table #4. Another consultation is set up for the following week to check progress.

Sharing the Social Contract

The social contract is effective because it serves as a communication mechanism for the teacher and the students in the classroom. Both the teacher and the students communicate their needs and expectations through the development of the social contract. Once completed, the contract serves to provide clarity and promote understanding of the rules and consequences. There are three other audiences who should also be part of the social contract communication process: parents, administrators, and substitute teachers.

Parents

Parents typically become involved in discipline matters with their children once a rule has been violated. Often, a parent, teacher, and student conference is one of the consequences used in the social contract. When parents are contacted by schools and/or teachers to deal with a discipline problem, some become defensive and protective of their children. Some become overly upset with their children while others apathetically ignore the event. We have found that it helps communication with parents to send them a copy of the social contract.

One method of parent communication is to write a cover letter explaining the social contract process, include a copy of your class social contract and enclose a return slip indicating that they have read and understood the contract. Enclosing a phone number for questions is also helpful.

Another method is to inform parents of the contract process prior to its development and invite parents to include any rules and/or consequences they feel might be helpful. Then include some of the parent rules when you and your class engage in the process. It is a good idea to include at least one parent rule if you use this approach to demonstrate your willingness to use parental suggestions. Once the contract is completed, you can follow the same steps as the example cited above.

A third alternative for parent communication is to use parents' night at the school to explain the contract process and to share your classroom social contract. You can use the mail method for those parents who do not attend.

Once parents have seen the contract and understand how it will work, you have increased your chances of parent cooperation when their child breaks a rule. They have an understanding of what is expected of their children and what consequences were agreed to by the class. Thus, they know exactly what their role is, should a child break a rule. Should you find that a parent is overly upset with you for "doing something to his child," you can refer to the contract and explain your decision from a point of mutual understanding. If the parents are needed to fulfill a consequence, the chances of the parents cooperating will be strengthened if they have a prior understanding of their responsibilities.

Administrators

Administrators, like parents, can be informed of your social contract process and should see your contract once it is developed. This is especially important if you include administrators as part of your consequences. You should reach a full understanding and agreement with your administration of any consequence that involves them. Even if they are not directly involved in your consequences, you can help yourself by informing your administration of your discipline plan. We find that clarity between teachers and administrators around the issue of discipline helps counteract the stress associated with feelings of isolation and lack of administrative support described in Chapter 3.

Substitute Teachers

Students' eyes typically light up when a substitute teacher takes over for an absent teacher. Armed with lesson plans left by the teacher and a "good luck" wish by the administration, substitutes must rely on patience, good humor, and a high tolerance for ambiguity as well as, in many cases, mild chaos. We have found a significant improvement when substitutes are given a copy of your social contract, so that the substitute will know exactly what is expected of your students and what he can do about it if your students break the rules. Most substitutes find they spend more time dealing with behavior than with subject matter. You can make life easier for them by providing them with classroom guidelines. If substitutes have been informed of your social contract the administrator can then support the substitute if a student or two becomes overly rambunctious in your absence. It is also helpful to include a rule in your contract that stipulates that all other rules are in effect if a substitute is present.

Social Contract Timetable

The following timetable is an example (which may be modified to fit your needs) of how to set up a social contract.

A. Before class starts:	Develop your flag and negotiable rules and consequences.
B. Day one (this may occur at the beginning of school, or during the year:	Explain to the class the process you will use to develop your contract. Share what makes a good rule and consequence. Assign for homework that each student develop one rule and consequence for you and for each other. Your "flag" rules are now in effect. (Approx. time: 10–15 minutes)
C. Day two:	Collect assignments. After school, organize the students' rules, eliminating duplications.
D. Day three:	Share all the rules and consequences, (including your flag rules) and negotiable rules. Discuss, role play, or define any rules that are unclear. (Approx. time: full class period)
E. Day four:	Use decision-making process to determine which remaining rules and consequences will become part of the contract. (Approx. time: 20–25 minutes)
F. Day five:	Administer social contract test. (Approx. time: 15 minutes) After school, correct test. Send letter home to parents, and inform your administration of your contract. Set up a meeting with administra-

	tion to discuss any consequences that involve them.
G. Day six:	Return tests, readminister test to any students who failed to get 100%. Post the contract in class.
H. One week later:	Renegotiate any rule and consequence that is not working. Add new rules and consequences as needed.
I. Once each following month:	Hold a social contract review meeting with class. Discuss how the social contract is working. You may add or delete rules and consequences at these meetings. Your students should have the same input as they did at the initial contract development meeting on day four.

The above example may be modified in many ways. One of the most common variations is to use small groups during class time for the development of student rules for teacher and for each other. This variation works more effectively than homework for younger students. With proper planning, a social contract can be completed in as little as two full class periods. By spending time during the first week of its development, you will find that the contract becomes an effective communication tool that will save you a great deal of time for the remainder of the year.

Examples of Social Contracts

What follows are several social contracts developed by teachers with their students. At the top of each is the grade level and type of class (regular or special needs). It is not our intent to judge each contract but rather to give you samples from some classes that have used the process in which the teacher has reported behavioral improvement attributed to the contract. One other important point needs to be stated. We have found that most of the power of the social contract resides in the process, not in the content (the rules and consequences). By this we mean that the involvement of students with the teacher in defining acceptable classroom standards and the process of reaching agreement on these standards are more important than the content of those standards. Once again, these samples are intended only as examples of the end point reached by various classes in developing their rules and consequences. The content of your contract may well be quite different from those that follow.

EXAMPLE 1   *1st Grade Low-Achieveing Class*

Partial Social Contract

RULE

We will sit together on the rug for story. Legs will be crossed, arms folded, and there will be no moving around once you sit.

Consequences:

1. Teacher places you on rug.
2. You must sit at your desk.
3. Time-out (removal out of the room).

RULE

Children will not fight, push, or scream on the playground.

Consequences:

1. Sitting on the bench.
2. The whole class goes inside early.
3. Not going out at all.

EXAMPLE 2   *2nd Grade Regular Class*

Rules and Consequences for Children

RULE 1

Children must not yell out. They should raise their hands and wait to be called upon.

a. The teacher will remind children not to yell out, but wait to be called on.
b. The teacher will not call on children who yell out.

RULE 2

Children must not fight, hit, or push in school. They should talk to each other instead.

    a. The teacher will remind children of our rule.

    b. The child will go to a time-out seat.

RULE 3

There must be no throwing of anything in the room. Hand things to each other.

    a. The child must pick up what is thrown.

    b. The child must apologize to others and clean up the floor.

RULE 4

Children must do their homework. This will help them learn. (They will be excused only twice.)

    a. The teacher will remind children of our rule.

    b. The child will have to make up homework.

    c. The teacher will call the parents.

RULE 5

All school work should be done neatly.

    a. The teacher will not accept any messy work.

    b. The child will do the work over.

RULE 6

There is to be no running in the classroom or hall. You must walk.

    a. The teacher will remind child of the rule.

    b. The child will have to walk instead.

RULE 7

Children may get drinks only when their work is done and only one child at a time.

a. The teacher will remind child of the rule.

b. No drinks will be allowed for a while.

RULE 8

Children may sharpen their pencils early in the morning or right after recess.

a. The teacher will remind the child of the rule.

b. The child will have to apologize to the group that's reading.

RULE 9

Children must hang clothing on hooks—not on floor. This keeps our room neat.

a. Child will have to pick up clothing.

b. Child will have to clean up whole clothing area.

RULE 10

Children must ask permission and not take other's things.

a. The child must return what he took.

b. The child must apologize to others.

RULE 11

Children must not walk around room when others are working. They should stay in their own seats.

a. The teacher will remind the child of the rule.

b. The child will sit in a time-out seat.

RULE 12

Children should have pencils and crayons in school every day.

a. The child will be reminded of the rule.

b. A child may have to sit without a pencil unless a neighbor loans him one.

Rule 13

Children must not copy anyone's work unless the teacher says it's O.K.

   a. Child's seat will be moved.

   b. Child will have to do work over.

Rule 14

There is to be no loud talking or noises when others are working.

   a. The teacher will remind children of the rule.

   b. Child will go to time-out seat.

Rule 15

All children must be quiet during a test.

   a. Teacher will remind child of the rule.

   b. Child will have test taken away.

Rule 16

When class work is all done, child may choose one idea from the morning or afternoon chart or he may sit quietly in his seat.

   a. Teacher will remind child of the rule.

   b. Child will lose free time.

Rule 17

Children must clean up after they use games or puzzles or art supplies.

   a. The teacher will remind children of the rule.

   b. Child will not be allowed to use games or art supplies for a week.

Rules for Each Other

Rule 1

Name calling is not allowed. You must call each other by their own names.

   a. Remind others to call you by your own name.

   b. Child will have to apologize.

RULE2

Children must ask permission to borrow something.

   a. Remind child to ask permission.

   b. Child will not be allowed to borrow that day.

RULE 3

Fighting is not allowed. Children should talk and tell each other they are angry.

   a. Child should apologize.

   b. Time-out seat.

RULE 4

Other children's desks and books are not for writing on.

   a. Erase or clean desks and books.

   b. Clean up all desks in row.

RULE 5

Children should be polite to each other.

   a. Remind child of rule.

   b. Child must apologize to other child.

Rules and Consequences for Teacher

RULE 1

The teacher must give homework only four nights a week and not on a Friday or holiday.

   a. Child should remind teacher of rule.

   b. No homework for a week.

RULE 2

The teacher must call on children by their names.

a. Remind teacher of rule.

b. Teacher will apologize.

Rule 3

Teacher must give jobs to different children each week.

a. Remind teacher of rule.

b. Teacher must choose different children.

Example 3 *4th Grade Bilingual Population Class*

Social Contract 1980–1981

In an attempt to promote a harmonious classroom, we the students and teacher of 4K have established and agreed upon the following social contract by means of discussion and through the use of a democratic voting process.

We agree to review this contract at least once per month or at any time the majority of the members feel it is necessary to do so.

Student's signature _____

Teacher's signature _____

Parent's signature _____

Rules for the Hall

1. Be quiet—whisper.
2. Always walk.
3. Keep your hands and feet to yourself.
4. Keep to the right in a single file.

Consequences:

1. The first time anyone breaks the above rules, that person will receive a warning reminder.

2. If anyone breaks any of the above rules more than once in any particular day, he or she will be given a ticket:

   - 1st ticket–$1\frac{1}{2}$ days after school session for practicing rules
   - 2nd ticket–2 days   ''   ''   ''   ''   ''   ''
   - 3rd ticket–3 days   ''   ''   ''   ''   ''   ''
   - 4th ticket–4 days   ''   ''   ''   ''   ''   ''

Rules for the Classroom

1. All daily assignments must be completed by the following day or a zero is placed in the grade book. If the assignment is not done by the second day after, the zero will remain. If the assignment is completed by the second day you will receive your regular grade. Students who hand in more than two late assignments in any one week may be kept in at noon to complete such work.

2. Use hand signals to go to the bathroom or for a drink.

3. During class work periods, the room is to be quiet; no visiting.

Consequences:

- Two warnings will be given to anyone who forgets to be quiet.
- If a person continues to talk, the offender will be asked to work in a separate work area.
- A 1/2 hour session of behavior practice may be given.
- Four violations of the rule and parents will be called for a conference.

4. Arguments should be settled by talking. No fighting. If you are angry, you can tell the teacher or write how you feel.

Consequences:

- Warning.
- Behavior practice 1/2 hour after school 1 day to a week.
- Check in behavior on the report card.
- Parent-teacher-principal-student conference.

5. Help keep our room neat and orderly by:
   - Keeping your desk clean inside and out.
   - Cleaning up the floor around your desk.
   - Doing your room job.
   - Hanging up your outer clothing and bags.

Consequences:

Everyone who follows our class rules during the week will receive one of the following:
   15 minutes free time or
   a popcorn party or
   a certificate to reward good behavior.

6. A student will be recognized to speak when he or she raises his or her hand and waits to be called on.

Consequences:

- If he forgets, he will be given a reminder.
- If he forgets a second time in the same discussion, he will not be allowed to participate in *that* discussion.

Student Rules for Students

1. Do not push.
2. No spit balls.
3. Do not tease or call people names.
4. Ask permission to use other people's belongings.

Consequences:

- The first time a rule is broken, the student will receive a warning reminder.
- If a student breaks one of these rules a second time in the same day, the student who has been offended may choose to give the offender one of these consequences:
  a. Miss your Friday reward.
  b. Receive one 1/2 hour of behavior practice.

Student Rules for Teacher

1. Do not say our grades aloud.
   Consequence: An extra popcorn party.
2. Teacher should keep calm—do not yell.
   Consequence: The teacher will be given a warning reminder. If the teacher yells a second time the same day, she will have to run around the field 5 times.
3. Teacher should check our papers in private.
   Consequence: Read two chapters from the current book she is reading to the class.
4. Remember to do the pledge.
   Consequence: If you forget, play Simon says 10 minutes before lunch.

5. Talk to the students in private when they have done something wrong.
   Consequence: Apologize to them with an ice cream or a treat.
6. Welcome us with a smile every morning.
   Consequence: Give us a smiley sticker.

EXAMPLE 4   *5th Grade Class*

Our Social Contract

RULES FOR EACH OTHER

1. People are not for pushing and shoving.
   a. Take away recess time.
   b. Time-out place—10 minutes.
   c. Send to principal.
   d. Notify parents.
2. Put-downs and name calling hurt feelings.
   a. Verbal apology.
   b. Written apology.
   c. Other person calls himself by that name.
   d. Put "I hurt" sign up.
3. Fights and other bothersome acts are to be settled by discussion.
   a. Write angry thoughts on a piece of paper and tear it up.
   b. Write a paragraph and read it to the class.
   c. Send to the principal.
   d. Contact parents.
   e. Loss of recess for one week.
   f. Talk about it—hear each side.
   g. Time-out place—15 minutes.
   h. Remain after school.
4. Try to remember what you are supposed to be doing "now."
   a. Warning.
   b. Write about it.
5. Tattling is forbidden except in an emergency.
   a. Warning.
   b. Teacher refuses to punish child tattled upon.

6. Permission must be asked of other and be granted by them before borrowing anything.
   a. Warning.
   b. Return borrowed item.
   c. Apologize as well as return item.
7. No pushing, shoving, or cutting in when lining up.
   a. Go to end of line.
   b. Hold teacher's hand.
   c. Remain behind for time specified.

RULES FOR CHILDREN

1. Homework must be done on time.
   a. Noon make-up instead of recess.
   b. Remain after school.
   c. Go to office to do it.
   d. Homework letter to parents.
2. Cheating does not help us learn.
   a. Re-do work.
   b. Subtract credit.
   c. Contact parents.
3. Only one person may speak at a time.
   a. Warning.
   b. Time-out—10 minutes.
   c. Write paragraph about rule.
4. Children must work and/or read when visitors enter room and speak with teacher.
   a. Warning.
   b. Extra homework.
   c. Write paragraph on courtesy.
5. Desks, chairs, and books are not for damaging.
   a. Clean assigned number of desks and chairs.
   b. Clean book and/or replace cover.
   c. Letter to parents.
6. Walk silently and to the right in the halls.
   a. Warning.

  b. Walk corridor a specified number of times.

  c. Go to end of your line.

  d. Go to end of last teacher's class line.

7. Gum chewing is not allowed.

  a. Warning.

  b. Write a story about gum using the encyclopedia.

  c. No recess.

Teacher: _____

Student: _____

Parent: _____

FLAG RULES

1. Pencils may be sharpened at the beginning and/or end of the morning and afternoon.
Permission is required at all other times.

2. Only *one* may be out to the bathroom at a time.

3. Teacher's desk is off limits unless you're asked to come by the teacher.

4. Should you return to the room from a resource room you must take seat quietly and continue with work.

5. Reading groups are not to be interrupted.

6. You may not leave your seat without permission.

RULES FOR TEACHER

1. No weekend homework.

2. Each child's desk is off limits for the teacher.

EXAMPLE 5   *Middle School Neurologically Impaired Class*

Social Contract

RULE 1

Students will arrive in class on time.

Consequences:

1. Three minutes will be allowed for those returning from gym or for an emergency.
2. After 5 minutes, the office will be notified and student will be paged over the inter-com.
3. After 7 minutes, student will only be admitted with a late pass.
4. Unexcused lost time will be made up after 3 P.M.

RULE 2

Students must arrive in class with a pencil.

Consequences:

1. One pencil per month (if needed) is issued to each student.
2. Student leaves a deposit (five cents or a personal item valued by student) for each additional pencil. Deposit is returned when pencil is returned to teacher.
3. Parent is asked to supply pencils which will be kept and issued to student by the teacher.

RULE 3

Outer wear must be left in homeroom or locker.

Consequences:

1. First infraction—student returns to locker or homeroom with garment.
2. Second infraction—time spent returning to homeroom or locker will be made up during recess period.
3. Third infraction—time spent returning with garment will be made up after 3 P.M.

RULE 4

Classroom assignments are to be completed in class.

Consequences:

1. Student deliberately wasting time will complete assignments during recess period.

2. Assignments not completed during recess period will be completed for homework.

3. Assignments not completed for homework will be completed after 3 P.M.

4. Students who complete a week's assignments will receive two tokens on Friday. Ten tokens may be redeemed for an ice cream treat.

Rule 5

Put-downs, 4-letter (swear) words, and name calling will not be tolerated in class.

Consequences:

1. Student must apologize for action to offended student.
2. Student must apologize to class for action.
3. Student may be sent to hall for "time-out" period.

Rule 6

Students must settle differences verbally.

Consequences:

1. Those engaged in physical fighting will be warned and separated.
2. At second infraction, student will be sent to "time-out."
3. If a student is hurt, one or both parties may be suspended at the discretion of the Vice Principal.

Rule 7

Students may change the location of their desks.

Consequences:

1. Student will warn teacher of the impending change. If there is room at the new location, teacher may not object.
2. If teacher cannot tolerate the new move, she must make students aware of her reasons for objecting.
3. Students may vote on the validity of her reasons. Teacher will abide by vote of class.

Rule 8

Teacher may not open student's desk or lockers without student's permission.

Consequences:

1. Teacher will be warned.
2. Student will have permission to open teacher's desk.
3. Student may ask for and receive public apology from teacher.

Rule 9

The chewing of gum or candy will only be allowed in the cafeteria.

Consequences:

1. Student will be warned and asked to dispose of the candy or gum in his mouth.
2. Student will share all remaining candy or gum with the class.
3. Student will throw away all remaining candy or gum in his possession.

Rule 10

Student will raise his hand in order to attract the teacher's attention.

Consequences:

1. Student will be warned that calling out is not the way to attract teacher's attention.
2. Teacher will not respond to student until hand is raised.

Example 6   *6th Grade Social Studies Class*

Social Contracts for Students

1. Each student is responsible for coming to class prepared with pen, pencil, notebook, and an assignment pad.
   a. Verbal reminder of rule.
   b. Classwork assigned for homework.
2. All homework assignments due on date established by the teacher.

   a. Verbal reminder of rule.

   b. Complete work on following day, accepting one grade lower.

   c. Accept a zero for lack of work.

   d. Three zeros in one marking period: conference with student, parent, and teacher to find a solution to the problem.

3. Only one person speaks at the same time during a class lesson.

   a. Verbal reminder of rule.

   b. Have student repeat what the interrupted person just said.

   c. Student must refrain from participating verbally during the remainder of the class period.

4. Student must raise hand and be recognized by the teacher before speaking in class during a lesson.

   a. Verbal reminder of rule.

   b. Student will apologize to the teacher.

   c. Student remains after school for a conference with the teacher.

5. Copying another student's work during a test is not allowed.

   a. Reminder—tap on shoulder.

   b. Remove the student to another location in the classroom.

   c. Accept a zero for the test.

6. Work considered sloppy and inappropriate by the teacher will not be accepted.

   a. Verbal reminder of rule.

   b. Paper rewritten for homework.

   c. Paper rewritten after school in class.

7. When teacher is talking to a guest in the classroom, student must remain quiet.

   a. Verbal reminder of rule.

   b. Student will apologize to the teacher.

   c. Student will apologize to the entire class.

   d. Student must rewrite the social contract he signed.

Rules and Consequences for Teacher

1. Teacher should not assign homework on Friday.

   a. Verbal reminder of rule.

   b. No homework on Monday.

    c. No homework assigned for the next two nights during the next week.

2. The teacher can call on students who raise their hands to avoid embarrassing those students who do not know the answers.

    a. Teacher cannot ask any questions for five minutes.

    b. The student does not have to answer.

3. The teacher cannot embarrass a student in front of the class.

    a. Warning.

    b. An apology.

    c. Five minutes free time for the entire class.

4. Teacher must allow students to work in groups with students of their choice at least once during a marking period.

    a. Verbal reminder.

    b. Students can form their own group for the entire next marking period.

5. Teacher must be understanding and patient, not yelling at a student for not understanding instructions just given, providing student was paying attention.

    a. Reminder of rule.

    b. Teacher apologizes to student.

    c. Teacher apologizes to the entire class.

6. Teacher should allow some class time for projects.

    a. Verbal reminder of rule.

    b. Allow entire period the next school day for working on the projects.

EXAMPLE 7   *Senior High English Class (partial)*
RULES FOR STUDENTS BY TEACHER

1. Students will be in their seats no later than three minutes after the bell rings.

Consequences:

- Reminder
- Warning
- Work will be made up after school
- A meeting will be held after school to help student learn to be in class on time

   • For each week of no tardiness, the students can choose any book they want (by vote) to discuss on Friday discussion time

2. Students will hand in homework on the day it is due.

   a. Homework must be handed in by the end of the day

   b. Homework must be made up after school

   c. Homework will not be accepted

3. No fooling around, which means no acting in a way which interferes with the class process; i.e., no hitting, fighting, touching, loud talking, dropping things, leaving seat without permission, making noises.

   a. Warning

   b. Discussion after class, student learns new ways of behaving including practice

   c. Discussion with parents and student

   d. Discussion with parents and principal

STUDENT RULES FOR TEACHER

1. Students can choose between at least four books for all reading assignments.

   a. Reminder

   b. No one has to read the teacher's selection (but a book must be read for the assignment)

2. Teacher must tell why something is good or bad, not only say good or bad.

   a. Warning

   b. Teacher must give up a class period and set up 5-minute interviews with each student who wants more feedback on their papers

STUDENT RULES FOR EACH OTHER

1. No copying homework.

   a. Teacher will be informed

   b. Principal will be informed

   c. Parents will be informed

2. Put-downs in class are forbidden, if you want to comment about an individual, you must say something nice.

   a. The person who made the put-down must do one nice thing for the person put down

   b. The violator will be assigned a book for the Friday discussion by the person put down

EXAMPLE 8   *High School Home Economics Class*

Social Contracts

TEACHER RULES FOR STUDENTS

1. Each student is responsible for coming to class with paper, pen, and text each day.

Consequence:

   a. First offense—will result in warning.

   b. Second offense—you must give collateral such as shoe, ring, wallet to borrow a pen.

   c. Third offense—student will be responsible for making up work.

   d. Fourth offense—will result in one point from the average.

   e. Non-offenders will earn one point toward average.

2. Teacher will allow any student to miss one homework assignment per marking period without being penalized.

   a. First offense—no penalty.

   b. Second offense—class time in order to get homework caught up.

   c. Third offense—deficiency notice sent home.

   d. Fourth offense—grade is an automatic failure.

3. Keep your hands and feet to yourself. Arguments and disputes are to be settled through talking rather than fighting.

   a. First offense—verbal reminder of rule.

   b. Second offense—time-out from group participation within classroom or until student feels ready to return.

   c. Third offense—removal to principal's office.

4. Only one person speaks at a time.

    a. First offense—reminder of rule.

    b. Second offense—no recognition for 10 minutes.

    c. Third offense—no recognition for remainder of lesson.

5. No smoking in Home Economics House or on school grounds.

    a. First offense—reprimand.

    b. Second offense—send to office of vice-principal.

6. It is the responsibility of each student to bring his own equipment.

    a. First offense—borrow equipment with understanding that student will forfeit his seat for the one-hour class.

7. Students must wear their aprons in order to cook.

    a. First offense—relegated to such tasks as setting the table.

    b. Second offense—does the dishes.

    c. Third offense—does all the cleanup, stove, table, cabinets.

8. Students must be quiet after bell rings.

    a. First offense—verbal discussion to be quiet.

    b. Second offense—when bell rings for lunch, use three minutes of their lunch period.

STUDENT RULES FOR TEACHER

1. Teachers may not use a degrading or insulting remark when disciplining a student.

Consequence:

    a. Student informs the teacher that she/he hurt his/her feelings.

    b. Teacher must apologize privately to the student.

    c. Teacher to apologize to student in front of whole class.

STUDENT RULES FOR EACH OTHER

1. Use other's property only with their permission.

Consequence:

    a. Apology as well as the return or replacement of lost/ damaged or borrowed property within a reasonable amount of time.

    b. Seat change.

2. Students will be in their seats when bell rings.

Consequence:

    a. Stay after school for late time or coming in for early detention.

    b. Bring a note in from home explaining why you can't get here on time.

3. All non-eaten food that students do not want and they made is to be refrigerated, not left in oversize pan and in the open to spoil.

Consequence:

    a. First offense—may not have leftovers next day.

    b. Second offense—practice cleaning after eating.

    c. Third offense—notify parents with threat of removal from class for a day.

4. Students should not annoy others by being a general nuisance.

Consequence:

    a. First offense—verbal agreement.

    b. Second offense—go to study hall until he was ready to come back and conform.

    c. Third offense—cannot make up work missed because he was a nuisance.

5. Students should not deface property: example, getting up at 4 A.M. and painting "Class of 1981" on the roof of school.

Consequence:

    a. First offense—apology to the Board of Education and fine of $400.00 to clean the roof.

6. Students should not cheat during an exam.

Consequence:

    a. First offense—have the exam removed; taking half of the grade obtained in the time spent on the exam; coming in after school and taking a new exam.

As you can see from these examples, social contracts come in a variety of forms, each with their own unique rules and consequences. There is also a great deal of similarity between them. From the variety of grades and classes, you can see that it is possible to develop a social contract for your class.

Conclusion

The teachers who have used social contracts tell us quite emphatically that they make a difference. They find that students break rules less and that they themselves can spend more time doing what they are paid to do—to teach. We encourage you to try as much of the process as you want and judge the power of the process for yourself. Ultimately, the process becomes easier and easier each time you and your students experience it. And the more it becomes internalized as part of your teaching style, the more effective you will be as a classroom manager.

For the Administrator

Social contracts are an integral part of the Three Dimensional Process. As the administrator in your building or district, you can be a helpful resource for those teachers who wish to develop social contracts in their classrooms. You can help the teachers by reviewing their proposed rules and consequences before they are introduced to the students. Help clarify any rules that are not clear, see if the list is complete, and check to see if the consequences are logical and natural (see Chapter 5, Consequences) rather than punishments.

Clarify with each teacher who establishes a social contract what your role will be should any student break a rule. Specify very clearly what you will do if a student is sent to you, and under what circumstances you will agree to see a student who misbehaves. You can use the social contract model to develop a contract between you and your teachers related to your responsibilities about discipline.

Once the social contracts have been established you can offer support by checking to see how it's going, by teaming up teachers who have tried the social contract with those teachers who are ready to try for the first time. You can set up classroom visitations so that teachers in the school or district can observe the social contract in operation. This process can be enhanced by choosing as a model for discipline one classroom, which you set up in close cooperation with the teacher. The model can be used for experimentation and to demonstrate the effectiveness of the social contract.

If you wish to set up a school-wide contract for your building, begin by reaching agreement on rules and consequences with your faculty. Then once you have worked through the school-wide issues (and this will be the most difficult part of the process), you can invite student input on the rules for both teachers, and for students. You might even encourage a rule or two for the administrators to follow. The key to the success of a school-wide contract is that everyone on the faculty agrees to honor it, even if it is not everyone's first choice. If you decide not to develop a school-wide contract, then you can check your school-wide rules for clarity and specificity and see that they state what should be done as well as what should not be done. Also examine your school-wide consequences to see that they are clear, natural, and logical and that they provide a range of alternatives. We recommend that if you do not already do so, you should give every student a test for your school rules to ensure that there is a clear understanding about what is expected from the students.

When a substitute teacher is assigned to a class, see that he is given a copy of the classroom social contract. If the teacher does not have a social contract, then at least provide the rules and consequences. Providing behavioral guidelines are equally important if not more so than providing lesson plans.

Finally, see that every parent in your school knows what each teacher's social contract is, what their rules and consequences are, or what their plan for discipline is. You might also see that every parent is informed about your school's rules and consequences. When a parent questions you about what is happening with his child, use the contract as a basis of mutual understanding and agreement. That way, you will always have a common ground to begin discussion, and there will be more of an emphasis on problem solving than on blaming.

References

1. White, R., and Lippitt, R., "Leader Behaviour and Member Reaction in Three 'Social Climates,'" In Cartwright, D., and Zander, A., eds, *Group Dynamics in Researched Theory* (2nd ed.), New York: Harper and Row, 1960.

2. Curwin, R. L., and Mendler, A. N., *The Discipline Book: A Complete Guide to School and Classroom Management*, Reston, Va.: Reston Publishing Co., 1980.

3. Register Print Shop Century Village.

FIVE

Consequences

*T*he social contract process depends on the development of effective rules and consequences. The rules clearly state what behavior is expected, and the consequences clarify what will happen if the agreed upon expectation are or are not met.

Classroom teachers often think of consequences after a rule has been broken. The problem with this method is that it leads to students' uncertainty, annoyance or anger, and does not help the students learn to be good decision-makers. It is, therefore, preferable to have your consequences spelled out in advance.

Many of the teachers we work with tell us that when they develop social contracts they have little trouble thinking of effective rules, but thinking of good, effective consequences is more difficult. Teachers are often without sufficient guidelines to aid them in having consequences that work. For a consequence to be effective, it must meet the following four criteria:

1. It is clear and specific. All students and the teacher know exactly what will happen when a rule is broken.

2. It has a range of alternative options for the teacher that enables him/her to implement a consequence consistently while treating his/her students as individuals.

3. It relates to the rule as directly as possible.

4. It is designed to teach, not to punish.

Let us examine these criteria in more depth, beginning with the last one. Much of the research that investigates the effectiveness of punishments tells us that punishments stop short-term misbehavior but are ineffective for long-term change. Most of us have experienced or know of someone who has received a speeding ticket. Usually the speeder slows down for a hundred miles or so, and then slowly builds up speed again, but is far more careful to look for police cars. Radar detectors are sold mostly to convicted speeders who prefer taking extravagant measures as a way to avoid getting caught again. Similarly, punishments in classrooms can work well for a short time but have little effect on improving behavior over a longer period of time. Punishment teaches the importance of not getting caught!

What is the difference between a consequence and a punishment? While they often appear to be similar, there are significant differences. The first significant difference is that a punishment is a form of retribution. Its goal is to make the rule violator pay for his misconduct. Punishments have their roots in the philosophy that students will avoid bad behavior to avoid being punished. Fear is the prime motivator.

Our view is that punishments offer an available release of tension for the person giving the punishment. Scolding, yelling, hitting, and feeling avenged are all common releases for the pent up anger we feel when disruptive students are constantly challenging us. They make us feel frustrated, agitated, and annoyed. None of us likes being confronted, accused, or defied; nor do we enjoy being cast in the role of the "disciplinarian." We find ourselves resorting to punishments that we "know" are ineffective as a way of expressing the negatively toned emotions that we feel when students misbehave. Punishment is not worth the short-term pleasure of ventilating our anger, which only creates resentment and ultimately more rule breaking in the future. Teachers need to find non-destructive methods of releasing their anger when working with difficult students (see Chapter 3).

Consequences are directly related to the rule. They are both logical and natural, and they provide help for the rule violator to learn acceptable behavior from the experience. Its intent is instructional rather than punitive because it is designed to teach students the positive or negative effects of their behavior. Let us look at some specific examples of the differences between consequences and punishments.

Differences between Consequences and Punishments

RULE

Students are not for hitting, fighting, or hurting.

Consequence	*Punishment*
Do one nice thing for the victim before the day is over.	Stay after school for two hours and sit in silence.

RULE

All trash must be thrown in the basket.

Consequence	*Punishment*
Pick your trash up off the floor.	Apologize to the teacher in front of the whole class.

RULE

Tests and homework must be completed by yourselves unless group work is assigned. There is no copying other students' work.

Consequence	*Punishment*
Do the test or homework again under supervision.	Write one hundred times, ''I will not copy other students' work.''

RULE

No talking when someone else is talking. If you want to speak, wait until the current speaker has finished.

Consequence	*Punishment*
Wait five minutes before speaking.	Sitting in the hall for the entire period.

RULE

You must be in your seat by five minutes after the bell.

Consequence	*Punishment*
You are responsible to get any missed information or make up any work missed while you are late.	Miss entire class sitting in the principal's office, then make up work.

The main differences between consequences and punishments in the above examples are that the consequences are simple, direct, related to the rule, logical (that is, they are natural outcomes of the rule violation), and instructive. The punishments are not related to the rule, are not natural extensions of the rule, and tend to generate anxiety, hostility, and resentment on the part of the student. Natural and logical consequences help teach proper behavior. Effective consequences are also direct and simple.

Multi-functional Consequences

Some effective consequences that can be adapted to many different rules are:

1. *Reminder of rule.* For example, "Mary, we raise our hands before speaking. This is your reminder."

2. *A warning.* This is a stern reminder. The consequence is for the student to hear the warning. It is not a threat that something will happen later although the assertive tone with which it is delivered should leave no doubt in the student's mind that the next infraction will result in a more active consequence. Notice these two examples: (a) "Johnny, this is the second time today that you have gotten out of your seat and bothered Mary. If you don't stop doing that, I warn you that you will have to stay after school for detention." (b) "Johnny, this is the second time today that you have gotten out of your seat to bother Mary. This is your warning." The first example is a threat that something will happen later. The student who hears this message learns that he has at least one more chance and who knows how many more after that. The second message is a clear statement. It is not a threat that something will follow. The warning is the consequence itself. If and when another infraction occurs, take action. Don't threaten!!

3. *Developing an action plan for improving behavior.* For example, "Johnny, you are out of your seat bothering Mary. I want you to

write for me how you intend to stop breaking this rule. List very clearly what you will do when you want to tell Mary something.''

4. *Practicing behavior.* Often students break rules because they either emotionally or behaviorally do not have the skills to match their cognitive understanding of what the rules are. In other words, sometimes students do not know how to behave appropriately even when they know what the rule is. Even for those students who do know how to follow rules, practice with the teacher can be a helpful and effective consequence if the teacher is not sarcastic or condescending. We have seen this consequence used effectively for teaching proper lunchroom behavior, for teaching effective nonviolent strategies for expressing anger, and for teaching effective and appropriate ways to get attention. The teacher in implementing this consequence may follow this sequence:

    a. Role play the inappropriate behavior first, or have the student role play it.
    b. Then demonstrate one appropriate way of following the rule.
    c. The student then role plays the appropriate behavior.
    d. Finally, the student practices other appropriate behaviors (where there is more than one optional behavior) until the student can do them easily.

These guidelines can be applied to every rule; they are natural and logical. We will show you some strategies for developing specific natural and logical consequences later in this chapter.

An example of practicing behavior occurred at Valley View Elementary School, which had developed a school-wide plan for having more orderly cafeteria behavior. Built into their system was a clear statement of the cafeteria rules, which were monitored by cafeteria aides who placed a check mark next to the name of a student when he broke one of the rules. There were various individual and class privileges and rewards built into the system for short-term and long-term behavior, but after a student broke a rule three times in any month, the student was assigned to a before-school or after-school cafeteria class. The class was designed to teach students how to behave acceptably in the cafeteria by practicing appropriate behavior. Students in the class "practiced" walking through the cafeteria line, getting their food, emptying their trash, and in some cases, eating with a fork (for those who threw food). After the students practiced these behaviors, they were offered a test to make sure that they understood the rules. When they received a 100% grade on the test, they were graduated from make-up class. The intent of the program was therefore instructional. School authorities needed to stop making assumptions that the children knew how to follow the rules and accepted that some might need extra help in learning these skills.

Range of Alternatives for Consequences

Another criterion for a good consequence is that it has a range of alternatives. This criterion is very important because it allows the teacher to be consistent by always giving a consequence regardless of the circumstances surrounding the violation of the social contract, while allowing the flexibility needed to meet individual needs. Imagine the following situation.

Miss Martin is a tenth grade biology teacher who has the following rule and consequence: "All homework must be done on time. If homework is not done, the student will stay after school and finish it." In early March, Susan, one of her best students who had never missed an assignment, told Miss Martin, "I'm sorry, Miss Martin, but my father was very sick last night. I had to babysit while he was taken to the hospital, and in the confusion, I didn't have time to get my homework done." Miss Martin now faces an uncomfortable dilemma. She can tell Susan that it doesn't matter what the excuse is and Susan still has to come after school and finish her homework—there are no exceptions. If she gives this consequence, Susan and other students in class will see Miss Martin as unfair and feel resentful.

Another option is for Miss Martin to accept Susan's excuse. She doesn't have to stay after school because her excuse is legitimate. This choice will teach Susan and the other students that a good excuse will get them off the hook when a rule is violated.

Neither option helps Miss Martin deal with the situation effectively on a short-term or long-term basis. She is caught in the classic bind that eventually erodes any system of discipline. The situation gets worse when, the next day, Tom tells Miss Martin that he didn't do his homework and presents his excuse. Tom is a student who has been late with his homework ten times in the last month. Now it is difficult for Miss Martin to be consistent with her policy and still deal effectively with Susan and Tom. How can she be consistent *and* treat Susan and Tom as separate individuals?

Our solution to this problem is to develop more than one consequence for any given rule violation. Miss Martin's range of consequences might have been:

1. reminder
2. warning
3. student must hand homework in before close of school that day
4. stay after school to finish homework
5. a conference between teacher, student, and parent to develop an action plan for completing homework on time

With this range of alternatives, Miss Martin could gently remind Susan that homework is due on time, and then discuss how her father is doing, etc. In this way she is implementing one of the prescribed consequences, yet she is not being overly rigid with Susan. With Tom, staying after school to finish his homework would probably be more appropriate.

The range of alternative consequences gives Miss Martin the flexibility to meet specific needs while consistently implementing consequences when a rule has been broken.

Sequenced and Unsequenced Consequences

If you develop a range of alternative consequences, there are two ways to organize them. The first is by sequencing them so that the first infraction of the rule earns consequence number one, the second infraction earns consequence number two, the third infraction earns consequence number three, etc. The second method is to simply list all of the consequences and choose the most appropriate one in any given situation.

If you use the sequencing method, you are less likely to play favorites, and both you and the students will have greater clarity about what will happen when the rules are broken. There will be fewer instances of students telling you that you are not fair because they got consequence number three when another student got number one for breaking the same rule. On the negative side, you must keep records of infractions, and even simple record keeping is usually frowned upon by already overburdened teachers. Not only that, but you give up your power of discretion.

Listing consequences is easier to implement and gives you more freedom of choice. But you run the risk of not being "fair" and being accused of playing favorites. We believe that both methods can work effectively, depending upon the needs of the students and the personality of the teacher. We recommend that you select the method with which you feel more comfortable, or try both methods and see which works best for you. You may even have some rules with sequenced consequences and some rules unsequenced.

Fair and Not Equal

One preventive and important strategy that we recommend you use as part of your preventive package involves the notion of "fair and not equal." This is especially relevant when you are using unsequenced consequences as part of your social contract. Because you may use different consequences with different students, even though they have each violated the same rule, you will be subject to the outraged cry of being unfair. It is important when you use different consequences that you make sure to explain your reasoning in advance.

We start this preventive strategy by teaching the concept that "fair is not always equal" before any issue related to that question ever occurs. This unit makes a wonderful first or second day class project for all grade levels, although it can be helpful at any point in the school year. Begin by telling your class a story similar to the following:

Imagine that I am the father/mother of two children. The first is a successful lawyer who has an annual income of over $100,000. He has found his dream house and needs $10,000 more than he has in savings for the down payment and asks me for a $10,000 loan. At the same time my second child, who is a college dropout and works in the local shoe factory, has decided to go back to school. He needs $10,000 for tuition and asks me for a loan. He has been accepted and is excited about getting his life together.

I have only $10,000 to loan. Who do I give the money to? Do I split it evenly, give all to one and none to the other, or make a different percentage split.

Most students choose to give most or all of the money to the second child. This leads perfectly to the concept that being fair means giving what people need, and when different people have different needs, they are given different amounts. This is fair—it is not equal. Another example of fair and unequal that you can share with your students takes place in a doctor's waiting room. Ask your students to imagine ten patients waiting for their turn to see the doctor. One has a cold, one has a broken arm, one has pneumonia, one has poison ivy, one has a sprained ankle, one has diarrhea, one has allergies, one has chicken pox, one has a splinter, and another came in for an annual checkup. All of a sudden, the doctor comes out and announces to the patients that today is aspirin day. All patients will be treated equally and given aspirin to solve their ailments.

A lively discussion can now ensue analyzing whether the doctor in this example is being fair although he is clearly being equal. There are dozens of other examples that you and your class can think of. Some are:

- Equal Rights Amendment
- Affirmative Action
- Some people are quarterbacks, others linebackers
- Some hitters lead off, others clean up
- Different aged children have different chores at home
- Homogeneous/heterogenous grouping in school

Once the class understands this concept, you can then write on the board or make a permanent sign which reads, "I will be fair, and I won't always be equal." We like the use of the conjunction "and" rather than "but" so that the second statement does not negate the first. When a student asks why you are being unfair by giving him a different consequence for the same violation (providing of course that the situation warrants it), you can point to the sign and say, "Because I am being fair and I am not being equal." That usually ends the protest. If it doesn't, and the student continues, you merely have to repeat the phrase over again until the student gets the message that his protest is not going to work. This strategy will work as long as you are really being fair with your inequality. If the students see you as being unfair and unequal, this strategy will backfire and cause anger and resentment in your students. However, if you are being unfair and unequal, your students will feel resentful with or without this strategy. We are proponents of Ed Pino's position that "there is nothing so unequal as treating unequals equally." [1]

Major Causes of Teacher Failure to Implement Consequences

We find that regardless of how good your consequences are, they must be implemented consistently for them to be effective. That means every time that you ignore a rule violation or threaten rather than actually give a consequence, you are giving the message to your students that you are not serious about your contract. You are also telling them that they have at least some chance of breaking the contract without any consequences. This will encourage them to break rules if only to define for themselves what your limits really are. Yet, there are a great many reasons why teachers do not implement consequences, even after they have gone through the trouble of developing them and reaching agreement on them with their class. Here are four of the major causes of failure to implement consequences.

1. THE CONSEQUENCE IS TOO HARSH OR INCONGRUENT

The teacher is not comfortable with a consequence because it is either too harsh or incongruent with the teacher's style. We are reminded of the teacher who told her class that if they didn't clean the room they would be refused a chance to go on the school field trip to the circus. She made this statement out of desperation and frustration, and the moment she said it, she knew she had made a big mistake. She wanted to take her class to the circus more than the class wanted to go. After her threat, she prayed that the class would clean up so she wouldn't be forced to either live with a consequence she did not want to implement or go back on her word. They cleaned up just enough for her to say, "Okay, the room's clean. Let's get on that bus."

To avoid facing this situation when your feelings are running hot after a rule has been broken, it is important to make sure that you can and will live with every consequence on your social contract. Even though you have alternative choices, you still must be willing to implement all consequences listed so that you won't find yourself regretfully implementing an uncomfortable consequence when the stakes are high.

2. RULE VIOLATION OCCURS AT AN INCONVENIENT PLACE OR TIME

The rule violation occurs in a part of the room physically distant from the teacher or at a time when the teacher is involved with other students. Frequently it seems like a lot of work to interrupt a lesson and quietly go over to a student who has just broken the social contract. This is especially true when the teacher is working with one group and the violation occurs elsewhere. It seems almost too much to interrupt the lesson to stop loud talking from the other group. In the long run more time and energy will be saved when the students see that you consistently implement consequences when the rules have been broken.

While we understand the difficulty of being in two places at the same time, there are ways to implement consequences that minimize their emergence as a disruptive factor. Develop some nonverbal cues; these can include touching, such as gently placing a hand on a student's shoulder or giving a student a specific look that has a prearranged meaning. These non-verbal cues can be the equivalent of a reminder or warning. Once the look or touch has been established as a cue, you can often use it in situations like those described above. Then it is simply a matter of catching the eyes of the students who are breaking the contract and giving them the look.

Another method that involves self-monitoring is to have each student that violates a rule write his own name on the blackboard. This can also be accomplished non-verbally, by pointing to the student and then the blackboard. Yet another possibility is for you to keep a simple daily chart that includes each student's name with the rules and place a check mark next to the student's name when a rule is violated. You can contact students when time permits and show them the chart. No matter which methods you use, be sure to specify all of these procedures in advance! If these non-interruptive methods do not work, then it is time to stop what you are doing and go over and deliver the consequence at closer proximity.

3. TEACHERS ARE NOT POLICEMEN

Teachers do not want the job of policeman and prefer to let the students get away with minor rule violations. We agree that the teacher should not always be trying to catch students breaking rules, and the teacher should not perceive of himself as a policeman. The students also should not see the teacher as primarily a policeman. However, we feel that prevention is the best solution to this problem. By that we mean that the teacher should only have rules that are important to be followed.

You won't feel like a policeman if you eliminate rules that you do not mind being broken and only keep those you feel strongly about. Then you will not feel that it is okay to close your eyes to a violation of the social contract.

It is also not always necessary to enforce the consequences yourself. One alternative is for your class to hold elections for sheriff and deputy sheriff. Tell your class that you need "officers" who have good eyes and ears, who are not afraid of others, and who are willing to help enforce the consequences. Make your "officers" responsible for keeping the behavioral records that are so important in having an effective social contract.

It is interesting that several teachers who have used this method have reported that the elected sheriff and deputy sheriff have often been "hard to reach" kids and they (teachers) have found this to be both effective in helping to manage classroom behavior and in providing an acceptable outlet for the difficult student's need to be in control. It is also a good idea to have biweekly or monthly elections so that different students share the responsibility for monitoring their peers' conduct.

4. TEACHERS SOMETIMES LOSE THEIR SELF-CONTROL

Teachers sometimes get angry and "out of control" themselves. When they feel extremely agitated they prefer to punish as a way of releasing their feelings rather than helping the child grow by implementing a consequence in a rational way. In this situation, the teacher ends up yelling, hitting (this is rare, but occasionally happens, much to our regret), or making up a new punitive consequence that is not part of the social contract. These kinds of reactions happen when the teacher has lost control and needs to express feelings in a very clear and direct way. It is obvious how negative this kind of behavior can be, especially when the class looks to the teacher as a model of appropriate behavior. You can avoid this kind of action by attending to your feelings regularly. Consider it to be part of your job responsibility so that anger, resentment, hostility, and other negatively toned emotions are released in positive and constructive ways (see Chapter 3 for suggestions on how to accomplish this).

Developing Effective Consequences

We are continually asked by teachers to help them think of good consequences. It takes skill and practice to develop effective consequences that are not punishments and that have a range of alternatives. Two important skills are needed for the development of effective consequences: creativity and the ability to see the logical extension of the rule violation. It also helps to know your students well and to know what works with them.

Creativity is an important part of consequence development. We know of a teacher who had trouble keeping her fifth grade students from running in the halls. She tried this creative consequence: "Any student who runs in the halls will receive a kiss from me." For her grade level this was a most effective consequence, although it might not have worked for younger children who love teacher kisses or secondary students who also might love teacher kisses for different reasons. The natural and logical aspect of this consequence was stretched a bit; she said that the reason she did not want students running was that she loved them too much to see them hurt themselves, and therefore she would direct an expression of love when she found them running. The consequence was creative, nonpunishing, humorously disturbing, and most importantly, it worked.

A junior high science teacher was fatigued by the frequent use of name calling (i.e., "your mother _____") that occurred daily. His solution was to announce that beginning immediately, anybody who said uncomplimentary things about someone else in a student's family would be required to call that person. They would have to tell that person what they said and offer an apology. One student tested the rule, the consequence was implemented, and name-calling in the classroom came to an abrupt halt. When he (the teacher) was asked why he decided to do this, he said, "I thought it would be useful for students to learn that another human being, not a thing, is on the receiving end of a put-down."

To help you create good consequences, here are five strategies that help you to get started.

1. READ YOUR RULE TWO OR THREE TIMES

Close your eyes and imagine a student breaking that rule. See it clearly in your mind. Do not think of it in words, only pictures. Now picture the result of the rule violation—watch it carefully. Often there are natural consequences that will "pop out" at you when you try this experiment. For example, one shop teacher reported that when she visualized students refusing to clean up their mess she saw that it would be impossible for students to find their tools and supplies. She then thought of the consequence of removing any supplies and tools found out of place and putting them in a large, old trunk. At the end of the week, any student that had left tools laying around, but who had three days (consecutive) of no mess would get their supplies and tools back. All work was required to be completed, and it was the students' responsibility to find new supplies and tools from home if theirs were in the "trunk."

A high school teacher visualized the problem of students breaking the rule, "People are not for hitting in this class." The purpose for the rule was that someone might get hurt. When he saw a visual image of a student coming to school with bandages, casts, etc., he had a brainstorm. He went to one of the local department stores and asked for a display mannikin that was no longer in use. He brought it to class, thought of a name for it with his class (the name turned out to be an acronym for the students in class). Everytime a student hit another student, the hitter was required to bandage the part of the body he hit on the dummy and then initial the bandages. For every week that the dummy had no bandages, the class was given a night of no homework.

While you may or may not like these particular consequences, you can see the process used to invent them. By visualizing the rule violation and thinking beyond the incident to what happens after, you can begin to find either symbolic or real consequences that flow naturally from the rule.

2. COLLECT EFFECTIVE CONSEQUENCES

Don't hesitate to collect effective consequences from other teachers and administrators. Often teachers feel that they must do everything for themselves when it comes to discipline, although they exchange subject matter ideas more freely. Other teachers may have one or two excellent consequences for you, if you systematically ask them. One or two good consequences from each teacher in your school could provide you with fifty to a hundred consequences depending on the size of your school. We suggest you list some of the rules you are having trouble thinking of good consequences for, each on the top of a blank dittomaster. Then send it around through your mail routing system with a cover letter asking each teacher to write in their favorite consequence for that rule, the one most effective for them. To thank them for their effort, tell them you will run the dittos off and send each teacher a copy for their own use. Include administrators, secretaries, nurses, librarians, substitute teachers, and anyone else in your school who works with the students. You may get better results if the responses are anonymous. You don't have to use any consequences on the list, but usually there are a few gems and many other effective ones to choose from. You might also try modifying some of the ones you reject to be more in tune with your educational philosophy so that they can become helpful to you.

3. Use the Students

Often your students can tell you the consequences that work best for them. There are three basic strategies we have used to get input from students. The first is to spend one class period brainstorming consequences with your students for all the rules that lack effective consequences. The second is to allow your students to brainstorm at least one consequence for all of your rules. Another way to accomplish this, without using class time, is to give each student the task of thinking of one or two consequences for a homework assignment. Then you can tabulate them on a ditto and give the students a booklet of their consequences as feedback for their efforts. We strongly suggest that you use as many of the student consequences as possible to show them that you value their input and to give them a feeling of contributing to the classroom environment. The third method is student input that has been solicited or asking students who have already graduated from your class. Ask them to help you think of consequences that would have been effective with them when they were with you. This strategy can be used by teachers at all grade levels. First grade teachers can ''borrow'' the second graders for a class period. High school students who have already graduated can be invited back during college vacation time for an evening meeting that will also include those students who did not go to college.

We find that some of the most helpful students in this process are those who had trouble following your rules. Make sure you include your chronic problem students in your group because they will provide you with many valuable insights, providing there is enough distance from the problems to make them willing to contribute.

4. Elicit Parent Suggestions

Whether through the mail, a telephone interview, or on parent night, ask your parents what the most effective consequences with their children are. You can use the same ditto technique as with the faculty and duplicate all responses. These booklets can then be sent to all the parents as a way of saying thank you for helping. Parents can always use good suggestions for consequences from other parents. This process also evokes good feelings on the part of the parents and helps them feel more positive about school and you as a teacher.

5. USE YOUR OWN EXPERIENCES

Recall when you were a student. Imagine yourself breaking the rules you have established in your class as a teacher. What consequences would help you to

1. stop the misbehavior
2. learn from the experience
3. be willing to be more cooperative
4. not feel embarrassed, angry, or resentful

If you were a student who never broke any rules (some teachers were like that), remember back to the time when you were the same age as the students you now teach. Picture a student from that time who was a troublemaker. Then imagine that you are this difficult student and go through the process outlined above. When you imagine breaking the rules as either yourself or another student, be as graphic as you can. Recall the actual classroom, the teacher, the other students, and the specific rules that were broken. Ask yourself, "What do I need right now to stop misbehaving?"

A variation of this procedure is to imagine yourself as a student the same age as your students whom you now teach. Then imagine yourself as a student in your own classroom violating one of your own rules. Again, see this as visually and directly as possible and avoid intellectualizing the process. Then think of what consequences would be effective for you.

Involving Others

If you have other people involved as part of your consequence, it is important for you to receive their support and agreement before you put the social contract into effect. We have seen consequences such as the following:

1. A meeting with the principal, student, and/or teacher to discuss the problem.
2. A meeting with the parent.
3. No library privileges for a week.
4. No school field trips.

5. The student will eat in the classroom, not the cafeteria.
6. The student will be required to make up missed work between classes.
7. The student will make up lost work during gym.
8. The student will sit in the principal's area for one class period.

Each of these consequences involves at least one or more people other than the teacher. Parents, administrators, librarians, and other teachers are all affected by these consequences. We find that you can avoid many problems by gaining the support and commitment from all third party people involved in your social contract. If a principal must keep a child in his office, or be part of a meeting to discuss ways of following the rule, then he must agree prior to your telling your students of this consequence. In gaining third party support, we suggest you ask the other people what they need from you to be most helpful in the process (usually they at least want a copy of your social contract when completed) and what you might do for them to be helpful in their dealings with your students.

Positive Consequences

Many schools approach discipline from the perspective of stopping misbehavior by developing punishments for rule violations. This perspective, many claim, is too negative because acceptable behavior is ignored while attention is given to those who misbehave. Behavior modification researchers believe that by giving most attention to the negative, the implicit message to students is that the way to be noticed and rewarded (with attention) is by breaking rules. Further, they claim, stressing the negative makes school a dreary place to be, setting up an adversarial relationship between students and teachers. Why should any student behave when all the implicit rewards go to the few students who drive the teacher crazy? These educators advocate the use of positive consequences, which reward students for following the rules.

Positive consequences can fit perfectly within the social contract formula. Each rule can state precisely what happens when the rule is broken and what good things happen when the rule is followed. Positive consequences can be developed for the class as a whole or for individual students who follow the rules. Some rules can have only positive consequences when followed. The loss of the positive consequence is viewed as the natural and logical consequence of not following a rule. For example, Bill Evans, a junior high history teacher had this rule and consequence in his social contract:

RULE

Paper airplanes are not for throwing during instructional time.

Consequence

For each week of no paper airplane throwing, the class will have a paper airplane throwing contest. Each student will use his best airplane and have three tries at shooting it across the room. The longest throws will earn points. The highest point total will win a free paperback book. Any unauthorized paper airplane throwing will eliminate the contest for that week. A second violation will eliminate it for the next week and so on.

The creative contract stopped paper airplane throwing for the entire year.

Some teachers believe that it is wrong to have positive consequences. They feel that rewarding good behavior is akin to bribing the students or paying them to do what they should do for nothing. They note that it is more important for children to learn to behave correctly and learn responsibility because it feels good intrinsically to do so. They cite studies that indicate that rewarding good behavior decreases it, rather than increases it.

Which point of view is correct? Frankly our view is relatively unimportant in helping you grapple with this difficult issue. We prefer that you choose which point of view works best for you, the one with which you can feel most comfortable implementing. It is our bias to have at least one positive consequence for each rule, but it has been our experience time and time again, that if you do not believe in what you are doing, it won't work. And as we stated before, we believe that the process of an agreed upon set of standards is the crucial factor—not the content of the consequence.

We suggest that you choose either one point of view or the other, depending on your view of what school should be teaching students, and more importantly what you want to teach your students. If you are comfortable with positive consequences, use many of the same techniques described earlier to think of good, clear positive consequences for each of your rules. If you do not believe in positive consequences, don't use them.

For those of you who are not sure, and we suspect that most teachers fall into this category, we suggest you experiment and see what happens. Choose one or two rules in your social contract that seem to lend themselves to positive consequences. Perhaps you can try one rule that has both positive consequences and negative consequences (unpleasant outcomes) and one rule with only positive consequences (like the airplane example above). Then keep a journal for about a month or two (shorter or longer depending upon your situation) and record how often each rule in your social contract was broken and which of the alternative consequences you implemented. Note how often you actually gave the positive consequences. Most importantly, record how you felt giving the positive consequences and how you felt giving the negative ones. See which was more comfortable for you and which were most effective. If you seemed to enjoy giving the positive consequences, pick one of the least followed rules without a positive consequence and add a couple of positive ones. Continue your journal and see if the addition of the positive consequences made the rule more effective.

One of the most common positive consequences is the use of praise. There are many pros and cons for using praise as a reinforcer. Along with some positive change in behavior, praise also has many negative side effects, which include conformity, stereotyped choices, students downgrading themselves (so that others will build them up), bragging, and role playing.

Praise Guidelines

Harmful Characteristics of Praise

Many responses encourage the sharing of positive feelings and support including appreciation, enthusiasm, caring, interest and sensitivity. But the kind of praise that can be harmful has each of the following characteristics:[2]

1. Praise is used so an individual will repeat behavior. By telling a person how good some action is, you increase the probability of

the person's doing it again. But this method of responding can be highly manipulative and has many harmful side effects. You're really saying, "You can have my approval only by doing what I decide is right for you."

2. It involves making a value judgment for someone else. In order to praise, unless you praise everything, you must make value judgments that reflect your value system and beliefs about right and wrong. These judgments may contradict the values of the other person, his parents, and, in many cases, his culture. For example, some teachers try to eliminate dialects by positively reinforcing only the child's "proper" use of language. By making decisions for people, praise-giving limits the opportunity for them to develop their own decision-making ability and their willingness to try new, unique behaviors.

3. Praise is always in the form of *judgments*, not *facts*. Praise is a positive interpretation of factual data. Judgments reduce the student's ability to self evaluate and eventually to make decisions. It is better to say what criteria might be used to make a judgment than to give the judgment itself. For example, you can tell your math student, "problems should be neat, show all work and clearly indicate the answer. How do you think you did?"

It is possible to respond to our students with encouragement, support, care and concern—without using these manipulative, judgmental tactics.

Can Praise Really Be Harmful?

This is a complex question. Many teachers like to use praise because students like it. These students often respond more positively to the teacher and to school. In many cases, the students do what the teacher wants—a pleasant departure from the usual struggle that teachers often face. As praise becomes more and more addicting (the more one gets, the more one needs), students naturally behave in ways that the teacher indicates are positive, for the teacher is the source of satisfying their habit. (Teachers who reduce praise giving don't have it easy. Withdrawal symptoms are difficult to accept, and by cutting down on praise, teachers may face the hostility and mistrust of students who want praise, but aren't getting it.)

Another reason for the general acceptance of praise is a reaction against the image of the schoolmarm with the hickory stick. For many people, the image of a teacher is punitive, critical, and negative. Praise is seen as an alternative to this unrealistic picture. The other side of the coin is that praise, like punishment, is still controlling and potentially dangerous. It is like a coin, one side (praise) is heads, the other (punishment) is tails. Regardless of which side is up, it is still the same coin. It's like choosing between the carrot and the stick—two fine choices for donkeys but not for children.

"New" People, New Expectations

People who do not need praise show certain characteristics, sometimes recognizable to only themselves:

1. They stop asking, "What does he want?" and ask instead, "What do I want?"
2. They begin to consider a wider array of choices, some of them different from the choices of the significant others, who are sources of praise.
3. They stop manipulating others for praise, and no longer play praise-getting games such as downgrading themselves, bragging in a way that encourages agreement, and living by the values of others.
4. They begin to discover their own unique, creative, individual and personal abilities, behaviors, and attitudes. They still try to please others, but their reasons change. They do it to feel good about themselves, and for more altruistic reasons, rather than to have others tell them how good they were to do it.
5. They like themselves better. In the long run, their self-concept is improved. They are better able to appreciate themselves without dependency on the approval from others.

Don't Eliminate All Praise

There are some positive effects of praise. Praise can help people master basic skills, work harder for certain extrinsic goals, and overcome extreme cases of poor self-concepts.

Students with special learning disabilities, emotional problems, and other disorders that make it critical for them to master basic skills may initially need a high dose of praise so that they can learn to feel good about being able to learn.

Alternatives to Praise

Use of I-Statements

An effective alternative to praise is the use of I-statements. An I-statement contains three components. It describes specifically what another person did (the behavior), it tells the other person how you *feel* about their behavior, and when possible it gives the person the *reason(s)* for your feelings. Whereas praise statements are judgmental and non-specific, an I-statement specifically says what can be appreciated about another's behavior. We believe that it is not only possible but also quite desirable to send students messages of appreciation regarding their performance.

A statement of praise would be, ''Billy, you behaved very well today.'' An I-statement of appreciation would be, ''Billy, I feel really pleased because you were able to settle your differences by talking with Mary rather than by hitting her, and you successfully completed three class assignments today.'' The latter message clearly tells Billy specifically what his teacher liked whereas the former statement lacks meaningful feedback. As a way of practicing the skill of communicating with I-statements, start by considering any behavior or performance of a student and complete the following:

1. (Student's name) _____When you did _____.
2. It made me feel _____.
3. Because _____.

It may become obvious that I-statements are appropriate not only in sharing appreciations but can also provide an effective alternative to yelling, scolding, lecturing, and threatening when students do things that make us feel sad, annoyed, angry, tense, or disappointed.

We suggest you think about the use of praise in your classroom, and see if you are comfortable offering appreciations and the use of I-statements instead of praise. If so, you may try to cut down your general use of praise and reserve it for those situations that really need it. Indiscriminate use of praise, not only increases dependency but also eventually becomes a meaningless message.

Other alternatives to verbal praise include non-verbal cues, touching or asking for self-evaluation such as, "Steve, what do you like about the way you have been following the social contract?"

It is important to understand the delicate difference between praise as a means to manipulate and as a positive consequence—a statement of appreciation for the effort shown by students to follow a rule. Positive outcomes that are naturally and logically related to positive behavior can be an effective method of classroom management.

Use of the Three Dimensional Discipline Method

A school where we recently consulted was experiencing considerable problems in managing the behavior of its students in the cafeteria. Their plan for solving this problem illustrates the use of consequences as well as the other factors that make for an effective social contract.

A discipline committee at this mid-sized, lower middle class elementary school worked on developing a school-wide social contract based upon the principles of Three Dimensional Discipline. The committee was comprised of two students, two parent representatives, one administrator, the school psychologist, two primary level teachers, and two intermediate level teachers. The discipline committee identified student cafeteria behavior as the school-wide discipline problem that required attention. As a result of their work, the following plan was developed:

CAFETERIA RULES

1. Students will raise their hands and are expected to receive the permission of cafeteria supervisors before they may leave their seats.
2. The cafeteria is a place to talk quietly; not to scream, whistle, or yell.
3. Food is for eating, not for throwing.
4. Fighting is not permitted under any conditions or for any reasons.
5. Each class will have an assigned table in the cafeteria. Students are to clean their area after they have finished their eating.
6. Students are to walk in the cafeteria, not run.
7. Students may go through the lunch line only once—with their class.

Consequences

1. Violation of any of the above rules results in a ↙ mark next to the student's name on a record-keeping form. (A list of names for each class is provided the cafeteria supervisors.)

2. A student's first infraction will result in a warning.

3. A student's second infraction will result in a letter being sent home to the student's parents by the student's teacher and the school principal.

4. The third infraction will require a parent-teacher-principal conference. The student will not be allowed to eat in the cafeteria until this conference occurs.

5. Each rule infraction requires the student to eat at a separate table for the remainder of his lunch period.

6. For "fighting," each infraction results in the immediate loss of cafeteria privileges until a parent-teacher-principal conference occurs.

7. The class that receives the fewest violations per week gets a banner, which is presented by the principal, cafeteria supervisors or "celebrity" guest at a school-wide assembly (two banners—one for primary and one for intermediate).

8. The class with the fewest violations per month is rewarded with a class picnic, field trip, or some other special outing.

Before this plan could be implemented, each teacher was expected to have a thorough discussion with his class. Following this discussion, a test for comprehension was administered to guarantee that each student knew what the rules and consequences were. The most common game that students play who misbehave is to claim that they were unaware of the rules. Since 100% is considered a passing grade, students who passed the test could no longer claim lack of knowledge.

Class privileges were tied to passing the test, and students who didn't pass could retake the test as many times as necessary.

The list of rules and consequences (School-Wide Social Contract) was posted in the cafeteria and in each classroom and mailed to parents. While this school's discipline problems have not been completely eliminated, the cafeteria is certainly a more pleasant place than it used to be.

The success of this program can be attributed to the specificity of the rules and consequences; school-wide support for the program; and clear guidelines for the teachers, cafeteria supervisors, and students. Each teacher thoroughly discussed the contract with the class, administered and scored a uniform test for comprehension, posted the Cafeteria Contract in the classroom, monitored the records kept by cafeteria supervisors, and consistently implemented consequences. The cafeteria supervisors knew how to keep accurate records of student violators and shared this information with teachers. Also of significance was the inclusion of positive consequences to reward classes which were able to follow the contract.

Cafeteria Class Test (Grades 4–6)

True or
False

1. _____ Students are allowed to go through the lunch line as many times as they would like.
2. _____ Students may move from table to table as they like.
3. _____ Students are allowed to talk quietly.
4. _____ Anyone can go to the library at lunchtime.
5. _____ Students will not be allowed to leave their seats without permission.
6. _____ The cafeteria supervisors can't tell you what to do, so you may talk back to them.
7. _____ We are not responsible for cleaning up our own area in the cafeteria.
8. _____ Spitballs and throwing food are not allowed in the cafeteria.
9. _____ Pushing a classmate off a seat is fun, so it is permitted.
10. _____ Going to the lavatory more than once, except in cases of real emergency, is allowed.
11. _____ Quiet games or school work may be done during lunchtime.
12. _____ Our feet belong on the floor and not on other people.
13. _____ We may climb on the tables and seats at lunchtime.
14. _____ People caught fighting in the cafeteria automatically have to sit at the table set off by itself.
15. _____ Only your own teacher can tell you what to do in the cafeteria.
16. How do students get permission to leave their seats?
17. Name 3 cafeteria rules that must be followed by all students.

18. What happens to students who continue to misbehave in the cafeteria?

19. Is the class that displays the best behavior in the cafeteria recognized in any way?

20. How can I improve my behavior in the cafeteria?

Conclusion

Developing effective consequences is an important part of the social contract and the prevention dimension. Whatever consequences you select, you must be willing to implement them consistently when rules are broken. Effective consequences are clear and specific; they include a wide range of alternative choices; they relate to the rule as directly as possible; and they teach rather than punish.

Consequences, like rules, are not cast in stone when they are included in the social contract. They can be eliminated if ineffective and others can be added. They can be modified at any point in time, *except when a rule has just been broken.* No consequence should ever be changed just before it is given to a student rule breaker. Creative consequences can be fun, instructive, and improve classroom communication between teacher and student.

For the Administrator

The following is a list of hints for you to help develop effective consequences for behavior in your school.

1. Help your teachers share effective consequences through the use of the mimeo sharing process described on page 126. Collect the best consequences from all the teachers in the school and publish them for all teachers to use. You can also organize groups of students who graduated from your school to meet with teachers to help brainstorm effective consequences. Remember to include a good number of students who were in your office much of the time for disciplinary reasons. These students usually have good ideas about effective consequences.

2. Find out from all your teachers how they plan to include your presence as a consequence. If you are to play a part in any consequence, make sure that you and your teachers agree with just what your role will be. Do not agree to any role with which you are not comfortable. If you cannot support a consequence, tell the teacher about this before you actually become involved. Our general principle is that if a teacher refers a child to you, then you can chose to do what you feel is acceptable to solve the problem. However, you should have a clear, specific range of procedures that are known to the teacher and the students before you receive a referral. It is most important that you inform your teacher of your action shortly after the student is returned to the classroom.

3. Recognize that a teacher's referral is usually an expression of his frustration. It is necessary for you to be a good active listener for your teachers, even when you receive referrals that you believe are unwarranted. We have found that many teachers want their administrator to be "tough" with students when they are referred to your office. You loom as an alternative for many who would really like to open their window and drop the student from the third floor. When you talk with the student and send him back to class, some teachers view this as being "soft" and "ineffective." It is therefore essential that you understand the frustration that teachers experience in response to disruptive student behavior. They need to know that you understand, that they will have your support, and that you also have limits just as they do, which will not always make it possible for you to do as they wish. A referral to the principal is more often an emotional rather than a rational response. Act accordingly.

4. Elicit a plan of action from the referred student. After it is clear to you as to what happened that led to the referral, be sure to have the student write up what he intends to do the next time a similar situation presents itself in the classroom that will prevent trouble from occurring. Share this plan with the teacher and, if possible, include the student in this process.

5. When students are referred to you, it is important to encourage the teacher and student to solve their own problems. Act as a resource or facilitator to help each party develop the plans stated above. It is not helpful to rescue either the teacher or the student. Let them do their own work. On the other hand, you can be very helpful by allowing the teacher to remove a student who can no longer safely remain in class. If a student will not allow a

teacher to teach or other students to learn, then that student
should be removed from class until he is willing to cooperate.

References

1. From a workshop by Dr. Ed Pino, sponsored by Educational Consulting
   Associates, February 1981, in Rochester, New York.
2. Curwin, Richard, "Are Your Students Addicted to Praise?" *Instructor,
   90(3)*, October 1980, pp. 61–62.

SIX

Taking Action

*T*he prevention dimension eliminates many incidents of rule breaking, but not all. There will be times when your students will violate the social contract. If you have established an effective social contract, then these disruptions can provide a healthy opportunity for you and your students to interact in a positive way. It is healthy and natural for students to occasionally break rules and test the limits; and that provides an opportunity to help them learn about the effects of their behavior. We find that classes in which no rule is ever broken are stultifying environments that appear to be teaching students to accept authority blindly. Passivity and seeking the approval of others are more highly valued than experimentation with students' own struggle to define who they are.

We are not suggesting that teachers encourage students to break rules. We find that through the social contract process, in which all the limits are clearly spelled out and which contains a strong component of student input and decision making, teachers can minimize the occasions when students break rules. If you view contract violations as an opportunity for generating positive interaction and communication with your students rather than as a personal affront to your authority, you will be well on your way to taking charge of your classroom. In this chapter we will examine how you can take charge by viewing discipline problems as opportunities and how you can help your students grow as a result of their experience.

The first step in developing the attitude that discipline problems are opportunities, not burdens, is to feel a sense of relaxation and a sense of control while you are teaching. Chapter 3 provides a number of activities to help you maintain a high level of relaxation and control. Practice these activities regularly and they will help you to have a healthy mental and emotional attitude when your students break rules.

Eight Principles for Consequence Implementation

Once a rule is broken, there are eight principles that will help you convert that situation into a growthful experience for you and your students.

1. ALWAYS IMPLEMENT A CONSEQUENCE

In the previous chapter we discussed at length the importance of developing consequences that are not punishments and that offer a variety of alternative consequences for each rule violation. Once a rule has been broken, choose the best consequence for the situation and implement it. If you have sequenced consequences, then choose the one that matches the frequency of the rule violation for that particular student.

By always implementing a consequence, your students learn that there is an order and predictability in your classroom, and that you will honor your contract and expect them to honor it.

2. STATE THE RULE AND CONSEQUENCE

By remembering that the student who broke the rule was not out to get you, you will minimize your need to punish. Strategies such as lecturing about why the rule is important, scolding by giving the student a guilt giving message, "How could you be so stupid to break that rule again?" or other forms of retaliation are unnecessary. Further they lead to an escalation of the problem by generating angry and hostile feelings in your students. All that is necessary in most cases is to state simply and gently the rule and the consequence—"Johnny, the rule in this class is that there is no talking when other students are talking. The consequence is that you will be silent for five minutes.'' The best time for explanations about the importance of the rule is when it is discussed as part of the development of the social contract. It is not appropriate to explain the importance of the rule immediately after it has been broken. These explanations are viewed as lectures and are generally not listened to by students. It is far more effective to be direct, simple, and to the point.

We often forget to be concise because we want to make sure our students have the same understanding as we do. It is a little like the old joke about the child who asked where babies came from, and after getting a long involved lesson on the facts of life, said, ''Oh, I thought I came from Cleveland.'' Long explanations do not help the student understand better, especially after a rule violation. If the student needs help in following the rules, provide instruction after school or when you both can be alone, and demonstrate how to follow it. Then have the student practice the correct behavior. This is far more effective than long lectures. Detailed explanations of rules and consequences are encouraged *before* misbehavior occurs, *not* when it's happening!

3. BE AS PHYSICALLY CLOSE TO THE STUDENT AS POSSIBLE WHEN YOU IMPLEMENT A CONSEQUENCE

The closer you are to a student when you calmly tell him the rule and consequence, the more effective it will be. We recommend for junior high and high school students that you calmly and quietly walk to the student who has broken a rule. Go as close as conversational distance, which is about arm's length away, then move one step closer. This is a safe, yet powerful distance to deliver your message. With younger children, you can move even closer, looking directly into the student's eyes as you state the rule and consequence. Touch is also an effective adjunct to eye contact with elementary age children.

4. MAKE DIRECT EYE CONTACT WHEN YOU DELIVER A CONSEQUENCE

As you repeat the rule and consequence to the student at close proximity, look directly into the eyes of the student and capture his eyes with yours. After you have finished delivering your message, maintain eye contact for a second or two and continue to maintain it as you slowly move away. Continue with your lesson.

5. USE A SOFT VOICE

Generally the closer you are to the student and the softer the voice, the more impact you will make on the student. In our workshops, we try the following experiment to demonstrate this principle. We ask a teacher to stand about twenty feet away from the experimenter. The experimenter shouts a consequence from that distance, then moves three steps closer and delivers the same consequence using a slightly softer voice. This sequence is repeated until the experimenter is about conversational distance using conversational loudness. Then the experimenter goes one step closer and delivers the message in a tone that is barely louder than a whisper. Once the experiment is completed, the teacher is asked which consequence would be the most effective in stopping a misbehavior. Invariably the closer, soft consequence is selected as the most effective. We suggest that you try this experiment for yourself with a colleague or friend and see what happens. Be sure to make your comments clear and slowly paced. Try being both the sender and the receiver of the consequence. In essence you want to deliver a consequence in a soft, yet well-modulated tone that is convincing without being intimidating.

6. DON'T EMBARRASS THE STUDENT IN FRONT OF HIS PEERS

One of the most significant reasons for using a soft voice and being in close proximity is that it is important to avoid power struggles that emerge when a student feels embarrassed and needs to save face with his peers. Public displays of consequence implementation embarrass the student and often make it difficult if not impossible for the student to hear the message. Privacy is always helpful in implementing consequences. If possible, implement them immediately after a display of misbehavior. Be brief. Remember, your goal is to keep teaching, and you need to minimize words and/or gestures to get the message across without worsening the situation. Preventing the rule breaker from public embarrassment will give all of the other students in class the message that their right to privacy will be maintained, that their integrity will be preserved, and that they are expected to behave in class.

7. BE FIRM AND ANGER FREE WHEN GIVING YOUR CONSEQUENCE

We have seen teachers who give consequences as if they are sorry that they have to give them, almost apologizing to the student for bothering him with an intrusion. These teachers are telling their students that they are fearful of them, and the students learn quickly that this kind of teacher is easily intimidated. Often this delivery ends up with the teacher asking the student to stop or a consequence will be delivered later. Notice this example: "Oh, Johnny, please stop talking, okay? Please, because, uh, if you don't, I will have to ask you to stay after school with me. Now please, won't you just be a bit more cooperative? Okay, then?"

This is an extreme example, but when the tone of voice and the body posture of the teacher reinforce the verbal apology, the message is loud and clear that this teacher does not mean business, is not serious, and can be intimidated by the students.

On the other hand, an overly hostile or aggressive delivery can create hostility, resentment, and fear on the part of the student. These are not emotions that lend themselves to setting up a growth producing interchange between the student and the teacher. Imagine a teacher pointing his index finger at a student and shouting in a loud voice, "Johnny, this is the third time today you have gotten out of your seat, now I'll see you after school, *buddy!*" We find that the most effective delivery is neutral and that it is devoid of either fear or hostility from the teacher. It is delivered assertively. Words are spoken slowly, and the teacher presents himself with assurance and confidence. The teacher can demonstrate seriousness, caring, and support to the student.

8. DO NOT ACCEPT EXCUSES, BARGAINING, OR WHINING BY THE STUDENT

If you are sure that the rule was broken, implement the consequence as directly and expeditiously as possible. If the student makes excuses, simply repeat the rule and consequence, calmly and softly, until he stops. Notice the following example:

Teacher: Roger, the rule in this class is that only one person may speak at a time. The consequence is five minutes of no talking.

Roger: But it wasn't my fault, Susie started it first.

Teacher: The rule in this classroom is that only one person may speak at a time. The consequence is five minutes of no talking. (Teacher backs away maintaining eye control). Now class, who can tell me what the square root of 16 is?

If the student tries to bargain with you, by promising never to do it again, or by offering you something else, it is better to ignore the offer and simply state the rule and consequence again. Or you can acknowledge his offer, and then restate the rule and consequence. Notice the following example:

Teacher: Sally, the rule in this classroom is that people are not for hitting. Your consequence is to come in after school and I will help you practice other ways of expressing your anger.

Sally: If I don't have to stay after school tonight, I promise I will never hit again, please.

Teacher: You promise never to hit again, and I'm glad. For this time, you hit Judy and the rule in this classroom is that people are not for hitting. To help you keep your promise, your consequence is to come in after school and learn some ways to express your anger besides hitting.

Younger students might whine when given a consequence. We allow students to whine as long as they want but not in a way that disturbs the class. Ask the whiner to go to your time-out area, and once there, he can whine until he has it out of his system, then he can return. Most whiners can only sustain whining for about five minutes and usually less if there is no reinforcement. Champion whiners can go up to ten minutes at best. Older students might challenge your tenacity, and you need to remain calm and firm to this challenge.

Don't Be a Victim

Often the way we communicate to students non-verbally is a more powerful message than our words. Your students read the way you walk around the classroom every day, and the message you communicate tells your students how much they can affect your behavior. The following was condensed from a news story that appeared in the Boston Globe, January 20, 1981.

How "Muggable" Are You? Clue Is Your Walk

by Judy Foreman, *The Boston Globe*

It's not your age.

It's not your sex.

It's not even the mere fact of walking alone in a high-crime area that appears to make some people more "muggable" than others.

It's the way you walk, according to research by a New York marketing professor and a group of dance analysts, that sends out easy-to-assault or hard-to-assault cues to potential assailants.

Hofstra University marketing and communications professor Betty Grayson became interested in the fact that some police officers and many imprisoned criminals seemed able to tell at a glance which potential victims would offer the least resistance to attack.

Were the cops and muggers just using some kind of intuition? Or were there specific behavioral cues—which no one seemed able to specify—to which they were responding?

Grayson began her study by using a fixed, hidden videotape camera to take frontal shots as people walked along the street. She kept the camera on each subject for about seven seconds, the length of time, she figured, it would take for a mugger to size up a victim.

She and three assistants sorted the subjects into four categories of 20 people each: young women (under 35); young men (under 35); older women (over 45); and older men (over 45). Armed with the videotapes, Grayson then talked to inmates at the Rahway, N.J., prison who helped her create a scale of "muggability"—or as she puts it, likelihood of assault.

For methodological reasons, Grayson needed two sets of inmates, the first to view the tapes and help her create a rating scale—in the criminals' own words—of "muggability," and the second group to rate the videotaped subjects on that scale.

Grayson first showed the tapes to about 60 inmates. She audiotaped their comments and listed the main reactions on the blackboard. She then asked the inmates to rank their responses in order, which ranged from, "Most assaultable, a very easy rip-off," to "Would avoid it, too big a situation, too heavy."

With this 1 to 10 "muggability" scale, Grayson then asked a second group of 53 prisoners—all convicted of violent assaults on strangers—to rate the 60 videotaped subjects on their potential "muggability."

Whenever more than half the prisoners agreed that a potential victim fell into the first three most-easy-to-mug categories, Grayson put the videotape into a special category, which ultimately contained 20 people, male and female, young and old.

With the help of Jody Zacharias, executive director of the Laban Institute of Movement Studies, Grayson analyzed the way these 20 people walked. The researchers used a movement-analysis technique created by an Austro-Hungarian dancer-choreograher, Rudolf Laban, born in 1879.

Upon analysis, the 20 most muggable people turned out to have a number of distinctive movements, five of which, Grayson says, were apparently crucial in signaling vulnerability.

The most muggable people tended to take strides that were of unusual length, either too short or too long. Instead of walking heel to toe, they walked flatfooted. Instead of swinging their left arm while striding with their right foot, they moved their left arm and left foot, then right arm and right foot together. Instead of the usual figure 8-like sway of upper body and lower body, the most muggable people seemed to move their torsos at cross purposes to the bottom half of their bodies.

By isolating the movements that seem to trigger "muggability," the researchers say, people, especially victims of multiple assaults, may be taught how to move without signaling vulnerability.[1]

Teachers, like the walkers described in this article, can communicate muggability and non-muggability. In the classroom, this means that an assertive gait and gestures communicate assuredness, confidence, control of yourself, and positive feelings of esteem. When you carry yourself in this manner, you are telling your students that you feel good about yourself and feel good about being in your classroom. If you are not sure about what your body language is communicating to your students, have yourself videotaped for a twenty-minute teaching segment. If your school system does not have the equipment, you can usually work out an arrangement with the teaching department at your local school of education.

Watch your tape and see how you walk, how you gesture, and what messages you are sending to your students. If you feel that your non-verbal cues are communicating muggability, change slowly. Being comfortable with yourself will help you feel comfortable with your walk. Practice breathing and muscle relaxation as described in Chapter 3. Books on assertiveness training may also be used.

Once you have learned to relax, let your walk flow naturally from a relaxed, yet confident, position. Practice walking in this relaxed way in your classroom when no one else is present. Imagine yourself teaching, interacting with students, implementing consequences. Feel yourself in charge of your classroom. Feel the power of being in control. It is a power you demonstrate through relaxed confidence, not force. It might be helpful to work with a colleague who wants to practice the same skill. You can observe each other teaching and give each other feedback to see if you have transferred the skills from practice to real teaching situations.

Avoiding Power Struggles

One of the most troublesome problems that teachers face is "the power struggle." The typical power struggle occurs when the teacher implements a consequence and a student refuses to comply. The cycle continues when the teacher, in a more adamant tone, demands that the student comply and the student once again refuses or makes a wisecrack. The following example is a typical beginning for a power struggle.

Teacher: Bill, the rule in this classroom is to do your own work. Your consequence is to learn how to do your own work after school under my supervision.

Bill: (In front of whole class) I'm not coming, I have a job to do after school.

Teacher: (Upset and wanting to show class who is in charge) Yes, You will! Be here at three o'clock, understand?

Bill: (Needing to save face in front of his peers) I won't be here at three o'clock, and you can't make me.

Teacher: (Now the pressure is really on. He feels he must win) You will be here or else.

Bill: (Aware that the whole class is watching him) I won't be here and that's final.

By the time teacher and Bill reach this point, nothing short of a Middle East negotiator will have a chance to get either of them off the hook. They have both risked their professional and personal pride on the outcome of this power struggle, in front of an audience of students. The stakes are high, and although neither wants to lose, it is impossible for either to win. If the teacher forces Bill to come after school, Bill will make the teacher pay with interest later. If Bill doesn't come, the teacher will feel ridiculed and will punish Bill later for it.

A power struggle is like a classical animal trap or con game trap; that is, it is a one-way street that gets worse the harder you try to win. Jeffrey Z. Rubin's article in *Psychology Today* describes an activity that shows how this type of trap works:

> The psychological principles of self-entrapment are very similar to those that con artists employ to ensnare others.
>
> One devilishly simple and effective example of entrapment is a game known as the Dollar Auction, invented about 10 years ago by Martin Shubik, an economist at Yale. As his proving ground, Shubik allegedly used the Yale University cocktail-party circuit. Anyone can make some money—but perhaps lose some friends—by trying it out at a party.
>
> Take a dollar bill from your pocket and announce that you will auction it off to the highest bidder. People will be invited to call out bids in multiples of five cents until no further bidding occurs, at which point the highest bidder will pay the amount and win the dollar. The only feature that distinguishes this auction from traditional auctions, you point out, is the rule that the second-highest bidder will also be asked to pay

the amount bid, although he or she will obviously not win the dollar. For example, Susan has bid 30 cents and Bill has bid 25 cents; if the bidding stops at this point, you will pay Susan 70 cents ($1 minus the amount she bid) and Bill, the second-highest bidder, will have to pay you 25 cents. The auction ends when one minute has elapsed without any additional bidding. . . .

Several researchers have had people play the Dollar Auction game under controlled laboratory conditions and have found that the participants typically end up bidding far in excess of the $1 prize at stake, sometimes paying as much as $5 or $6 for a dollar bill. The interesting question is, of course, why? What motivates people to bid initially and to persist in a self-defeating course of action?

Thanks primarily to the extensive research of Allan Teger, a social psychologist at Boston University, the question has been answered. Teger found that when Dollar Auction participants were asked to give reasons for their bidding, their responses fell into one of two major motivational categories: economic and interpersonal. Economic motives include a desire to win the dollar, a desire to regain losses, and a desire to avoid losing more money. Interpersonal motives include a desire to save face, a desire to prove one is the best player, and a desire to punish the other person.

Economic motives appear to predominate in the early stages of the Dollar Auction. . . . As the bidding approaches $1—or when the amount invested equals the objective worth of the prize—the tension rises. At this stage Teger has found, the participants experience intense inner conflict, as measured by physiological measures of anxiety and nervousness; about half of them then quit the game.

People who remain in the auction past the $1 bid, however, typically stick with it to the bitter end—until they have exhausted their resources or their adversary has quit. Interpersonal motives come to the fore when the bid exceeds the objective value of the prize. Even though both players know they are sure to lose, each may go out of his or her way to punish the other, making sure that the other person loses even more, and each may become increasingly concerned about looking foolish by yielding to the adversary's aggression. Teger found that this mutual concern occasionally leads bidders to a cooperative solution to the problem of how to quit without losing face: a bid of $1 by one player, if followed by a quick final raise to $2 by the second, allows the first person to quit in the knowledge that both have lost equally.[2]

We have used the Dollar Auction game in our workshops with teachers to show how difficult it is to get out of a power struggle. We have slightly modified the auction, using a twenty-dollar bill instead of a one-dollar bill and starting the bidding at ten dollars. We also go up in fifty-cent increments. At the end when the bidding has escalated to between twenty-five and thirty dollars, we stop and talk about power struggles.

Generally there are only two ways out of the Dollar Auction trap. The first is for both remaining players to stop at twenty dollars and twenty dollars and fifty cents respectively. Then they can share their losses and gains together so that each loses a net of ten dollars and twenty-five cents. The second is for one player to stop and accept his loss (losing twenty dollars is better than losing forty dollars). These two options are the basis for stopping all power struggles in the classroom.

Steps in Avoiding Power Struggles

1. BE AWARE OF HOW POWER STRUGGLES CAN ENTRAP YOU

Commit yourself to avoiding them, even if it means initially backing down. Remember that continuation of a power struggle does not make you appear to "win." Continuation makes you look foolish, out of control, and at the same level as students who are arguing about whose mother wears red underwear. You must be prepared to see long-term victory (a cooperative, positive classroom climate) as more important than short-term winning. By victory we mean defusing a potentially escalating negative situation between teacher and student and changing it into an opportunity for positive communication and mutual trust.

2. TAKE CARE OF YOURSELF EMOTIONALLY

We have stated time and time again that it is critical for you not to carry anger, resentment, and other hostile feelings once a discipline situation is over. If you are angry with a student from an incident that happened the day before, you might enter a power struggle just to flex your muscles and show who is boss. Don't! Start fresh each day.

3. IGNORE STUDENTS' INITIATING POWER STRUGGLES

When a student tries to engage you in a power struggle, back off and ignore his attempt. Often, by simply ignoring the student's "hook" (catch the teacher), the power struggle is over before it starts. Notice the following example.

Teacher: (Walks slowly over to Ralph). Ralph, the rule in this class-room is that people are not for hitting. The consequence is for you to stay after school today and practice other ways of showing your anger.

Ralph: It wasn't my fault and you can't make me come after school.

Teacher: (Maintains eye contact with Ralph for a few seconds and returns to the front of the room) Now class, who can tell me who was the only president to resign from office?

In this example the teacher listened to Ralph's protest but did not acknowledge it in any way. If the teacher had said, "Yes, you will have to stay after school!" Ralph would have had to show the teacher and all of the other students in class that he was not going to show up. By ignoring the hook, the teacher has opened the door for Ralph to comply with the consequence. Before the class was over for the day, the teacher waited by the door and said privately in a calm, yet firm, voice, "Ralph, I expect to see you here after school!"

4. ACKNOWLEDGE THE STUDENT'S FEELINGS

In the above example, the teacher simply ignored the hook put out by the student. If the student had persisted, or if the teacher preferred to interact more directly to the hooking statement, she might have acknowledged the student's feelings, by active listening and reflection.

Teacher: (Walks slowly over to Ralph) Ralph, the rule in this classroom is that people are not for hitting. The consequence is for you to come after school today and learn some other ways to express your anger.

Ralph: It wasn't my fault, and I am not coming back after school.

Teacher: Slowly begins to walk back to resume teaching position.

Ralph: I said I'm not coming back after school.

Teacher: (Returns to close proximity to Ralph) Ralph, I can see that you are upset and angry, and that you feel that the hitting wasn't your fault. I understand how you might feel. However, this is not the time to discuss it, so let's get back to our lesson, and we can discuss our problem later.

By accepting that the problem was theirs and not only the student's, and by indicating that he understood Ralph's feelings, the teacher in this example prevented what might have escalated into a classic power struggle.

Becoming an active listener requires skill and practice. You must be able to step inside the student's experience and develop a sense for the feelings that are motivating the student's obnoxious behavior. Many troubling situations can be defused by listening with empathy to a student. Active listening means that you must make an educated guess about what a student is feeling and you then paraphrase these feelings by restating them to the student.

Louis, a student who demonstrated his power by loudly accusing Mr. Neilson of running a boring class, was shipped out to the office for such disruptive behavior. Mr. Neilson feared losing control of the class and felt a need to assert his power. Sending to the office was his solution and it was effective in removing the source of the problem, except Louis was always back for more the next day. One day, after Mr. Neilson had learned how to actively listen, Louis did his thing. But instead of using the standard threat of classroom exclusion, Mr. Neilson approached Louis as he continued his lesson and quietly said, ''Louis this class is probably the most boring, awful class you have to attend. It must be a real drag for you to be here. You probably wish you could be doing something else, and after class today, if you would like, I would be willing to discuss with you some ideas that you might have about how you could enjoy this class more.'' After this exchange, Mr. Neilson immediately returned to the day's lesson, and after the class, the two began a constructive process of discovering how Louis could be more stimulated and what he needed to be less disruptive.

5. PRIVATELY ACKNOWLEDGE POWER STRUGGLES

Tell the student directly that a power struggle is developing and you want to stop it. Often, you can defuse a potential power struggle by recognizing it and pointing it out to the student.

Teacher: Sally, the rule in this classroom is that only one person may speak at a time. You have chosen 5-minutes in Siberia (time-out area).

Sally: I was just asking what the homework was, it's not fair. I can speak if I want to.

Teacher: Sally, it seems that we both have a need to show who's boss, and we both can't win. You want me to know that you can talk if you want to, and I want you not to talk for five minutes to help you learn to follow the rule. I think that if we both try to prove who is the winner, neither one of us would like that very much, and in the end we would both lose. Let's calm down and talk about it later when neither one of us feels as angry as we do now.

In this example, the teacher explained to Sally what might happen if they each escalated the situation and suggested they discuss it later. This effectively ended the need on the part of the student to show her power, and in the end, both the teacher and student won.

6. DO NOT TRY TO EMBARRASS STUDENTS INTO SUBMISSION

Keep all communication private between only you and the student. Do not embarrass the student in front of his peers. Power struggles are created when two parties need to win. The stakes are always increased when the struggle is publicly displayed. The teacher feels a need to show the other students who is boss, and the student needs to show the other students that he is not intimidated by the teacher. Often, both teacher and student make statements when others are present that they are both sorry for later but are locked into with no way out. If you can keep most of your communication private, you eliminate much of the need for you and the student to save face.

We have stated that when a power struggle is imminent, it is better to stop before it escalates into an unsolvable problem. We do not feel this is a sign of weakness, but strength. However, we feel that follow-up is critical when you either ignore or acknowledge feelings to avoid a power struggle. If the student still refuses the consequence, then it is critical that you not allow him back into your class until he has accepted the consequence. One rule you can include in your social contract that helps is, ''Students who do not accept a consequence will not be permitted to stay in class until they have done so.'' You need to check with your principal and/or vice principal to let them know that you intend to have this policy prior to including it in your contract. Most principals will cooperate with your request and set up a system for out-of-school suspension, in-school suspension, or some other short-term arrangement. When you explain your need for this policy, make it clear that you will not abuse it by asking for suspensions from your class unless it is absolutely necessary for you to maintain control. You might also ask what you can do for your principal to help him make your new policy work from his perspective. We have found that the vast majority of principals are thrilled when a teacher provides any sensible discipline program to them, and most will be supportive.

In the example cited earlier, if Ralph had not come in after school, then he would have been met by the principal or vice principal before school the next day and informed that he could not return to Mr. X's class until he honored the consequence. Furthermore, Ralph is responsible for all of the work missed during his absence. It is now Ralph's choice to accept the consequence and return to class or wait it out. Most students will accept the consequence and end the matter rather quickly. By not publicly flexing his power, the teacher has shown the other students that he will not embarrass them or allow them to hook him into a power based game. He has quietly and confidently taken charge. By not allowing the student into the class without accepting the consequence, the teacher has shown he means business and that in the long run it is better for students to follow the social contract (assuming of course that the student has an investment in being there). When Ralph did not appear in class the next day, all of the students wondered where he was. Ralph's absence made a strong statement of the authority of the teacher, one which was much stronger than if he had tried to win a verbal argument with Ralph in class.

There is one other strategy that is helpful for avoiding power struggles. We find that if you can identify students who are prone to engage in a power struggle, you can develop a mutual plan to deal with the problem through prevention. Meet with the student at a time when you can both be alone and when you have no problem between you. Tell the student that you know that when you ask him to accept a consequence, he sometimes has a problem accepting it. Ask what you can do when this happens to make it easier for the student to accept it. Such students usually want the teacher to be less public and are often willing to accept a non-verbal cue, such as a head nod, so that he will know, but the other students will not. Brainstorm three or four strategies together that the student can agree to, to help both of you to avoid power struggles in the future. When you must implement a consequence with the student, be sure to follow your agreed upon guidelines.

How to Implement Consequences when More than One Student Is Acting Out

So far in this chapter we have focused on situations in which the teacher has dealt with a single student who has violated the social contract. Sometimes you may be faced with three or four students who are acting out at the same time. The better you know the dynamics of your class, the more effective you will be in handling this type of situation.

The first step is to pick the one student among the acting-out group who is the most prominent opinion maker for the class. This student is the one who the other students either respect the most, or fear the most, or are amused by the most, or in some way is looked up to by other students. Stop the misbehavior with this student first.

Often that is enough to stop it for everyone else. When you stop the misbehavior with the opinion maker, then the others will follow suit. If you have two opinion makers acting out at the same time, pick the more prominent one first, and stop the misbehavior with him; then go over to the second one and repeat the same process.

Occasionally you can be effective dealing with a group as a whole. The best time to try dealing with an entire group is when they are in close proximity with each other, perhaps working together at a table. Walk over to the group slowly and calmly. Make eye contact with each student before you speak. Then state the rule and consequence scanning the entire group slowly with your eyes; maintain eye contact. When you are finished, scan the group one more time with your eyes to make sure they know you are serious and mean business.

Usually it is not effective to deal with groups of students by yelling at the class as a whole. This only leads to more confusion and noise. If you continue to have problems with groups of students, it might be worth your while to have a class meeting and see if you and your students can think of any preventive strategies for minimizing the problem.

When several students in a class are acting out, it becomes necessary for you to acknowledge a mismatch between the needs of your students and what you are doing or not doing. Sometimes a solution is as simple as cruising (walking about the whole room as you present a lesson to keep in close occasional proximity with all students), while other times you may need to be willing to substantially modify your curriculum or method of presentation for substantial change to occur. When you are confronted with a large-group classroom discipline problem, you must maintain an attitude of calm, a security about yourself, and a willingness to explore change.

For the Administrator

Teachers and administrators need to take direct action when rules are broken. The best action is to choose the most effective consequence from the range of pre-established consequences related to the broken rule. When a rule is broken, it is not the time for lectures, scolding, bargaining, accepting excuses, moralizing, or making a public display of the student. You can be a role model for effective consequence implementation in working with both students and teachers. You may also demonstrate effective consequence implementation at a faculty meeting, or preferably at smaller group meetings such as a support group (see previous chapter) or department meeting, so that teachers will be less inhibited to ask questions and try role playing themselves.

When you observe your teachers in the classroom you can use the list of eight principles for effective action (page 142) as a feedback instrument. As with any observation, it is important that you share your plan with the teacher prior to the observation and receive agreement that this type of feedback will be helpful. If a teacher is not interested in using the list for feedback, it will not help to do so anyway. Remember that your goal in using the principles is to improve discipline, not to collect information for a formal evaluation.

You can use the Dollar Auction technique described on page 149 during a faculty meeting to introduce the topic of a power struggle. Once the auction is complete, discuss how various faculty handle a power struggle once they are in them, and what they do to stop getting caught in the first place.

When you see a power struggle playing itself out between a student and teacher you can serve as a "fact-finder" or "mediator" to help bring an end to a dispute. Recognize that power struggles are caused by two people having a different set of "wants" with each believing that the other is unwilling to compromise. Try to get the student and the teacher to identify their demands to each other, and then try to solicit a commitment from each to do one thing for the other. It is sometimes helpful to serve as a third person in helping to resolve such disputes.

References

1. Foreman, Judy, "How Muggable Are You? Clue is Your Walk," Boston Globe, January 20, 1981.

2. Rubin, Jeffrey, "The Psychology of Entrapment," *Psychology Today*, March 1981, pp. 58–59.

SEVEN

Creative Discipline for Out-of-Control Students

*I*t seems that every year most teachers have a few students who defy all efforts at becoming constructive members of the class. Instead, these students appear to enjoy setting up one power struggle after another as they engage in a series of behaviors that disrupt the learning process. They are the students who loudly complain of the teacher's unfairness, who make various noises and sounds constantly, who show up to class unprepared, and who simply refuse to take responsibility for their actions. Their behavior is always somebody else's fault. These are the students with whom the teacher finds himself at "wit's end" and who often proclaims, "Somebody's got to do something with that kid!" They are likely to be referred for diagnostic services and often, although not always, turn out to be from homes in which parental conflict is the norm. They often believe themselves to be inferior, inadequate, and unworthy, yet hide this from themselves and others through destructive efforts that make them feel in control. It is typical to find these students functioning well below grade level despite adequate intellectual potential. They have been identified as failures, believe this to be true, and go about living up to these expectations. They take comfort in surrounding themselves with others who mistake inadequacy for power.

Although factors outside of school are often at the foundation of such problems, these students generally find the school environment to be unresponsive to their needs. Because their life is often rooted in confusion and powerlessness, they resent a system that tells them what to do, how to do it, and how well they have done. When they come to school with their primary concern being how to belong with others and they are expected to do math, they become bored.

Some Alternatives within the School System

We have found that the social contract process has been very effective with many of these students because for the first time in their lives they are asked to shape the environment in which they live. And they are involved as a member within a community that teaches them how to share decision making. They are often much more responsive to following the rules and accepting the consequences within this arrangement than they are when the teacher presents himself as an authority figure and demands compliance from them. Such students are generally in need of a teacher who mixes democracy with authority, is soft and warm as well as tough as nails, who responds with immediacy to untoward behavior, and who is both predictably consistent as well as loose and unpredictable. In short, working with chronic misbehavers and out-of-control students requires a broad repertoire of behavioral skills and ways of being.

One of the problems in dealing with these students is that they know their own reputations. Because they have been successful in building these reputations (for some, over many years), they want to maintain and even enhance them. This is the one area of school where they misguidedly achieve a degree of success. Usually many methods have been attempted with these students, and for some, positive changes have occurred. Unfortunately, there are still some who have been actively listened to and who have been positively reinforced yet continue to misbehave. One solution for these students is to find another educational environment that will be more suited to their needs. We are firm believers in the principle that school is not for all students and that there are some students who need more than we can give. If it is possible, we urge you to work with your administration and mental health team to properly place such students in smaller, more individualized programs.

Unfortunately, many states and school systems are not as responsive to alternative placements as they need to be for helping difficult students. Complicated policies, bureaucratic red tape, and lack of resources all lead to a delay at best and often a refusal to remove these students from your class. When this happens you are often left with little choice but to try to do your best and meet the needs of all students, including the most troublesome, as best you can.

In addition to the extreme cases mentioned above, there are some students who act out enough to make you feel that they are totally uncontrollable, but because of the nature of their misbehavior, or because it runs in cycles, you may believe that removal from class on a permanent basis is too radical. You just wish there was something you could do to keep those students under control more effectively.

Each of these student types are difficult to work with because of their history of locking into power struggles with teachers and other authority figures. They have already formed an established pattern of, "You do this, then I'll do that, and then when you try this, I'll escalate with that." The one positive aspect of teaching these students, and it is significant if you choose to feel its power, is that you have very little, if anything, to lose. Because all of the traditional methods have proven ineffective, you are free to try anything you want, within reason.

In spite of the freedom that difficult students allow, many times teachers continually try strategies they know from prior experience are ineffective. Yet it is very difficult to abandon these unsuccessful methods because (1) teachers are often unaware of other, more unusual options, and (2) emotions often run high when teachers are confronted with these students. We know that students who challenge authority make teachers aware of many feelings that are difficult to accept: anger, frustration, sadness, feelings of failure, and helplessness. These feelings make it difficult to try new strategies and behaviors.

As we have said, teachers have the most power to change their tactics in working with out-of-control students because they have nothing left to lose! They have tried all of the conventional methods and none of them worked, at least not for very long. Feeling defeated, their tendency is to grit their teeth and bear it, counting the days, hours, and minutes until Friday. Although there are no surefire ways to effectively manage the out-of-control student, there are an assortment of survival strategies that can build confidence and add excitement to the often draining process of attempting to control the behavior of a student who seems principally motivated to drive you crazy. Other chapters have described a comprehensive process for discipline prevention and effective action(s) to be taken when students break rules or refuse to accept consequences. But when these methods fail, it is time to try new, creative methods that have the potential to at least change the way you feel and respond, which can give you a new way to perceive your interactions with these difficult students.

The resolution dimension contains positive confrontation strategies that are negotiated between you and a student (sometimes one or more resource personnel, teachers, or parents are included) in an effort to make life more pleasant for both you and the student. Also included within the resolution dimension are numerous unusual strategies of classroom management that we term "creative discipline." These strategies are recommended for use with those students who have repeatedly shown a low probability and willingness to change their behavior.

What Is Creative Discipline?

Our concept of Creative Discipline involves examining the transactions between the out-of-control student and the teacher. As we said earlier, this transaction is usually controlled by the student because he knows exactly how to "get the teacher." Teachers often relate to out-of-control students in very predictable ways because of limited options and strategies available to them. Thus, teacher and student are often trapped in their own little game, with no one winning in the long run. The main goal of Creative Discipline is to offer the teacher some ways to make those transactions less predictable. The idea is that when a disruptive student is faced with unfamiliar responses by the teacher, he might open up his willingness to try to develop a new pattern. Many of the activities suggested here are designed with that goal in mind. Some strategies are helpful over a long period of time while others are for short-term use.

Another way we can look at dealing with disruptive students is to focus on the difference between teacher change and student change. Unless the student is willing to try new behaviors to improve his relationships with the teacher and/or class, the responsibility for change belongs to the teacher.

There are two different kinds of steps you can take. The first is designed to help you grow, to help you develop more options, and give you more strength. The second is designed to open the door to a new pattern of interactions between you and your students. We also wish to remind you that the activities in Chapter 3 relating to stress reduction are critically important in dealing with difficult students. While trying some of the strategies outlined in this chapter you should be taking very good emotional care of yourself to keep your stress at a minimum. Use these two chapters hand in hand when dealing with out-of-control students.

Individual Negotiations

The social contract, which involves a total class decision-making process regarding rules and consequences, is often effective in preventing misbehavior among a large number of students who had previously created classroom disruption. However, there are some students who repeatedly violate the rules of the social contract. These students need individualized help in learning how to follow the classroom rules. Positive confrontation involves setting aside some time to meet individually with the student and attempting to resolve differences through negotiation. The process of confrontation is patterned after often used processes of mediation that attempt to resolve disputes between management and workers.

Although individual negotiation through positive confrontation can be accomplished by a meeting or series of meetings between the teacher and student, we recommend that a third person who is neutral to the conflict be called upon to help mediate a resolution of the conflict. This third party can be another teacher, a guidance counselor, an administrator, resource person, or even another student. The important attributes of the third person are (1) being a good listener, (2) being neutral to the conflict, and (3) somebody who can remain calm when the going gets rough.

Individual negotiation involves giving both the teacher and the student an opportunity to state resentments or dislikes to each other ["What do you dislike about what Billy (Mrs. Smith) does?"]; stating appreciations or behaviors that are liked or appreciated ["What do you like about Billy (Mrs. Smith)?"]; making demands upon each other ["What do you want from Billy (Mrs. Smith)?" or "How do you want Billy (Mrs. Smith) to behave that is different from what he (she) is doing now?"].

After each person to the conflict states resentments, the other is asked to repeat the statement to ensure understanding. This is done for each step in the process. After all of this information is presented, the teacher and student are requested to negotiate with each other ("Which of Mrs. Smith's demands are you willing to meet?" "Which of Billy's demands are you willing to meet?"). When a plan of action is settled upon through agreement, each person is requested to sign the contract and another meeting is scheduled to check how well the plan is working.

Individual negotiation requires from the aggrieved teacher a willingness to (1) share directly with the student, (2) take the risk of hearing unpleasant things from the student, and (3) consider program modifications for the student.

While extensive involvement between the teacher, all school resources, and the home is not always essential to the success of this kind of contract, it certainly helps and is strongly suggested.

The following example of an individually negotiated contract at Morristown High School (New Jersey) provides an excellent view of how a well-integrated plan of action negotiated between home and school with a student's involvement can effectively deal with the problem of chronic class-cutting. Although not all schools have the good fortune of extensive resource services, the principles of involvement and responsibility are applicable to all situations (the Morristown plan is called the "Comprehensive Social Contract").

The Comprehensive Social Contract *

What is the Comprehensive Social Contract?

The Comprehensive Social Contract is basically a resolution dimension contract between the student, school personnel, and the student's family.

The unique aspect of the Comprehensive Social Contract is that everyone claims ownership to the student's problem; specific tasks are outlined for each person to carry out to ensure a positive change in the student's behavior.

To effectively help a student, not only should his responsibilities be carefully outlined but also the responsibilities of all others involved in that student's life inside and outside of school.

---

* We wish to thank Rocco Feravolo, principal of Morristown (N.J.) High School for submitting this material.

Features of the Comprehensive Contract

In writing a Comprehensive Social Contract, the following guidelines should be an integral part of it:

- Everyone claims ownership to the problem. (not only the student.)
- Be honest and open with the student and his family.
- Focus on the feelings of the parents and student.
- Show faith in the ability of the student to correct his behavior.
- Present alternate plans if necessary.
- Set realistic goals for the student.
- Establish an on-going communications system between home and school.

The Comprehensive Social Contract is being used at Morristown High School to deal with chronic class-cutting.

An efficient attendance policy is one of the most important factors to an effective code of behavior for high school students. Our attendance policy has been specifically designed to help students understand the importance of regular school attendance as the key to success in school.

The concept of the attendance team was developed several years ago and has proven successful. The attendance team consists of the teachers of the student, the guidance counselor, the attendance teacher, an attendance coordinator, a clerical assistant, and a class administrator.

The *classroom teacher* keeps accurate records of the students' attendance and counsels students who do not attend class regularly.

The *attendance teacher* is responsible for taking the official attendance for the day and is the first classroom teacher with whom the student is scheduled daily.

The *attendance coordinator* is a classroom teacher with no more than two teaching assignments—the balance of the school day being devoted to attendance matters.

The *clerical assistant* helps the attendance coordinator to telephone parents and keeps student records.

The *guidance counselor* is the person assigned to the student.

The *class administrator* is one who has been assigned to oversee the attendance for a particular grade level.

Jim's Comprehensive Social Contract

1. Jim agrees to attend his algebra class on a regular basis. If he feels that he wants to discuss his feelings about the class, he will make an appointment for a conference with Mr. Arthur, his algebra teacher.

2. Mr. Arthur agrees to help Jim during his free period with any of his assignments. Mr. Arthur will set the time and place for the extra help.

3. Mrs. March, Jim's guidance counselor, will arrange an appointment with Jim every Friday during the sixth period for the purpose of discussing the week's work with Jim.

4. Mrs. Koch, the attendance coordinator, will arrange a conference with Jim each Monday during the sixth period to review his week's responsibilities.

5. Mr. and Mrs. O'Brien, Jim's parents, will call Mrs. Koch, the attendance coordinator, every Friday at 1:30 P.M. to get a progress report on Jim's attendance during the week.

6. Mr. and Mrs. O'Brien will monitor Jim's homework period at home for the next two weeks to be certain that all assignments are complete.

7. Bill O'Brien, Jim's older brother, will check his algebra assignments to be certain that Jim is prepared for the next day's work.

_____

Student's Signature

_____

Attendance Coordinator's Signature

_____

Parent/Guardian's Signature

Social Contract Approved by

_____

Class Administrator

It is therefore a tenet of the Comprehensive Social Contract to involve all parties to a conflict in its resolution and to specify very

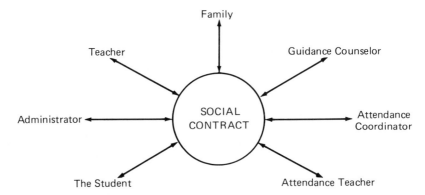

FIGURE ONE *Everyone has a part in the development of the Comprehensive Social Contract.*

clearly what each person is responsible for. Jim's Comprehensive Social Contract illustrates these principles.

Goals of Creative Discipline

Creative discipline contains strategies that involve both a new way of perceiving classroom interactions and a series of strategies that do not fall into the normally accepted area of classroom management. Teachers who behave creatively with their out-of-control students are not as concerned about things not working out as they are with taking the risk of doing something new with the possibility, not certainty, that the situation will improve. They have exhausted their supply of traditionally learned behavior management techniques and are not afraid to experiment with new ideas. They believe that there is little left to lose, and therefore, they are willing to explore the use of rather unusual and extreme techniques, which are needed to preserve the integrity of the classroom.

The goals of creative discipline are:

1. To stop a student's misbehavior in such a way so that there is little interruption in the flow of the lesson.

2. To insure that the out-of-control student is stopped from preventing others from learning what you have to offer.

3. To refuse the student's efforts at hooking you into a power struggle.

4. To defuse tense situations by using humor including poking fun at yourself.

5. To define yourself as having the capability to remain calm in the face of "shocking behavior."

6. To occasionally say and do unusual things so that you are somewhat unpredictable to the student and may therefore be seen as somewhat different from the masses of other teachers whom the student views as the enemy.

7. To search for methods of communication that may lead to a new pattern of interaction between you and the student(s).

8. To offer the student substitute outlets for expressing feelings that interrupt the learning process.

9. To learn how to appreciate those students who are intent upon driving you crazy.

Using creative discipline is not easy because it requires ways of being that most of us have had no experience or practice with. Many of us are unable to be truly creative because of the blocks that have been placed in our path while we were becoming socialized.

Blocks to Creative Discipline

Nevin, Nevin, and Danzig have listed fourteen blocks to creativity.[1] We have found that teachers are most affected by nine of these blocks in searching for creative solutions to problems posed by the "out-of-control" student. These nine blocks are defined and followed by strategies that are designed to help you cope more effectively with the out-of-control student.

1. FEAR OF FAILURE

Fear of failure prevents teachers from trying something new. Failing in the old way with disruptive students is preferred to failing in a new way. It can be scary to try something novel, even when the old behavior is predictably ineffective. The adage, "I know what I have but I don't know what I'll get," keeps teachers locked into habitually ineffective response patterns with disruptive students. Yet with out-of-control students we have very little to lose. Failure has already occurred.

2. RELUCTANCE TO PLAY

This block relates to the tendency to be too serious and literal in confrontations with problem students. Often the seriousness of the situation, especially when violent students are involved, leads the teacher to a fixed pattern of responding rigidly to all student misbehavior. "If I give an inch, they'll take a mile" becomes a prominent belief in dealing with students. We recommend that teachers be firm when problems occur, but that they allow themselves to play in their interactions with these students when things are going better. Also, humor is one of the most effective disarming strategies in potentially explosive situations.

Paul was loudly chattering with some classmates in his junior high school class. He was told three times to be quiet, and when he persisted, Mr. McCarthy said, "Paul I want to *see* you after class." Paul's sarcastic comment was, "Is there something wrong with your glasses?" A conventional teacher's response would be to write a referral, to give Paul a zero, to threaten him with a parent conference, etc. Mr. McCarthy, with a half-smile, retorted, "Paul, my glasses are just fine. When I have them on, I can *hear* all the loud talking coming from your end of the room." This resulted in momentary classroom laughter, which defused what could certainly have become a teacher-student power struggle.

Amy, a senior high music teacher, was confronted by an awkward male student who demanded to use a guitar. Amy refused because she wanted to lock up the music room. The student, agitated by her response, blurted out, "Fuck you." Amy, trying to divert a probable tense situation, answered in an obvious non-serious tone, "No thanks." The student laughed and apologized to her. She took a risk by using humor rather than power.

Play is also extremely important in the problem-solving phase of discipline when new ideas are generated. By playfully looking at the situation, many new options can be considered, which might be missed with a more serious attitude.

3. RESOURCE MYOPIA

Failure to see one's inner strengths and to recognize external resources are the effects of this block. When nothing seems to work, feelings of inadequacy or self-failure occur. Feeling frustrated, we become irritable; we keep our tension hidden within or blame ourselves and others for not correcting the situation. One way to help overcome this block is to identify the strengths that you have. Each day that you do something related to discipline that gives you confidence, making you feel positive about yourself, note what you did or what skills you have that helped you feel this way. Make a personal list of strengths which says, "I am strong because _____." It is also helpful to learn how to create effective support from school resources so that help is available when things are not going as well for you as you would like.

4. FRUSTRATION AVOIDANCE

This block involves giving up too soon and short circuiting potentially effective approaches that, given more time and/or realistic goal-setting, would have the desired result. Resolving problems with out-of-control students takes time! Many teachers set themselves up for frustration by expecting wholesale changes in students and give up even when small improvements are visible. Small improvements often go unnoticed because they are usually overshadowed by a continuation of a wide range of misbehavior. But if you and the student are to experience any feeling of success together, you must clearly define what it is you want from the student in very small increments and be prepared to share appreciations when these improvements occur. You must also have a lot of patience for the misbehavior that continues. It is not realistic to expect the student who communicates through the put-down to cease entirely, but a pattern in which such language gradually diminishes can be met with a sense of accomplishment by the teacher. Being blocked with frustration avoidance interferes with such a sense of accomplishment.

5. CUSTOM BOUND

Teachers are custom bound when they emphasize the traditional way of doing things. This happens not because these methods are better but because that's the way things have always been done. Many school customs, such as giving detention and sending to the principal, are ineffective with the out-of-control student. If these traditional methods had worked, then the student would not be a problem for you. If you become aware that this block is limiting your potential responses, then it may help just to ask yourself two questions: "Am I doing this because it's a habit or custom?" and "Does it work?" If the answer is "yes" to the first and "no" to the second, it's time to replace those methods with more creative and fresh ideas.

6. IMPOVERISHED FANTASY LIFE

This block means that objective reality is over valued. In relation to out-of-control students, we reject some of our more creative ideas and insights because we do not see them as realistically working; yet many of them may either work or lead to other ideas that will work. If you find yourself continually saying, "Yes, . . . but the reality is that. . . ." or "That sounds good, but. . . .", then this block is limiting you and your creativity. Remind yourself, or ask a good friend or colleague to remind you each time you use this type of expression, and then change the "It sounds good, but . . ." to "It sounds good and I'll try it."

7. Fear of the Unknown

Fearing situations that have unknown outcomes can predictably prevent you from many successful options in dealing with out-of-control students. Many approaches that appear at first glance to be too radical may be just what is needed for your most difficult students. Begin by listing all of the possible outcomes, so that the unknown becomes known. ("If I did _____ then _____.") Be as imaginative, ridiculous, and far-out as you wish. Remember, nothing was ever discovered that did not at first appear totally improbable. Try the new strategy. Your experiences more than your lists will give you a wider knowledge of the consequences of your actions, and there will be less unknown to fear.

8. Reluctance to Exert Influence

Sometimes we are afraid to actively confront disruptive students because we do not want to risk losing the confrontation. In more extreme cases, we fear challenging students who might make our lives more difficult, or who may cause physical harm. The result of this block is to come across as wishy-washy or weak. This gives the disruptive student the message that he can get away with whatever he wants, and the other students get the message that they have a teacher who is not in control.

It is far better to learn how to effectively confront a student who is frequently disturbing so that there is no personal humiliation, power struggles are avoided, and your demands are clear and understandable. Tell the disruptive student(s) exactly what you want him to do, and exactly what will happen if he doesn't do it. A matter-of-fact, non-condescending tone should accompany the message. This discussion is best served when only you and the student are present so as to avoid the predictable battle of wills that is most likely to occur when "saving face" in front of others becomes the primary issue.

To be able to achieve this goal, you will need to prepare by listing exactly what your demands are, what consequences you have for not meeting your demands (these can be extreme for extreme cases), and by building your base or support. You should also indicate what you are willing to do for the student when demands are met. Support should include the principal, who must be willing to back you in your demands and consequences, resource personnel, and teachers who will give you emotional support, which you may need. The additional time with the student can also be used as a way of finding out what the student needs in class, and you might choose to allow the student to make some demands of you.

9. ONE-SIDED IDEAS

This block results from having polarized ideas and from seeing issues in either/or terms when it is more appropriate to see things in a more integrated fashion. We often see only the negative side of disruptive students. Yet all students who are hard have a soft side, and all students who are mean have a kind side. By conceptualizing the other side of these students and seeing them as having the potential to be the opposite of what they usually are, we can help them become kinder, softer, and more willing to not disrupt in class. Just by letting these students know that we appreciate these other sides and that in some ways we can appreciate the "bad" as well, we will be setting the stage for them to improve their behavior. Ask yourself, "What is there about the disruptive behavior that I can appreciate?" For example, appreciations for fighting might be (from the student's viewpoint):

1. wanting to show yourself to be strong
2. letting go of anger and not allowing it to build up
3. not taking other people's guff
4. being desirable to your peers
5. showing the teacher that you hate feeling stupid

It is not your intention to sanction the misbehavior, but by learning how disruptive behavior can be appreciated and through communicating this understanding to the student, the need to act out is reduced. When disruptive students begin to feel connected to a teacher who can appreciate them, their need to do damage diminishes.

Eliminating any of these blocks can be a significant factor in increasing your ability to behave creatively when confronted with out-of-control students. The first step in adopting a new way of behaving creatively is to inventory your own behaviors in relation to these common blocks. Try the following self-evaluation to see how these blocks affect you. Do this now and then again after you have finished reading this chapter. It is important at this stage of the process not to judge yourself in either positive or negative terms. Try to understand fully which are your particular trouble blocks but avoid putting yourself down or seeing yourself as not creative. Every one of us has the ability to be creative, just as each of us blocks our own creativity in many ways. The important thing is to learn how to reduce these blocks and to create new alternatives for confronting out-of-control students.

Creative Discipline Inventory

The purpose of this inventory is to give you a better understanding of how you block your creativity when confronted with out-of-control students. Before writing, close your eyes and imagine your classroom and your feelings and actions when the out-of-control student misbehaves. Think of more than one student, if you had more during the last few years. Once you have an accurate picture in your mind, fill out the following form:

STEP ONE

Rank each block as follows:
Rank 1 the block that you believe is your personal biggest block, 2 the second biggest block, and the rest until 9 is the least significant for you.

1. Fear of failure _____.
2. Reluctance to play _____.
3. Resource myopia _____.
4. Frustration avoidance _____.
5. Custom bound _____.
6. Impoverished fantasy life _____.
7. Fear of the unknown _____.
8. Reluctance to exert influence _____.
9. One-sided ideas _____.

STEP TWO

For each of the highest ranked blocks, fill out the following statements:

1. (Name of block) _____.
   a. List two specific examples from your teaching (with out-of-control students) of this block.
      (1)
      (2)
   b. List two specific examples from your teaching of your not being blocked in this way.
      (1)
      (2)
   c. List three specific steps you can, and will, take to reduce the influence of this block in your teaching.
      (1)
      (2)
      (3)

STEP THREE

Keep a simple record of how effective each of your steps was in reducing your blocks by noting

1. whether you actually did them as planned
2. whether you did them enough
3. how you felt doing them
4. what effect did they have on your out-of-control student
5. what effect they had on how you feel about yourself and your ability to handle difficult students.

Creative Discipline Techniques

Once you have reviewed your creative discipline results, you will most likely find areas where you can allow yourself more creativity. You are now ready to try some new techniques with out-of-control students. Try some of the following suggestions.

School-Wide Inventory

Write out a situation or problem you face on a dittomaster and leave off the ending—like a mystery puzzle. Distribute copies to any of the teachers in the school whom you trust, or who you feel has a good reputation for dealing with out-of-control students. Include either the principal or vice-principal and one or two resource personnel, such as the school psychologist. Have each of them write in their ending, or how they would handle the situation. Ask them to be specific.

After you collect the responses, rank order them in order of most to least preferable. Each time a situation similar to the one in your inventory occurs, try each of the trial solutions in order, until you have tried them all. Each time you have tried one, write at the bottom of the paper how you felt doing it and how successful the strategy was. It is important to try all of the suggestions without prejudgment. Once you have gone through the entire list, eliminate any suggestions that didn't work or made you feel very uncomfortable. Review the blocks to creativity to see if you gave each suggestion a full opportunity to be successful. Refine and try again any strategy which either worked with the student or made you feel better.

The Discipline Institute

Imagine that you are the leader of the famed *Discipline Institute*, a creative institute dedicated to solving the most difficult discipline problems. In fact, you only accept severe cases, referring the more common problems and easily resolved ones to the local discipline expert. Your specialty is the most difficult cases the *Institute* accepts, and your caseload has as its number one priority your own biggest classroom problem. Write it up in an impersonal way as if it belonged to somebody else. Gather your *Institute* colleagues (friends or staff members at a team or faculty meeting), and role play your *Institute* staff meeting. Use the staff meeting to think of as many off-beat, seemingly crazy ideas as you can. Stay in your role as members of the *Discipline Institute* throughout the role play.

Once you have generated a list of solutions, imagine that you are the teacher client, and list all your objections to the suggested ideas. Now return to your role as the *Institute* leader and refute, in writing, all of the objections, and explain why the ideas will work. Try as many of the ideas as you can. Be certain to pick at least one that you are convinced is so extraordinary as to not be believable, and do it. The sooner you realize how little you really have to lose, the more quickly will your creativity flourish.

Role Reversal

The technique of allowing a student to play teacher for a short time has been used by many teachers. This strategy is designed to carry that concept one step further. Give the student the responsibility of teaching your class for a significant time period. Younger students might have fifteen minutes, middle grade students an hour or two, and older students one-half or a full day (this is a lot of time to give up, but we feel that improvement with out-of-control students may well be worth it). You take the student's place and act the way the student usually does. After the experience, meet privately with the student to try to creatively solve your conflicts, but stay in your role reversal. In other words, you continue to play the student, and the student continues to play the teacher as you creatively try to find ways for both of you to resolve the conflict. Once agreement has been reached, honor your agreement in your real roles.

Using Humor and Nonsense

Write down various jokes, phrases, sayings, and statements that you find funny or nonsensical. Try to include in your list some that are certain to get a rise from many of your students. At least once per day for one week when a student behaves disruptively, respond with one of your "funny" statements. For example as Jack comes to class late for the third day in a row, tell him wryly, "Jack! Did you know that Peter Piper picked a peck of pickled peppers?" Contrast Jack's reaction to this with how things are when he's told, "Jack, where's your pass!

While humor will neither defuse all explosive situations nor produce long-term behavioral change, it does set up possibilities for relationships to be formed that lessen the likelihood of power struggles. Moscowitz and Hayman found that those teachers rated "best" by inner-city high school students used more humor than did those rated "typical." Other characteristics of "best" teachers were discussing current events in class, not yelling while disciplining, and empathizing with students' feelings.[2]

Behaving Paradoxically

Behaving paradoxically can be a very effective method with anti-authority students. It is based upon a psychotherapeutic technique developed by Victor Frankl.[3] Frankl found that some people resist changing even when they want to change. Because they resist change, they respond to suggestions for change by continuing to behave maladaptively. He discovered that many people can be helped by having somebody strongly suggest that the person continue to behave exactly as they have been and to even suggest that they exaggerate their maladaptive behavior. This is called "siding with a person's resistance."

For example, a therapist might suggest to a person who is afraid of the dark that tonight when it is dark they should be sure to feel extremely terrified and to make sure that their fear keeps them awake. Frankl found that for various reasons, this method can be highly effective in creating more adaptive behaviors for people. It is similar to the old-world adage of using reverse psychology (suggesting the opposite of what you want a person to do in order to have them do what you want). In a school situation, the message of the teacher is firmly, "I want you (student) to try to keep behaving exactly as you have been. You are just being yourself!" This is in contrast to, "The way you are behaving is unacceptable, and I expect or demand you to change." The former paradoxical message may have the effect of eliciting a challenge to the student who may then defy the teacher and behave in a desirable way. Consider the following typical and paradoxical messages:

EXAMPLE   *Typical:* "This is the third day that you have not done your homework. The consequence is that you will have to remain after school."

Paradoxical: "This is the third day that you have not done your homework. This is terrific! (genuine) Your assignment for tonight is to try hard to forget your homework tomorrow."

EXAMPLE   *Typical:* "Larry, stop throwing erasers! That will be five minutes of time-out for you."

Paradoxical: "Gee, Larry, you have a great jump shot with that eraser. You ought to try using it more often because I know that you cannot talk out your problems when you are throwing erasers."

Example   *Typical:* "Jane, I will tolerate no more swearing in this class. If you use those words again, you will not come with us on the field trip."

Paradoxical: "Jane, you said, "_____." Tell me how you are defining that right now, and I will write the definition on the blackboard."

The contrasting styles are probably obvious to you. The *typical* responses will work with most students who respect the voice of authority. They do not work for anti-authority kids. The paradoxical message sets up a challenge to the student whose behavioral mode of functioning is contradictory to the message. If a student does the homework assignment in defiance of your instructions to him to forget it, then you have motivated him to do a valued school task. If he forgets it, then he has behaved appropriately according to your wishes. You can reward his compliance. Either way, you win! The same can be said for Larry. As an anti-authority youngster, the five minutes, or for that matter, five hours of time out will make no impact on his undesirable behavior. By acknowledging his ability to throw erasers as a strength, you have taken away this weapon of control and have challenged him to learn to talk as well as throw things. By telling him that he cannot talk, you have potentially motivated him to prove to you and himself that he can. "If that lousy authority figure thinks I cannot talk, well then, I will just have to show him that I can." The process involves setting up a situation where the student has to behave more appropriately as a way of defying your authority.

There are situations in which we would not advise this technique in a school setting. The most obvious is fighting or hard hitting (as opposed to the camaraderie shoving that most junior high school students use to express the combination of friendship and manhood). Obviously it is too dangerous for a teacher to encourage a student to hurt another student.

Sometimes, the other students will feel threatened and angry by the use of this technique. They may perceive their "out-of-control" peer as receiving preferential treatment and will experience more hostility toward the student and the teacher. It is often helpful to have a class discussion (when the identified student is not present) to explain the purpose of this "preferential treatment" to the class members. The concept of fair and not equal can be very useful in this process, see page 120. This can also be a good time to enlist the support of students, particularly those who are not intimidated by the out-of-control student, to help you with your program.

Use of Mime and Non-verbal Messages

Most out-of-control students have been verbally reprimanded thousands of times every year. They eventually become immune to verbal messages, which are tuned out. Try using mime to demonstrate your message the next time you deal with a chronic rule breaker. Mime is a form of non-verbal communication in which messages are conveyed with body movement and no words. First, mime the action that the student did that is bothering you. Use no props, simply act out his hitting another student, throwing paper on the floor, or jabbering to his neighbor. It may be helpful to practice these movements in the safety of your own home before trying them in your class. Next, act out your feelings about the action, such as anger, sadness, frustration. Learning to express feelings without voice can be difficult, but it is a helpful and important tool.

Finally, act out the consequence for the violation, or what you expect the student to do differently. You may have prepared in advance some written instructions to each phase which may say: YOU DID, I FELT, NOW I WANT YOU TO , AND YOU MUST. Or you can write these instructions on the blackboard. If you are good at miming, you can ignore these and let your actions speak for themselves.

Audio- or Videotaping Your Class

If you have access to a video recorder (preferable) or an audio recorder (acceptable) try taping your class for an entire period. Focus on those students who give you the most difficulty. After class, when you have captured an incident or a series of disruptions, meet with the student(s) who are causing the problems. Show them or let them listen to the tape and discuss their feelings about the way they looked to themselves. When given a chance to actually see or hear themselves, students often gain an awareness of their negative impact and are willing to try something new. To help make this procedure more effective, it is helpful if you can also agree to try something new with these students. Your and your students' suggestions for change should be specific and manageable. Meet again in a couple of weeks to discuss how things are going.

Audio Playback

Some students are unfortunately committed to denying all responsibility for being disruptive. Furthermore, a phone call home may well be greeted with a parent defending his child's actions. When you are confronted with such a situation, it can be helpful to tell the student that ''beginning today, I will be keeping the tape recorder on record. Since I think that it is important for both you and your parents to understand the problems that we have here, I will make the tape available to your parents when we come together to discuss your school progress. Good luck!'' This method has been extremely effective in curtailing a wide range of inappropriate behaviors (especially verbal abuse, put-downs and swearing).

Using Older Students as Resources

Often older students who have been ''in trouble'' in school are wonderful resources for dealing with younger disruptive students. If you teach in a school that is close enough to a high school, try setting up a program for the disenfranchised high school students to work in yours and/or other teachers' classes. Select those students who have been in trouble and need a healthy outlet for feeling good about themselves. The principal or school psychologist as well as high school teachers should be able to help you select the best candidates. Arrange for freeing up these students on a regular basis during the week. Short times work best because you do not want to give the student helpers too much of a rigid burden. An hour every week is sufficient.

Prior to coming to your class, meet with your student helpers and explain that you want their help in guiding some students who seem to be on the wrong track. The student helpers' job is to come to class and to work individually in a comfortable private spot with the troubled student. Work can include actual lessons in the form of tutoring, or they can focus on social issues. Try to provide a flexible structure so that the helper has an idea of what to do but is not required to deliver your lesson plans. It is important for the helper to feel like a worthwhile person who is given a special privilege to help another student. Meet with the helpers each month for an hour or so to help them get new ideas and listen to their observations and feelings.

Creative Limitations

We believe that there need to be limitations even with ''creative'' approaches. As mentioned previously, we believe that all students have a right to attend school so that their safety and security is guaranteed. Dangerous or violent behavior that includes fighting or carrying weapons cannot and must not be tolerated in a school setting. We feel strongly that fighting should be dealt with swiftly by excluding the student from school until such time as he can return with an action plan that specifies what he will do (other than fighting) the next time a similar situation presents itself. It is also a fact that carrying exposed or concealed weapons is a legal matter, and the solution to this problem should always include legal authorities.

A Fresh Start

The suggestions in this chapter are not going to work all the time for all people. Creative ideas are not designed to be perfect solutions but rather to begin an exciting new adventure into the unknown with the hope that both you and your students will learn more about yourselves and each other. By unblocking yourself and venturing into the unknown, you have the capability of changing old patterns and making an important difference in the lives of your most troubled students.

For the Administrator

There are usually a small percentage of students who can be legitimately called "out-of-control," but they require a large percentage of time—from the teacher, from the support personnel in the school, from other students, and from the administrator. The best role you can take is to help the student to be placed in the best educational environment possible. This might mean transfer to a special school or class either in or outside your district. Proper placement helps the teachers and students alike as well as freeing the teacher to spend more time and energy with the other students.

However, often the reality is that there are no special school or classes available, or that there is a long waiting list, or that there are no available funds for a given student. Even when special placement is a possibility, the time it takes to secure the placement because of red tape, paperwork, and due process requirements can involve many months. The teacher must still work with the out-of-control student during that time. Thus, in spite of your intentions to properly place students, you will have teachers in regular classes who must deal with chronic problem children.

Teachers need a lot of support when working with the "out-of-control" student. We propose the following ways in which you can support your teachers' efforts.

1. Administer the Creative Discipline Inventory to your faculty during a faculty meeting. Do not collect them but use them as a springboard to generate a discussion about the use of creative approaches in solving seemingly insurmountable problems. These inventories are personal, and all material must remain confiden-

tial. However, faculty can share perceptions and ideas on a voluntary basis.

2. When you have chronically disruptive students, their parents must be involved on a continuous basis. Do not be afraid to call them at home and at work when you need to. If you have a student who must be sent home for disciplinary reasons, insist on parental support. If your teachers need a parent to come to school, intercede when there is a problem and use the weight of the school to get them in. If a parent claims that they cannot leave work for school, tell them that you are sure that their child is very sorry for the inconvenience and that he will be waiting in the hall in twenty minutes for pickup. Keep parents of disruptive students informed of their progress.

3. Allow your teachers freedom in dealing with chronic problems. Remember that nothing has worked with these students for a long time. Teachers have nothing to lose when trying creative strategies, but they often fail to try creative strategies because they fear administrative non-support or disapproval. Let all your teachers know that you will support most of their plans that are non-punitive in nature and as long as the teacher shares them with you in advance.

4. Be vigilant with all follow-up to any problem with a disruptive student. Keep teachers, parents, and students informed of all of your actions.

5. Working with difficult students is frustrating! You need to understand that when a teacher is calling a student names, is making demands of you for swift action, or is in some other way behaving "unprofessionally," that this is the time for support, not debate. You can help your teachers feel less frustrated by sharing information concerning the student *and* by being a good listener who can express empathy.

References

1. Nevin, E.; Nevin, S.; and Danzig, E., *Blocks to Creativity: Guide to Program*, Cleveland: Danzig-Nevin International, Inc., 1970.

2. Moscowitz, E., and Hayman, J. L., "Interaction Patterns of First Year, Typical and 'Best' Teachers in Inner-City Schools", *Journal of Educational Research, 67(5)*, 1974, pp. 224–230.

3. Frankl, V. E., *Man's Search For Meaning: An Introduction to Logotherapy*, New York: Pocket Books, 1963.

EIGHT

Special Problems

*B*ecause Three Dimensional Discipline is a flexible, eclectic process, it can be applied to any situation that involves teachers and students. However, we are frequently asked to discuss how to utilize Three Dimensional Discipline for special problems. The most frequently asked questions deal with

1. working with handicapped students in a mainstreamed class
2. applying Three Dimensional Discipline specifically to an inner city school
3. minimizing drug and alcohol use in school

The basic principles of Three Dimensional Discipline were developed and field tested in inner-city environments. Teachers of mainstreamed classes who have used Three Dimensional Discipline report that the model and processes are effective with both the handicapped and nonhandicapped students in their classes. Teachers of special education report similar results. Students who use drugs and alcohol should be dealt with in similar ways to any student who does not behave appropriately in class. Thus, each of the chapters and activities in this book are written for use by teachers who teach in the inner city, who teach handicapped students in special education and mainstreamed classes, and who deal with students who use drugs and alcohol. We do not suggest that an entirely different approach be used in these special areas. Social contracts, consistent use of effective consequences, minimizing stress, utilizing creative approaches for out-of-control students, and avoiding power struggles will help you to take charge of your classroom whether you teach in an inner city, suburban, or rural school; they will help you regardless of the type of students you teach.

However, each of the three special problems mentioned above is of sufficient importance to discuss in more depth; in addition, there are specific knowledge, awareness, and strategies that might help you cope with discipline problems associated with these issues. In this chapter we will explore additional activities and information that apply to these special situations.

Handicapped Children

Federal law PL 94–142 mandated that children with handicapping conditions receive the "most appropriate education" in the "least restrictive environment." The law is designed to prevent the indiscriminate dumping of children into special classes or schools. It is becoming common practice in most school districts to conduct rather extensive diagnostic evaluations that identify students for placement in special programs and establishing IEPs, (Individualized Educational Plans). Many school districts require rigorous arguments to be made in support of special services for fear of violating the "least restrictive environment" clause. This all means that it is more difficult and time-consuming to secure special placement and more likely that "handicapped" students who have previously received instruction in special classes will return either part-time or full-time to the mainstream. Whether you are ready or not, trained or untrained, you can expect more of these students to be in your class.

There are a variety of reasons why some students are referred to special classes: physical, emotional, behavioral, and learning disabilities. Because the educational and emotional needs of "handicapped" or disabled students vary so greatly, it is impossible to discuss how to set up an effective program of discipline for each potential problem. Moreover, many disabled children do not behave any differently than students considered to be normal. However, some disabled children have special behavior problems that makes dealing with them doubly difficult. What follows are descriptions and suggestions for teachers who have handicapped students who are also behavior problems in their mainstreamed classes.

Disabled children are often referred to special classes and remedial units because their behavior is considered to be unacceptable in the regular classroom. They may be viewed as hyperactive, distractible, argumentative, surly, rude, immature, or irresponsible. Youngsters who are ultimately enrolled in special education classes usually have many common characteristics. Except for those who are mentally retarded, they are generally of average intelligence or better (although some are slow learners) but experience learning problems in reading, spelling, writing, and/or arithmetic. They have been either retained in one of the early elementary school grades or referred for remedial services to supplement instruction in the regular class. At this early time in their school lives, teachers often use descriptions such as, "lazy," "could do better if he worked harder," "needs to develop good study skills," "seems unmotivated," "has better ability than he shows," "is bossy and can't share with others." From the fourth grade through the eighth grade, they usually have great difficulty competing with the rest of the class. The more difficulty they have, the more likely they are to act up in class, lack enthusiasm, skip class, and become rather predictable fixtures in the office of the school disciplinarian.

For many, the experience of academic success is unattainable, and the special student seeks other methods of gratification. Excuse-making, failure to take responsibility for one's own actions, a tendency to project blame onto others, and refusal to work or to follow guidelines for acceptable behavior are common. Without the help they need, such students often drop out of school, much to the silent relief of school guardians.

Disciplinary problems among handicapped students are therefore strongly associated with their inability to compete with others in class, to get the attention of other students, or to feel equal to them. Everyone, including handicapped students, needs to feel important, whether it is for acting up in class, for being the best swimmer on the team, for being a good musician, or for being a top notch math student.

Since we are focusing our discussion on handicapped students who exhibit unacceptable behavior, changing behavior needs to be one of the primary focal points in planning for the handicapped child's integration into a normal setting. If you work in a school that has the good fortune of extensive remedial and support services, then the major responsibility for preparing a student for life in the mainstream resides within the specialist. But if you do not, and you are a regular classroom teacher, then the burden of responsibility falls squarely on your shoulders. Like it or not, the student is placed in your class. Your choices are to continue teaching as if he was not there, in which case the probability is high that inappropriate behavior will occur (or worsen), or to make adaptations in your program to accommodate his special needs.

If you are teaching a special education class, or if you have handicapped students in a mainstreamed class, we suggest you set up a social contract with your students and follow the other guidelines outlined in this book. In addition, we offer the following suggestions that will help you both prevent discipline problems with special students and resolve them more easily when these problems occur.

Take Care of Yourself

The first step in working with special students who have behavior problems is to do some work with yourself. You need to be in touch with your feelings; you need to recognize them, acknowledge them, and find outlets for expressing them. Teachers of learning-disabled or emotionally disturbed kids must be willing to give and give and give, and in return, often receive frustration, criticism, defeat, and failure. Despite many hours of extra planning and an inordinate amount of instructional time, complaints abound such as, "You never work with me like you do with the others." A good day in which the child behaves may be followed by two or three days of off-the-wall behavior. An "aha" experience in which Sammy finally "gets" subtraction is followed by a blank stare the next day that tells you it's back to step one. Inattentiveness, rudeness, messiness, and forgetfulness may be the norm for such a child. Some of the finest teachers resort to name-calling, acting like marine sargeants, pleading, whining, or withdrawing as ways of dealing with such students. In short, such children can be a constant drain, who deplete our energy reserves. If you have children such as this in your class, you need a support group of colleagues who can understand your feelings while avoiding "Ain't it awful" games.

Provide Responsibility

One common complaint from teachers of older handicapped students is that previous teachers, often in special classes and day or residential schools, did more for them than was needed in the long run. They tried to compensate for the disability by making sure that students got to class on time, had their work completed, were dressed and washed properly, and in general saw to it that the students experienced no failure, even if failure was a natural consequence of a choice they made. It is understandable why many special education teachers try to be overly protective. Their students are in need of a boost to their self-image and need to live and learn in a positive, supportive environment. Furthermore, special education teachers, simply through the natural selection process, tend to be patient and humanistic and are trained to see that the child is more important than the subject matter and that even small gains in achievement are worthy of pride.

However, these qualities and values can be undermined when they lead the teacher to take responsibility for the child's behavior. Taking responsibility means that teachers (or administrators or parents) accept excuses that are not legitimate. They find solutions to the child's problems. They offer easy ways out of difficult situations that the child has created for himself. They set expectations too low for both behavior and ability to learn, which tends to limit the child's potential. For example, some teachers do not follow through on agreed upon or previously stated consequences because the child uses his handicapping condition as a reason for not living up to realistic expectations. This situation often creates a vicious cycle when parents, stricken by the guilt associated with a disabled child, try to compensate for "apparent" behavior problems by doing too much for the child; in so doing they take responsibility away from the child and with that an opportunity for growth. By the time the child goes to school, he may not know how to take responsibility for himself. The next phase of the cycle is for his teachers to convert this diagnosis into a strategy, i.e., if a child cannot accept responsibility, then it might be harmful to thrust responsibility upon him. This confusion between a diagnosis and a strategy is common given the prevailing attitude of "taking a child where he is, and help him grow from there." Unfortunately, this view can end up reinforcing the inability of the child to ever begin to take responsibility for himself. Obviously, age, ability to understand, maturity, and other social development factors are all important in determining how much responsibility a child can handle. It is important to teach responsibility by allowing students to live with their decisions.

We find that a great many of the behavior problems associated with disabled children come from the lack of responsibility these children have been given throughout their lives. We suggest you give students responsibility as soon as possible, without overwhelming them to the point of agitation. Begin by giving the child choices whenever possible. For example, allow him to select which reading book he wants that period. If the child needs to go to the lavatory, ask whether he wants three minutes now or next period. If the child wants to play a game, give him three choices. Once the child has made a choice, let him live with it. Don't come to his rescue if the choice does not work out. Give him the opportunity to learn from bad choices within the limits of physical safety by allowing the natural consequences to occur and by asking the student evaluative questions, such as:

1. How did it turn out for you?
2. What did you learn from that experience?
3. What other choice could you have made, which may have been better?
4. What will you do next time?

For those children who cannot make open-ended choices easily, use close-ended choices. Do you want to read your book, or review your math problems? Do you want to play checkers, or chess? Slowly build up to more open-ended choices, but never stop giving as many choices as possible.

The second part of teaching responsibility involves the same principle upon which we based the whole notion of the social contract. Set clear limits and expect the children to follow them. You might need different limits in some cases with disabled students, but once they are established and mutually understood, live by them. Excuses and explanations are not acceptable reasons for failure to comply with realistic and previously understood expectations. Using the handicap as a reason or excuse for failure to meet expectations is one of the most self-defeating concepts that keeps disabled students handicapped. The difference between a handicap and a disability is that a disability is a physical, emotional, or behavioral impairment, while a handicap is other people's response to that impairment. For example, deafness is a disability, but difficulty in communication is a handicap. Be "kind and understanding" in setting up realistic expectations that challenge, but don't overwhelm the student. When it comes time to ensure that the expectations are met, it is time for your more demanding self to take charge.

The third aspect of teaching responsibility is to encourage and support problem solving and planning on the part of your students. When they come to you with a problem or excuse, use that opportunity to help them gather information, identify alternatives, make decisions, and analyze the consequence of those decisions. When they behave inappropriately, ask them for a plan of action for changing their behavior. Once they have thought of possible solutions and have developed their plans, hold them accountable for doing them. Sometimes students will fail to behave according to plan. When this happens, they sometimes need to experience an unpleasant, but non-punitive, consequence and be re-directed to developing a new plan. You can evaluate the plan to see that the student lived up to his part. Then allow the student the opportunity for self-reflection by encouraging him to evaluate how successful the plan was in solving the problem. Self-evaluation of planning is a critical skill for increasing responsibility. You need a high tolerance for broken promises and misunderstanding as well as lots of patience!

Learn to Communicate with Handicapped Students Who Have Communication Difficulties

Many disabled students have communication problems. For example, hearing impaired, visually impaired, and learning disabled children might be missing critical information that other students are receiving. Deaf students, for example, often miss much of the incidental information that most other students learn as a natural part of overhearing conversations in their environment. Much of this learning involves manners, social know-how, and implicit expectations of peers and teachers. Students who have communication problems might act out to express their confusion, anger, disconnectedness with the group, or they may lack understanding about what constitutes appropriate behavior. They might also withdraw and try to avoid being noticed at all.

If you have students who you suspect have a communication problem, find out what the extent and nature of the problem is. Find out what the ramifications are of that problem for the child's ability to learn and his potental for picking up the subtle social cues of the classroom. Find out what you can do to learn how to reach the child and communicate directly with him. If you have support people in your class such as notetakers, interpreters, tutors, speech therapists, or readers, take the time to talk with them about their roles, about how you can work together to make both your jobs more successful, and about how to coordinate your functions to help the child.

Level with Them

Everyone has personal hang-ups and most people put out quite a lot of energy in hiding their ''deficiencies'' from others. The people who become intimate friends are those who appreciate successes and encourage strengths. They are also genuinely able to accept imperfections, which no longer have to be hidden. People who are close, level with their friends by recognizing the balance of what they are: a person who has both strengths and limitations.

One reason that praise is differentially effective with handicapped students (or for that matter with anybody) is that it does not provide adequate balance to the complexities of the human condition. It *only* emphasizes the positive and ignores the effectiveness of feedback that is holistic and balanced. Tom, a fifth grade student who was ultimately referred to a learning disabilities class, illustrates the limitations of *not* leveling with children in a balanced way. He was not completing assignments nor doing his homework when his teacher and parents decided to praise any movement that he made in the desired direction. They were perplexed to discover that the more they praised, the *worse* he got. Despite their good intentions, they failed to recognize that Tom was afraid of praise because deep down he felt that he could not consistently meet their expectations. So he saw praise as a reminder of his inadequacy, which led to behavior that showed everybody just how inadequate he felt.

He needed honest feedback, which might include praise, but not praise *exclusively*. The fact is that students who are failures in school feel they have a big secret that needs hiding. You need to sensitively let them know that you know the secret and are prepared with a plan to provide needed remedial assistance as well as face-saving mechanisms to protect the student from the chastisement of peers.

Don't Ask Why

If Billy fights, doesn't do his work, makes excuses, etc., don't ask him why he behaves the way he does unless you like to hear "I don't know." Have a talk with him at a time of mutual convenience and list for him, using impersonal pronouns, the reasons why *you* think he does what he does. For example, you might say,

> Billy, I cannot accept your refusal to do your work. Although I don't know for sure what the problems are, *other* students who don't do their work may be feeling: (1) unable to do their work because they don't understand it, in which case, I'm willing to offer extra help; (2) afraid to look stupid in front of their classmates, in which case, I'm willing to call on you only when your hand is raised; (3) feel pressured to achieve by their parents or by me, and they don't work because they really feel angry, in which case, you can write me a note that tells me how you feel or let me know after class or talk to the guidance counselor; (4) simply

do not understand why they need to learn certain things, in which case, you can ask me and I'll try to explain or offer you a different assignment that makes more sense to you.

Such an approach is generally far more effective in making contact with the troubled student than asking "why" questions. Although your hunches may be off-target, they do let the student know that you have an in-depth understanding of young people, which makes it more likely that you will see evidence of compliant behavior(s). Students are more likely to consider the needs of others when they feel understood. As a way of concluding your talk with Billy, tell him, "Billy, I don't know if any of this is true for you, and what I want you to do is to consider what I said, the choices that I offered, and let me know either through your words or actions, what you are planning to do to get your work done."

Adopt a "Friend"

Taking risks to explore new skills is both scary and essential to personal growth. It is even more difficult for the student who has grown accustomed to failure. But everyone, no matter how limited, can stand out in certain ways. Those who are more fortunate have a variety of mentors along the way who help to identify strengths and provide support in undertaking new and difficult learnings related to these strengths. This gives confidence and encourages risk taking.

Many educators are in a position to be mentors, but it is often the case that those selected are students who have already demonstrated their skills. Few want to be involved with children who do not (on the surface) appear to have much going for them.

We advise each of you to adopt one "friend" for a year and to make a commitment to real involvement with such a student to draw out a special talent. Expect more than your share of disappointments when your adoptee retreats to familiar territory such as poor motivation or antagonistic behavior.

Mr. McKane's relationship with Joe illustrates the immense possibilities for gratification. Joe was a repeating seventh grade student and he was identified as learning disabled; Mr. McKane was an industrial arts teacher. Early in the school year Mr. McKane took Joe aside and told him that because he had already completed the seventh grade shop curriculum, he would be allowed to work on special industrial arts projects. Joe, who had demonstrated some prior talent (although nothing extraordinary), made a list of projects that he wanted to make, and Mr. McKane offered some of his time and help to participate with Joe in making these.

By mid-year, Joe had made a children's play table, a chair, and a small stool, and his work was placed on display in the window of the school library. Mr. McKane and Joe grew close to each other, which enabled Mr. McKane to discuss various problems that Joe had in other classes and made Joe receptive to considering other means of behavior. Joe's behavioral turnabout became the school's success story. Mr. McKane was both saddened and joyful to see his adoptee move on.

Permit Yourself to Make Mistakes

Disabled students have repeatedly experienced failure in school, which is one of the causes for their "handicap." They secretly see others as more worthy and competent than they so they often retreat to the safety of doing nothing as a way to avoid the risk of being wrong. You can help this child by allowing yourself permission to acknowledge your mistakes and by assuredly stating your utter lack of perfection loudly and publicly. By correcting your errors, you are also sending the message that mistakes are natural and are usually not permanent.

Provide Clear Structure

The learning disabled student in particular is often disoriented in relation to time and space; he is inattentive and is more often than not, hyperactive. As noted earlier, the social contract works well with such students because it specifically and clearly defines acceptable and unacceptable behavior. Your special needs students should be expected to follow the contract but may need some extra help from you in learning to do this.

Many special education students do best in environments that are structured and predictable. Because of their time and space disorientation, it may be insufficient to simply state a rule along with consequences. You may be enforcing rule violations all day! To help you and the student enhance your chances for mutual success, we offer the following tips:

1. If you have a hyperactive child in your class, keep him seated close to you and place masking tape on the floor around his desk that defines acceptable parameters of movement during "seatwork" time.

2. If you have a distractible child in your class and you want him to focus on a given task, have his desk face a wall to minimize classroom distractions, or, if feasible, arrange for one or more study carrels that block out visual distraction.

3. If the child responds excessively to auditory distraction when working at his desk, have him wear headphones to block out sound, or if you have the facilities, pipe in some soft, soothing music.

4. Provide a list of specific activities (hourly or less) to be done in class and tape this list to the child's desk. Make him responsible for placing a check mark next to each activity following completion.

5. Catch the child being good and formally acknowledge this through verbal reinforcement or, in more extreme cases, through activity or concrete reinforcement. You would do well to familiarize yourself with principles and practices of behavior modification, which have often been used with good classroom success for hard-to-reach students.

6. Use parents, volunteers, or other students (those with a high tolerance for frustration) as tutorial aides.

7. Accept that progress will be slow and find ways to show the student visible proof of his progress. Have him chart the number of times he raises his hand rather than blurting out an answer. Keep a monthly folder of the child's work so that he can check his own progress. Keep a running record of all new spelling words learned, successful solutions to math problems, and other accomplishments.

8. Some of the characteristics of learning disabilities include poor memory and sequencing skills. Be sure to break down each task into its components because the child's lack of organizational ability prevents him from doing this himself. Each step of a task needs to be emphasized, such as:

   a. get your math book (pause)

   b. open to page 23 (pause)

   c. do problems 1, 2, and 3 (pause)

   d. raise your hand when you are finished

   If you give more than two or three steps at a time, the child is doomed to confusion, and you are on the path to greater frustration.

9. Find and acknowledge the child's strengths. When students are

slow, disgruntled, or defiant, it is indeed difficult to find ways to appreciate them by acknowledging their strengths. We are reminded of a time when one of the authors while teaching seventh grade was challenged to a game of chess by an L.D. student. The teacher was surprised by how slow the game proceeded, and was even more surprised when he lost. It was a good reminder that "slow" does not equate with "dumb." Some students who are slower thinkers are not necessarily inferior thinkers.

If you cannot see a person's strength, then there is no way for you to improve his weakness. Even behaviors that seem to defy appreciation can be appreciated. Let us take fighting for example. Fighting cannot and should not be encouraged in the classroom, and we are advocates of stiff consequences for such behavior. But consider the following two messages after Jason has punched Susie.

a. "Jason, I told you not to fight. Now go down to the principal's office at once."

b. "Jason, people are not for hitting. I can appreciate that you probably felt angry and fighting is one way that you know to stand up for yourself, but you have chosen to go to the principal's office. When you return, we can discuss other ways besides fighting that you can use to stand up for yourself."

Example b shows how an unacceptable action can be both appreciated as well as limited.

10. Learn and practice reflective listening skills. When students accuse you, swear at you, threaten you, or refuse your demands, active listening helps to defuse the emotional situation while maintaining good contact with the student.[1]

11. Give the student responsibility that he can handle and that meets with success. Jim, a fifth grade emotionally disturbed youngster, showed an affinity for younger children. He was sent to a kindergarten classroom to be a "helper," and this become the focal point of his day. It also provided much needed relief for his weary teacher.

12. When you do make special arrangements for a handicapped child, explain your purposes to the child. Students who are treated differently usually know they have a problem, and you will earn the respect and a connection with them when you let them know that some special considerations are being made. Explain the purposes of each special strategy.

13. Set up the classroom to be most advantagous for disabled students. Many disabilities require special considerations when setting up the classroom. Students with visual or hearing problems often need to sit in certain locations that maximize their ability to receive classroom information. Hyperactive students need more room around their desks and more space at their worktables. Deaf students need to avoid looking at back lighted subjects because they cannot see enough detail to see signs or to speechread (lipread). A very stimulating environment can be unsettling for emotionally disturbed and hyperactive children. Colors in the room and on the walls should consist of soft pastels. Objects should not be left on the floor where physically disabled students or blind students could fall over them. The aisles and areas between seats should be kept clear.

    If you have a disabled student, take the time to contact the professional association associated with the disability. Ask questions about classroom arrangements that will provide the best possible learning environment for that particular student. You should also ask the student what special needs he may have. If you have support personnel in your district or in your class, be sure to confer with them about the most appropriate classroom arrangements.

Summary

Disabled students who are prone to behavior problems can drain your energy, create more work for you, and generate feelings of inadequacy and frustration. They will demand, either implicitly or explicitly, that you employ skills you have not been trained for and that you devise both learning and behavioral strategies which might not have been created as yet. You can improve your effectiveness by reducing the overall scope of the problem into smaller, more easily attainable goals.

    Set clear limits for these students and expect them to follow them. Provide clear consequences and implement them consistently. Provide decision-making situations with clear and understandable choices. Appreciate the students as fully functioning human beings who are capable of joy and success. Above all, remember that both you and your special students have feelings, and these feelings are the most powerful motivators of behavior. Learn to express your feelings in helpful ways: the joys and frustrations. Teach your students to feel their feelings and provide acceptable outlets for expressing them.

The Inner City

Inner-city schools often lack many of the luxuries their more affluent neighbors consider necessities. Often, inner-city schools are older and scarred from the battles of seventy-five to one hundred and fifty years of serving students. Many schools are overcrowded, with little of the needed space for students and teachers to feel comfortable. In some instances, the schools are located in neighborhoods that are threatening and hostile to the children who attend them. One school we visited had a problem because many of the third and fourth grade students had their sneakers stolen off their feet on the way to school.

The visual and metaphorical picture of the inner-city school is bleak, reminiscent of the burned-out wasteland of a war-torn city. Once, when we were asked to assist an inner-city school in the New York area, the first words we heard as we entered the building were, "Move your car before it is stripped or stolen." No wonder many teachers would like to see their inner city schools razed and rebuilt in a safer, more stable environment.

Yet, once you get beyond the obvious environmental problems, inner-city schools can offer a rich, rewarding experience for teachers and students alike. The city itself offers a variety of resources that cannot be matched in the suburbs. The arts, business and industry, parks, museums, and a multitude of different kinds of people are all within arms length of the creative inner-city teacher. For every turned off "street student" there are dozens of eager youngsters who want to learn. While the equal opportunities and education acts have not produced the results hoped for by their creators, more and more inner-city students believe that they can reach their potential, albeit with a struggle.

The authors were touched by the humanness of an eighth grade class in a human relations course at an overcrowded school in a poor neighborhood in the Bronx. One student shared that their family had their extra money hid under their living room rug. A classmate was curious as to why this girl would reveal such confidential information, fearful that his classmate's money might be stolen. The girl replied, "But in this class you are all my friends, I trust you." The sigh from all her classmates indicated the closeness of the moment.

Differences in Dealing with Discipline

One of the biggest differences in dealing with discipline in the inner city is that the types of problems are greater in intensity and are more destructive than their suburban counterparts. Violence, vandalism, fights, drug use (see page 204 for a more complete description of this problem), thefts, and extortion are reported as part of the daily routine of many inner-city schools.

Another difference is that the culture of the students is very different from the culture of the teachers and administrators. Even city schools with a high percentage of minority teachers often suffer from cultural clashes. Minority teachers and administrators who have "made it" and have graduated from college may be seen as different by the inner city students who do not view college as part of their world.

A third difference is the overcrowded and physically older school buildings. Many of these schools look more like jails than places of learning. Students often complain that they are prisoners, not students, and this attitude has a direct relationship to their physical environment. Further, these schools are often magnets for undesirable teenagers who are no longer in school and show up to cause trouble. Many schools have reported that their biggest problem with vandalism, drugs, physical abuse, and thefts are the result of teens who do not even attend school. It is difficult to learn and teach when physical safety is not ensured.

A fourth difference is the lack of trust that often permeates the school environment. The example of the trusting student described above is unfortunately not the norm. Students do not generally trust teachers or other students. Teachers are fearful of many students, especially those who are bigger and have reputations for violence. Even parents can generate fear in teachers. One teacher in a Rochester, N. Y. school was hospitalized by an angry parent who came to school and attacked the teacher. Some teachers have been killed in their classrooms. While these problems are certainly imposing, they are not impossible to deal with. As we stated earlier in this chapter, Three Dimensional Discipline grew out of our initial work in the inner city.

Using Three Dimensional Discipline

We recently (1980–81) did a controlled study with inner-city elementary school teachers in Rochester, New York, which provided them with a five-session, ten-hour Three Dimensional Discipline program, which attempted to reduce teaching stress associated with disruptive student behavior.[2] The finding from this study was that Three Dimensional Discipline was effective in significantly reducing anxiety felt by teachers at the end of a school day, as well as reducing the stress associated with a six-item discipline cluster (managing disruptive behavior, supervising behavior outside the classroom, target of verbal abuse, theft and destruction of teacher property, maintaining self-control when angry, threatened with personal injury).

These teachers generally found the social contract (because of its structure and flexibility) and the relaxation activities (see Chapter 3) to be most effective in improving discipline and diminishing their negative feelings associated with disruptive student behavior. But perhaps more importantly, the training program provided a forum in which teachers could share mutual concerns and learn how to become a support network for each other. Nowhere is this need greater than in the inner-city, where teachers are more often confronted with serious incidents of acting out and where they must have strong leadership, a high level of trust for each other, as well as skills to deal with student misbehavior. The 1979 New York State United Teachers' survey found that nearly three times as many inner-city teachers are experiencing high levels of stress as compared to those in suburbs and rural towns.[3]

Our experience in working with these teachers and other groups of inner-city teachers suggests that they often feel alone in tackling overwhelming problems, and that the communities in which they work are frequently lacking the values that lead to school success because of the problems described above. Violence is more likely to be viewed as an acceptable means by which to settle disputes in these communities, which may lead to a proliferation of fighting and, in more serious instances, stabbings and shootings.

It is unrealistic to expect major changes when we do battle with a society that theoretically provides equal opportunity for everybody, but realistically divides itself into the "haves" and "have nots." The net result of such a condition is the manifestation of intense anxiety and frustration among those in the lower socioeconomic classes. The anxiety and frustration is often expressed through violence, or apathy. Our responsibility is to provide a clear and firm policy of rules and consequences that provide safety for those students who want to learn, as well as many alternative non-destructive ways to express the negative emotions that are so much a part of many students' lives in the inner city.

STEREOTYPING THE INNER CITY CHILD

Teachers in the inner city must first be able to let go of the many stereotypes regarding the inner-city child. A series of studies (Hawkes and Koff, 1970;[4] Hawkes and Furst, 1971;[5] Hawkes and Furst, 1973[6]) has elucidated the many misconceptions held by teachers regarding the inner city child. Hawkes and Koff (1970) conducted a study in a large mid-western city, comparing the responses on anxiety scales by 249 children in the fifth and sixth grades of one inner-city elementary school to the responses of 211 children who were attending the fifth and sixth grades of a lab school connected with a large urban university. A content analysis was done of the responses to an anxiety questionnaire. It was concluded that the difference in the manifestation of anxiety was significant regardless of the type of anxiety being tapped. The inner-city child showed *more* concern than his suburban school peers on items that tapped objective fears, anxiety, general worry, concern about school work, and concerns of self-adequacy. Hawkes and Furst (1971) replicated these findings using as a sample 704 black fifth and sixth graders predominantly from the inner city and 495 white suburban children from public and private schools. This study was done on the eastern seaboard.

Hawkes and Furst (1973) studied the responses of 628 pre- and in-service teachers who were asked to respond to a sixteen-item questionnaire that was used in the two previous studies cited. The finding was that teachers significantly underestimate the anxiety levels of inner-city students and exaggerate the anxiety from upper middle class students. The authors (1973, p. 26) conclude that the following *inaccurate stereotype* is held by many teachers:

> The inner-city child who lives in a hazardous environment becomes accustomed to that environment, he reacts to that environment by becoming psychologically tough and resilient. He is unlikely to admit to fears and concerns about his daily existence, indeed he is unlikely to have such concerns. He doesn't care as much as his middle class peer does about getting ahead in life or school, his parents haven't trained him to care or be concerned about doing well in school, he doesn't mind being scolded by his teachers, he is not as likely as his middle class peer to worry, and he is unlikely to manifest symptoms of anxiety.

These investigations noted that teachers with three or more years of experience in teaching inner-city or suburban students were more accurate in their predictions, although still not predictive of the reality of the situation. This study raises the possibility that at least some classroom discipline problems result from the teacher's inability to recognize and address student anxiety. The teacher, thinking that his students are unmotivated, worry free, and unconcerned about their school work, fails to address these emotionally focused areas of student concern. Because the students' anxiety fails to be addressed in the classroom, they become unruly and disruptive in response to their anxiety. The teacher, faced with losing control of the classroom, may become dogmatic and inflexible in response to his increasing experience of stress. A real cause of discipline problems (high student anxiety and worry regarding school performance) is left unaddressed.

SPECIFIC SUGGESTIONS FOR THE INNER-CITY TEACHER

We suggest that the inner-city teacher use the processes of Three Dimensional Discipline, as described in this book, by placing a strong emphasis upon prevention. The following ten suggestions are offered to help the inner city teacher deal with discipline:

1. KNOW YOUR STUDENTS AND LET YOUR STUDENTS KNOW YOU

Because of the cultural differences between teachers and students and because of the potential for lack of trust in the inner-city school, we strongly suggest you know your students well before you begin to focus on content. You need to know how your students naturally communicate with you and with each other. Make sure that you are not offended by language that is natural for your students but may sound rough or uncouth to you. Learn your students' likes and dislikes. Find out what classroom privileges are meaningful to them and which are perceived as hokey or as undesirable chores. The more you learn about your students' interests, the more you should structure your instructional units around them. City students have a strong need for relevancy and meaningfulness in their school experience.

In addition, it is equally important for your students to know you. Many inexperienced inner-city teachers erroneously think that they must keep their guard up at all times. While it is a good idea to be on guard when in a potentially hostile environment, doing so with your students will guarantee that your classroom will have walls between you and them. The more your students trust you, the less they will make unfounded assumptions about you. Research has pointed out time and time again that students learn best when they trust their teacher. Use open communication and establish an atmosphere of information sharing to build trust in your classroom.

2. STATE YOUR RULES AND CONSEQUENCES CLEARLY

Regardless of whether or not you use the entire social contract process, state your rules and consequences clearly to your students. Inner-city students come from a variety of family structures, some very tight with strong parental structure; others come from broken or single parent homes. Trying to discipline twenty or more students with such a variety of school and family experiences is difficult at best. Start with a firm and clear structure that all students understand. Once you have firmly established your contract you may be flexible about changing it, but make your changes gradually. Your students will behave more appropriately when they always know what is expected.

3. DEVELOP CONSEQUENCES THAT WORK

It is important that you develop consequences that work. The best consequences are non-punitive and relate to the students' lives as directly as possible. Ask other teachers and older students to help you think of the best consequences for your rules. Consequences that are too harsh will alienate and break down trust, while consequences that are too lenient will be seen as a sign of weakness. Your students must respect your ability to control your class, and effective consequences are a must. Once you have developed good consequences, it is crucial to implement them consistently. While occasional lapses of consequence implementation in the suburban or rural school may make a teacher's life more difficult, inconsistency in the inner city can spell disaster.

4. PROVIDE APPROPRIATE OUTLETS FOR EXPRESSING FEELINGS FOR BOTH YOURSELF AND YOUR STUDENTS

Many inner-city students believe that they must put on a "front." They try to appear cool and detached as if nothing bothers them. This is considered a sign of maturity and strength. But the reality is that inner-city students have feelings just like anyone else. And because these feelings are often hidden under the guise of "cool," they can and do intensify. Learn the language of "coolness" and provide acceptable outlets for feelings to be expressed. Make sharing a regular but optional part of each day. The use of anonymous techniques, like a gripe box, is especially useful.

Teaching in the inner city generates many feelings of inadequacy and fear. It is most important for the inner-city teacher to learn how to deal with his feelings and to learn strategies for reducing stress. Our study showed that inner-city teachers can learn to minimize stress and feel better about teaching.

5. CAPITALIZE ON THE RESOURCES WITHIN THE CITY

Working independently or with a group of other teachers, use the city, itself, as a teaching laboratory for experiences related to your content. Visit places of business, hospitals, the police station, museums, libraries, planetariums, historical landmarks, and other city spots, which are sometimes taken for granted. Arrange trips to the nearest rural areas whenever possible. Some city children never see a live cow until they are adults.

Bring city resources into your school if you cannot take your students out. One school made an arrangement with a local college to let its architectural students rebuild a hallway into an arboretum, another hallway into a library, and time-out areas in five classrooms. Both the school and the college students were enriched by the experience.

6. IMPROVE STUDENTS' READING ABILITY

All teachers, regardless of subject, are reading, writing and English teachers. Make a point to improve every student's reading ability regardless of whether you teach math, science, or physical education. Lack of reading ability is directly associated with poor achievement and poor behavior. Find out what your students' reading abilities are and provide challenging reading and writing practice at their grade level. This should be a regular part of each class period. Continually reward efforts and improvements in reading and writing regardless of how small. Your students need to feel that they can and will become better readers.

7. FOCUS ON THE POSITIVE

While it may sound hokey to say that the positive should be stressed, we believe that it is incumbent on all teachers of inner-city students to focus on the positive. If a student gets two right out of ten, tell him he got two right, not eight wrong. Limit your corrections on writing assignments to one or two manageable corrections. Once the student has mastered the corrections noted, find one or two more improvements to work on. Continually build on success. Inner-city students need to feel that it is possible to be successful in school. They need to feel in a very direct way that the pay off at the end of the rainbow is potentially for them as well as their more affluent neighbors. Give them success every day as part of your teaching style.

Focus on the positive with your fellow teachers. Look for ways to make the school a better, safer place to be. It is better to suggest an improvement than it is to comment on what is wrong. By increasing the positive energy of the faculty and most importantly, of yourself, you will be reducing your own stress related to working in the inner city and making the school a better place for you and your students to live.

8. DEVELOP GROUP SUPPORT WITH OTHER TEACHERS

Share your feelings openly. Teaching is traditionally done alone, with the teacher isolated from the rest of the faculty, except for informal discussions in faculty lounges or lunchrooms. Because of the intensity of the inner city, it is important to minimize isolation as much as possible. As we stated earlier, one of the most important reasons for the success of our in-service training programs is the process of teachers sharing with other teachers how they feel, what their problems are, and what can be done to make the school a better place.

9. DEVELOP A STRONG WORKING RELATIONSHIP WITH YOUR PRINCIPAL AND OTHER ADMINISTRATORS

The Safe School Study (page 3) indicated that the safest schools had a strong principal. Meet regularly with your principal and offer your support. Ask what you can do to make his job easier. Tell him what you need to be successful in your classroom. Problem solve together. The more your principal feels important to you and your students, the more he can support your efforts.

10. ENLIST COMMUNITY LEADERS

Contact as many community leaders as you can and ask to meet with them on a regular basis. Every city has both formal and informal groups who try to help the community people. Some examples might be the local YMCA, the NAACP, a church group, or a Mexican cultural center. These leaders take responsibility for improving the lives of the people they serve. Find out what their programs are, what support they can give you, and what support you can give them. Invite them into your class to talk with your children. Ask them to review your social contract and offer any suggestions for improvement. Use them to better understand the subculture of your students.

These ten suggestions are offered to help make your teaching in the inner city a more positive and healthy experience for you and your students. It is not impossible to be successful in the inner city. You must feel that success is attainable for you if you expect your students to feel that success is attainable for them. The self-fulfilling prophesy works equally for teachers and students. Do not let your prophesy of your teaching experience be negative or you will ensure that it will be so. Many inner-city teachers would never change their environment. They feel that the energy, the challenge, and the needs of their students cannot be matched in any other environment.

Drug Abuse in School

Drug abuse in school is cited by teachers and administrators as one of their most difficult problems. Teachers have noticed that the incidence of student experimentation with drugs is on the increase and that the age of students who take drugs is decreasing. Although there is little hard data to support these claims, there is little doubt among those who work in schools that while drug use among pre-adolescents has not reached epidemic proportions, children are experimenting with drugs at earlier ages. The popular myth that drug use is limited to those from disadvantaged urban areas is simply not true. A recent article in the *New York Times magazine* concluded that young people are experimenting with drugs at earlier ages.[7]

Drug use is a complicated phenomenon full of facts and fiction; it evokes hysteria and fear, as well as economic concerns. Drug use creates a youth versus adult battle of the ethical and legal concerns. Educators have trouble distinguishing between the use of drugs by school-age children from the drug problems of our society as a whole.

Drugs affect student behavior in school. Some drugs act as stimulants, most notably amphetamines, which dramatically increase restlessness, excitability, and hyperactivity in students. Others act as depressants, such as barbiturates and cocaine, which make students lethargic and apathetic. Angel dust makes behavior erratic and often dangerous, leading to sporadic outbursts of violence. Regardless of the drug (and alcohol is included in this discussion as the leading abused drug), one thing is clear. Drug use in school blocks learning and creates either overt or hidden behavior problems for the teacher.

The problem of drug abuse in school is complicated because it is integrated with confusion and conflict in society as a whole. Students who take drugs do so for a host of reasons only some of which are school related. In the discussion that follows we will first explore the relationship between the drug use of students and society's attitudes in general about drugs, and then discuss the relationship between drug use of students and school. Finally, we will explore what you, the teacher, can do in your school and classroom to deal with misbehavior associated with drug abuse, and we will suggest preventive strategies for minimizing drug use among your students.

Drug Use in Society

The greatest contributor for drug abuse is the unrealistic, schizophrenic attitudes society has about them. Drugs are condemned and condoned. They are advertised and made illegal. People use them and criticize others for using them. Parents fear images of the pusher hanging around the schoolyard with an assortment of drugs in his trench coat, while the real pusher may be the good-looking kid next door, an older sibling, or a parent's liquor cabinet.

The image of the drug pusher is that of a Mephistophelian figure who poses a greater threat than did the communists in the mid-fifties. But the doctors who collectively write out forty million prescriptions a year for valium are viewed as saviors for reducing tension and removing headaches. The mixed messages children receive even go beyond these images.

Professional athletes are cheered when they win, and people close their eyes to the amphetamines, steroids, and other wonder drugs that are a daily part of their lives. Parents hoot and holler when they see their children modeling their heroes by taking the same wonder pills. Athletes and Rock stars, the two most powerful role models for our children, openly talk about cocaine use. Drugs are emphasized on our children's blasting stereos, as they work on tomorrow's homework.

Society tries to explain rationally to children that marijuana is decriminalized in some states while at the same time other states are making it a crime to sell rolling papers and other drug paraphernalia. The results of these mixed messages are clear. Children don't believe that drugs are harmful. They can see right through the double messages. There are probably a significant number of teachers who are mandated to teach about the abuses of drugs who themselves are drug users. Ray Birdwhistell's research says that when a person is communicating, 70% of his message is sent by body language, 23% by the tone or inflection of his voice, and only 7% by the words he uses.[8] For example, if the teacher believes that marijuana use is not especially harmful, it is likely that between 70–93% of his message will be that marijuana is okay, while only 7% of his message will consist of the harmful aspects of marijuana use.

Another example of a confused message involves smoking cigarettes. The Surgeon General reminds smokers that each puff of a cigarette is dangerous to health. And yet most faculty rooms in America have the blue haze and stale odor of cigarettes clouding the atmosphere. Each day after work, responsible teachers and parents stop off at the local bar for a few moments to drug away the tensions of the day before they get into their cars with enough alcohol in their blood to be considered intoxicated. There are many educators who cannot function without that first or second cup of coffee in the morning, despite the well-documented harmful effects of caffeine intake. Psychotropic drugs by prescription have become an integral part of society. Drug companies spend billions of dollars yearly advertising pills to lose weight, pills for headaches, backaches, muscular tensions, and other stress-related conditions. The fact is that drugs are an inherent part of our culture. Groups that practice strict abstinence from drugs, such as Mormons, Jehovah Witnesses, Christian Scientists, Moonies, and Orthodox Jews, are viewed by some people as backward, and out of the mainstream of American life.

School Causes of Drug Use

In the preceding section we explored how society at large contributes to drug abuse by sending children confusing mixed messages about drugs. Children have learned to mistrust information that tells about the dangers of drugs. But these children believe their friends when they hear that getting high is an exciting, fun-filled way to reduce stress and feel good. In this section we will see how the structure of the typical school contributes to the misuse of drugs.

All students need to feel that they are worthwhile, liked by, and important to someone who is important to them. They need to succeed at important tasks that are reinforced by their environment, and they need to feel that they have the power to influence the environment within which they live. Students who naturally feel good view themselves as important to others, capable of successfully meeting challenging tasks, and in control of themselves and the world around them. They achieve a natural high when they are class monitor or helper because they feel important when their outstanding achievements are noticed and appreciated. They feel good when they can use and enhance their power by making decisions that affect their lives. When one or more of these basic needs are unaddressed, the seeds are sown for drug abuse. The students in class who seem bored, inattentive, daydreaming, poor achievers, or lacking friends are all receiving negative messages from their environment and may begin to feel inadequate, incapable, and incomplete. They are likely to turn to drugs as a way to escape recognition of a poor self-concept.

Some schools tell children that they are not as important as teachers, principals, and the curriculum. For six hours every day they are told where to go, what time to be there, how long they are allowed for even basic biological necessities, which learning is relevant, what to learn, and how well they have learned it. How often do the students decide what rules should exist in the school for themselves, for each other or even for the teachers? How often are students consulted on what they want to learn, on how they should be evaluated, and on what activities they want to participate in? The answer is: not often enough! On the other hand, when students are given the opportunity to participate actively in the school, they are often given total unstructured freedom to do what they want rather than actively participating as part of the total school community.

One of the reasons for the frequent failure of the open school concept, which proliferated throughout the sixties and early seventies, was that most of the structure that children need (from a developmental perspective) was taken away. We feel that it is imperative for schools to give their students a say—a loud, clear voice in what happens in their school. The curricula need to be examined so that they truly reflect the needs and concerns of students. Schools cannot afford to be a place that puts young minds to sleep with trivia, busy work, and boredom. At the same time, students need clearly defined structure, one which they have a part in developing, but one which is consistently adhered to, so that they feel that their school is safe and predictable and at the same time adaptable and concerned with their welfare.

Another way that schools contribute to students' need for drugs is through pressure. Students are pressured to perform, often to standards that they have had no say in developing. They are pressured to be like everyone else. They are pressured to like what teachers have decided is good for them. Tension in students is no less common than tension in adults, and for the same reasons. And as we stated earlier, students often reduce their tension in the same way parents reduce theirs—through drugs.

What Can Be Done about In-School Drug Abuse (Alternatives to Drugs)

Changing the drug picture is no easy task. It requires an investment of time, energy, and money that has as its primary goal *prevention*. An effective drug program should begin in kindergarten and should address the underlying motives that are known to lead to drug abuse. Opportunities for experiencing ''good'' feelings need to be built into the curriculum daily and must emphasize units on decision making, problem solving, and stress reduction.

More importantly, drug prevention means

1. being aware of yourself and how you communicate yourself to students
2. being aware of students and setting the classroom climate that allows for feel-good experiences
3. teaching yourself and your students alternative ways to relax
4. teaching children how to assert themselves (especially how to say ''no'' and still save face with their peers)
5. presenting accurate information on the effects of various drugs
6. avoiding the use of threats with children who you suspect are using drugs

Threats rarely help to stop drug use. A school cannot completely end drug use without becoming a total police state. Schools can and should provide very clear consequences for drug offenders, both for those who use them and especially for those who help to distribute them.

We do not believe that these concepts will completely eliminate drug use in the school. Drug use is symptomatic of larger social problems, and our society is still struggling to deal with these problems successfully. The point is that teachers can limit the use of drugs. Faculty, parents, and students can effectively define policy regarding drug use that is firm, consistent, and clear.

An effective drug prevention program helps students learn that there are alternatives to drugs that are viable and can offer similar benefits.

Start by identifying those students who are now taking drugs and do something for them. However, once a child is married to the drug subculture, it is hard to divorce him from it. Begin by accepting the child as he is and building on his strengths. Offer him the opportunity to meet his basic needs for feeling good about himself, for achieving in school, for making meaningful decisions, and to feel that he can have an impact on his own life. Diminish the causes for stress and tension, while at the same time teach how to better handle the stressors that are part of the process of growth and development.

We offer the following strategies that are meant to represent what we believe to be essential components of a school-based drug prevention program. We encourage you to use the strategies as presented, to adapt them according to your classroom situation, or to create new ones. The bibliography at the end of the book offers other practical resources that can be of help.

ENCOURAGING USE OF THE IMAGINATION

Because of the curricula demands associated with emphasizing the 3-R's, we sometimes forget the importance of child's play and retreat into fantasy as a necessary and important developmental occurrence. And yet we often discourage the development and expression of fantasy ("stop daydreaming", "pay attention") in favor of the realism of cognitively defined classroom expectations. It is as if fantasy and imagination have no place in the world of the classroom.

As early as 1935, Griffiths' interviews of 50 five-year olds concluded that "fantasy or imagination provides the normal means for the solution of problems of development in early childhood".[9] Eric Klinger reminds us that most of us "normal" people spend between 30 and 40% of our waking hours entertaining daydreams.[10]

Today's young child whose significant others criticize his daydreams and who is provided no outlet for the expression of his fantasy learns to mistrust his own perceptions. Although his fantasies often "feel good," the equation of fantasy being equal to wasting time valences negativism around what is and can continue to become a source of a natural "high" for kids. Stripped of fantasy and not too successful with the reality demands of the classroom, the stage is set for drug use.

"Hey, Billy, want to toke-up?" becomes the cue for a return to the enjoyment of fantasy that had been earlier submerged to demands that attention be paid to "reality." There are many ways in which fantasy can be encouraged in the classroom and made consistent with other "reality-oriented" instructional goals. The following activities provide a sample of such methods.

Guided Fantasy   The teacher can select one of many fantasies from references such as *The Second Centering Book* (Hendrick and (Roberts), *Mind Games* (Masters and Houston), *Passages - Pilgrims to the Mind* (Andersen and Savery). After presenting a fantasy, it can be processed in a number of different ways including

1. encouraging students to share their fantasy verbally

2. having each student draw a picture of something from their fantasy

3. having students do a group drawing in which at least one aspect of each person's fantasy appears

4. writing a story based upon the fantasy and developing a class "book" of fantasies for all students to read

5. having one or more students act out or role play their fantasy

Children's artwork and stories can be prominently displayed in the classroom.

Daydreams   In our task-oriented schools and other institutions, daydreaming is often thought to convey escapism or avoidance of the task at hand. Most teachers have at least a few children that are obvious "dreamers" by observing such actions as doodling, staring out the window, having head resting on desk, and "forgetting" directions. Less obvious are many more students who may be seated upright with hands folded on their desks, appearing attentive, nodding their heads up and down in apparent agreement and understanding of the material, but who like their overt counterparts are silently daydreaming. They are simply better at playing the "game" than their less fortunate classmates who are likely to receive reprimands for their inattentiveness.

Many of the same methods suggested in processing guided fantasy material can be used with daydreams. The wise teacher is one who recognizes the non-verbal, body language messages sent by children and who modifies his style accordingly. If each question asked during a lesson is met with little or no participation, if students are seated upright with their heads straightened rather than slightly cocked to one side, if students are staring out the window, *stop* what you're doing and say, "My guess is that many of you are bored with the lesson. Probably you're thinking about other things. While your bodies are here it looks to me as if your minds are not. Your assignment for tomorrow is to write down all the places that your mind has been during this class. Tomorrow I'll collect your work and read each paper out loud. You don't have to put your name on your paper unless you would like others to know what you wrote.''

As it is neither desirable nor possible to eliminate students' daydreams, it makes sense to legitimize this ''misbehavior'' by attending to it. Using open-ended questions that contain no right or wrong answers, using imagination instructionally such as, ''If you were Christopher Columbus, Alice in Wonderland, et cetera, how would you have felt, what would you have done,'' are other methods that indirectly and clearly validate one's fantasy life. George Brown's work with confluent education provides many ways in which the teacher can effectively integrate instructional goals with the personal experience of each child.

Stress   We often forget that school for many children is a tension-prone, stressful experience. Academically successful children often feel pressured to continue their positive performance, middle-of-the road students are often struggling to stand out in some way, and poorly performing children are often exhorted to work or try harder. The result is that the school experience for all children can become a key source of stress.

Recently, a parent of a 14-year-old boy was perplexed in trying to understand why her straight A, exceptionally athletic son had dropped from the wrestling team and had plummeting grades. In further discussion it became clear that he had always put a lot of pressure on himself to excel in everything he did. Although his mother wasn't sure, Andy's red eyes, blank facial expression, lack of motivation, and flat, expressionless speech confirmed his use of marijuana. He had become sick and tired of living up to everybody's expectations of perfection.

Schools simply do not do enough, and in many instances, do nothing, to attend to student stress. It seems indisputable that the art of relaxation is a critically important skill for young people, and one that is not reflected in course curricula. Schools are claimed to be expert at transmitting information and training intellectual skills, but we have for the most part failed to recognize the influence that tension, anxiety, and stress have in negating such training. If children arrive at school feeling tense about events occurring at home or on the streets or have developed a set of expectations about themselves that allow no room for failure, or who chronically receive a series of messages that reinforce their feelings of incompetence, then the energy and motivation for learning is diminished. A preventive drug program should teach children a variety of methods that they can use to induce relaxation and hence alleviate tension. Adopting widely known strategies such as meditation and body relaxation, and by encouraging students to identify and express their feelings may make later drug use unnecessary.

Meditation   A study conducted by Joseph Morris in which he trained inner city third graders in how to meditate found a decrease in off-task behavior following training. Children had two 20-minute weekly periods of meditation.[11] We recommend Benson's *The Relaxation Response* and Carrington's *Freedom in Meditation* as excellent guides for easily teaching the reader how to meditate and—by extension—how to teach your class to meditate. And if you work in a school that frowns upon meditation, do it anyway and call it something else.

Tension Relaxation   Many students who become involved with drugs are observed to be ''anxious,'' ''tense,'' ''sitting on a powder keg,'' ''aggressive,'' ''hostile,'' and ''hyperactive.'' By learning not to express feelings verbally, these students keep their resentments and other feelings inside and convert these feelings to muscular tension. As a way to help them drain off this tension, we offer the following activity.

ACTIVITY   I'd like you each to find a comfortable seated position either on the floor (rug or mat if possible) or in your chair. Try to face away from each other. Let yourself relax and pay attention to your breathing. Listen to yourself breathing in and out. Now picture yourself in a very quiet, peaceful, happy place where you can do whatever you want. Nobody is going to tell you what to do unless you want somebody to do this. Close your eyes if you wish. What are you doing? Where are you? Just let yourself be wherever you are. Now again pay attention to your breathing.

I would like you to think of one word that makes you feel very peaceful and relaxed. Words such as friend, love, peace, quiet, calm are but a few that might be relaxing words for you. Now choose your relaxing word. Take in a deep breath and as you let it out, say this word quietly to yourself. Now let yourself breathe naturally and each time you exhale say this word. Keep your eyes closed or, if you insist upon opening them, find a spot right in front of you and keep your eyes fixed on this spot. Continue breathing and quietly saying this word as you exhale. Keep doing this until I tell you to stop.

Some students will find both their eyes and minds wandering. Tell them that when this happens, to just let themselves wander. Then when they are ready to return their attention to their fixed spot, tell them to continue their breathing while quietly saying their word.

We suggest this as a daily activity, not to exceed ten minutes with older children or five minutes with younger children.

GRIPE BOX

The purpose of this activity is to provide an on-going, daily account of difficulties and annoyances that students are experiencing during each day. It is important that little daily annoyances and resentments are not allowed to accumulate but are rather dealt with each day. It is the accumulation of resentments, often minor, that ultimately lead to blowups, chaos, confusion, and discipline problems.

We suggest that you use a shoe box or cardboard box and decorate it with the words "gripe box." Explain to your students that each day various things happen to us which leave us feeling upset, sad, annoyed, or angry. These events can occur on the school bus, playground, in the cafeteria, or in the classroom. Explain that students may feel resentful toward you, other students, hall monitors, security guards, or other people in the school. But from now on, when they think that they have been mistreated and they are feeling resentful, angry, sad, or upset, you would like them to write down on a piece of paper what happened and how they feel. After they have written this down, suggest that they put their gripe in the classroom "gripe box." Then explain that during a prearranged time you will read each gripe and together with them see if there are some things all of you can think of that would help the student with his or her problem. It is important that you, the teacher, participate in this process as well and contribute your annoyances to the "gripe box" along with your students.

Follow-Up   After you or a student has read each gripe, we suggest that you encourage your students to brainstorm as many solutions to the described problem as possible. You might direct the discussion by saying, "Billy felt angry when Mr. Paulsen scolded him in the hall today. If you (class) were Billy, what are all the things that you could do to make yourself feel less angry?" We suggest that you list all proposed solutions on the blackboard (even the silly ones) and leave it to Billy to either publicly or privately choose those which best fit for him. It has been our experience that publicly stating a problem is often sufficient help for students. The empathy and concern they experience from their classmates serves to help them feel that they are not entirely alone with a problem and that the classroom can be a place to receive emotional support. If support is lacking, then this may indicate the need for you to devote time to helping build a stronger community spirit within the classroom.

APPRECIATIONS

Students who are prone to drug abuse are often lacking in self-esteem. When a child feels uncared for and unappreciated, he learns not to care for himself and not to appreciate others. Particularly in the early elementary school years, it is important for all students to feel cared for and appreciated by both their teacher and their peer group. Students who do not get enough warmth will learn not to give any and will gradually distance themselves emotionally from others. They may well resort to drugs to reinforce their protective shell. Following are some suggestions for appreciations.

1. *Appreciation day.* Place a picture of each of your students along with his name on a large sheet of newsprint. Explain to your students that each day one child's picture will be hanging on the bulletin board. Tell them that at any time during the day (free time or play time might be preferred to minimize distractions) any student may go to the poster and write a statement beginning with "one thing I like about you is _____," or to draw a picture expressing their caring and appreciation of this student. No put-down statements are allowed. Before the end of the school day, take a few minutes to allow students to file past the poster and encourage them to read each statement or describe a drawing that they made on the poster. When you have finished doing this, ask if there are any further expressions of appreciation. When the process is completed, put the child's poster away until his turn comes up again.

   After two rounds, allow the student the option of taking home the poster or displaying it in school.

2. *Self-appreciation.* We believe that one important desired outcome for students is to gradually shift their dependency on support from their environment to support within themselves. It is rare in our society for people to express genuine appreciation for each other, and unless one learns to value and appreciate his own worth, he will often bitterly wander from person to person seeking a sense of security.

   This activity can be done once a day, once a week, or several times each day. Have the students complete the following aloud: "Something I did, felt, or said today that I'm proud of is _____ ." "Something that I like about myself right now is _____ ."

3. *Expressing feelings through art.* Give the students crayons,

paints, and/or thick pencils and tell them, ''Right now I'd like you to draw or color in a way that expresses your feelings. If you feel sad, draw sad; if you feel angry, draw angry; if you feel happy, draw happy. These are your pictures and you may keep them when you're finished or show them to the class.'' Be sure to provide no more structure than this. The less structure you provide, the more likely the students are to express their feelings as they feel them.

Students may be given the option of displaying their work in the classroom. This can be done by having an ''art gallery'' in which all participating students hang up their work and then browse through the ''gallery'' to observe each other's work. Comments are encouraged by helping each commenting student to recognize his feelings. This is not a contest but rather an opportunity to facilitate a feeling discussion among the class. You might provide a little structure by suggesting that students say, ''When I look at this drawing I feel (think, am reminded of, etc.) _____.''

Feelings of competence can be enhanced through instructional use of Aronson's ''jigsaw technique.''[12] This technique assigns students to work with each other in small groups and makes each individual responsible for one piece of a total project. All group members are dependent upon each other for the project's totality and must work closely together for its completion. As an example, segments of a story may be assigned to each member of a group. Their task is to understand the story in its totality, to answer various questions that test comprehension, and to report their findings to the class. Students are thereby forced to interact with each other because they are dependent upon their partners for information. Pairing highly and poorly motivated students or skills proficient and deficient students together is effective at generating improved interpersonal skills and feelings of accomplishment and competence for all.

Attending to Behaviors Associated with Drug Abuse

Students who take drugs may or may not exhibit overt behaviors that will tell you that they are taking drugs. Some signs of drug use are missed homework accompanied by a multitude of excuses and broken promises for improved behavior. A sudden or steady decline in achievement on tests, in class work, and in projects are other common symptoms of drug use. Students who take drugs often lack motivation and become passive in class. They appear to have many secrets to tell their friends and occasionally make drug jokes in class and snicker when words associated with drugs are mentioned. The suggestions above are designed to provide alternative options to taking drugs. But if you notice symptoms in some of your students, which indicate students are already using drugs, we suggest you try the following suggestions.

1. DO NOT ACCEPT EXCUSES

Do not accept excuses or empty promises when work is not completed. Demand that all work be done on time and done properly. At the same time, be sensitive to the needs that drug-using students might have to avoid pressure and tension. Offer suggestions for dealing with tension and pressure, listen carefully to your students' feelings, and offer them an opportunity to discuss their needs. Students need to learn that drug use cannot be explained away or that promises are the equivalent of performance. The most natural consequence for drug abuse is the inability to complete work, and this consequence should be continually adhered to.

2. POINT OUT CHANGES IN BEHAVIOR

Without making accusations, point out to the student, in descriptive language, what changes in behavior you have noticed. If you hear slurred speech or see red eyes more than occasionally say something like the following (privately): "Mary, I notice you are having trouble saying your words and that your eyes are red." Merely pointing out the symptoms is enough to tell the student that the secret is out. Many students feel a false sense that nobody knows what they are up to. It is important not to accuse or make assumptions that may be false. Notice the difference in the statement above and the one which follows: "Mary you look stoned. What did you do, take a toke in the girls' room before class?" By reporting only the observable in descriptive terms you minimize the potential for diminishing trust, while at the same time, letting the student know that the secret is out.

3. DISCUSS YOUR SUSPICIONS WITH THE STUDENT

If your suspicions are strong enough, and after you have communicated descriptively, you might take stronger action by stating that you are wondering whether or not the student is taking drugs. At this time it might help to let the student know that further action may be necessary. Notice the following message Mr. Calkins told Liza, a tenth grade student that he suspected of drug use in school.

"Liza, I have noticed that your homework has been missing for two weeks and that you have been daydreaming in class. When I call on you to answer, you have asked me to repeat the question and then you are still not sure what we are talking about. Last week your speech was slurred and you seemed to laugh in class for no apparent reason. I have been thinking that maybe you are becoming involved with drugs. It's not my place to demand that you tell me whether or not this is true, but I am concerned. So I am planning on telling you exactly what I need from you in class. I want you to do your homework, be attentive, talk normally, have clear eyes, and answer class questions. If you can do this then I will assume my feelings are incorrect, but if your current behavior continues, then I will think that I am correct and it will be time for me to share my suspicions with your parents and try to work with them to help you out."

In this statement Mr. Calkins might have alienated Liza if she was taking drugs, but he honestly shared his perceptions and outlined what he needed from Liza to be different. He gave Liza a chance to save face and stop using drugs, while letting her know that further action was pending. The key things he did were, (1) stated his observations, (2) offered choices, (3) stated consequences, (4) kept the demands related to classroom performance, not drug use, and (5) let the student know his suspicions without accusing her.

4. CONFER WITH OTHER TEACHERS ABOUT THE STUDENT

Find out from other teachers and professionals in the school if the student you are concerned about has exhibited erratic behavior in other classes or school settings. If the student has, then set up a meeting with those involved as a team and discuss what the changes in behavior are and what you can do to help. In these meetings be sure that the student is not tried and convicted on circumstantial evidence. Many adolescents go through changes in behavior that are associated with growing up and not drugs. Keep your information-sharing descriptive and develop a plan designed to improve school and classroom behavior, not to eliminate drug use.

If your suspicions are strong enough, find one person in the group or in the school who has a good, trusting relationship with the student and who can try talking with him about his problem. Often a former or older student can be helpful in making contact. When meeting with the student, the most important message to convey is that someone cares and is willing to listen. Accusations, threats, and punishments tend to push new drug users into a position of needing or wanting more drugs to deal with feelings of shame, alienation, or guilt.

5. DON'T TRY TO BE A RULE ENFORCER FOR IMPOSSIBLE RULES

Remember that you cannot enforce a rule that says students cannot take drugs. Rules of this nature are seen as a joke and tend to weaken the entire discipline system of your class. However, you can and should set limits that describe behavior. In other words, you can state clearly that students who come to class smelling of pot, with slurred speech, or who behave erratically will be sent to the nurse. This type of expectation is more effective than a rule which says, ''no smoking pot before class.''

Summary

In the final analysis, schools and teachers can limit drug use by limiting negative behaviors associated with taking drugs; by offering a multitude of choices that help students to relax, feel good, energized, and excited; and by making school an interesting and exciting place where young minds and spirits come alive to the energy of feeling and learning. If you can give these experiences to your students and if they still take drugs, then that is a choice the student has made that is beyond your control to change. You need to appreciate that some students can and will choose destructive paths and your ability to help them rests solely on whether or not they want your help.

Conclusion

In this chapter we have explored three special problems related to discipline. As we have stated in the discussions, each of these problems is part of a larger social issue. But because of their impact on students, teachers must often deal with special behavior problems associated with handicapped students, the inner-city environment, and students who take drugs. Three Dimensional Discipline is built on the foundation that prevention is far more effective than intervention. Many activities were suggested that help teachers to set up a preventive atmosphere related to each of the problems.

For the Administrator

Disabled Students

Aside from all of the paperwork involved in setting up special classes and special placement for disabled students, the administrator should see that the needs of the special student are met. This involves securing support services as necessary including interpreters, notetakers, readers, tutors, aides, psychological support, and physical support. Teachers need training in the use of support people. You should provide information about support people and a clarification of function.

In addition, teachers need training in methods of teaching students with disabilities. If there are special schools in your area that focus on a particular disability, arrangements can be made for visitations, exchanges, and information sharing. Local and national professional organizations are also helpful.

Be aware that teaching disabled students may create stress in both the teacher and other students. Be sure that each teacher who has either a special class or a mainstreamed class has regularly scheduled breaks during the day. Provide a place and time to practice stress reduction techniques, and make this practice legitimate. Many students and teachers might have irrational fears about interacting with a handicapped student. These fears need to be recognized and dealt with before positive interactions can occur.

When a disabled or emotionally disturbed child creates a discipline problem, it often requires the teacher to meet individually with the student to resolve the problem. You can help by providing either a substitute teacher for an hour, or by arranging for the teacher's class to be covered while the teacher works individually with the student. This might also be a good opportunity for you to teach. Use the list of suggestions beginning on page 192 as a checklist for helping teachers deal with discipline problems related to their disabled students.

Above all, be ready to listen and understand the pressures and demands in working with special children. The rewards are hard to see; and progress is slow, intermittent, and often goes backwards as equally as it goes forward. Encouragement and support from the administration can go a long way in making the year more rewarding.

Inner City

Like the teachers who teach in the inner city, it is most important for the administrators to know their students well. Knowing the students means understanding their culture, norms, and values and knowing the family history of each student. For those children who have a weak family structure, the school administrator often replaces the father or mother and becomes a parent figure. This responsibility must be taken into account when dealing with students, especially those who have broken the rules. When setting up school policy, it is important that the students have a voice in determining what their school will be like. Ownership of the rules and consequences is especially important in the inner city where most students feel powerless. However, once the contract has been established, it is critically important to consistently enforce every rule violation. Students must see order and learn that there are consequences for their actions.

One difficulty that administrators face in dealing with any discipline problem (which can be even more intense in the inner city) is whose side to take when the student and teacher are in disagreement. You can help both teachers and students by not taking sides when this happens but acting as a mediator and allowing the two to solve their own problems. Make it clear to all your teachers how you will handle referrals and what role you see yourself playing when a situation goes beyond what the teacher can handle. Have an emergency plan for those rare, but possible, situations when a student commits a violent act or threatens to commit a violent act in the classroom. Be prepared for situations in which the teacher demands that a potentially explosive student be removed from class, but the student refuses to leave. Your plan should have input from the faculty as a whole, and all teachers should know how to use it when necessary. This plan might never be used, but most teachers feel better knowing it exists.

Involve as many community resources in your school as possible. Invite parents, business people, local chapters of minority organizations, and others to be a regular part of your school community.

Encourage teachers who wish to use alternative teaching styles and who wish to use the city's resources as a learning environment.

One of the most helpful things that you can do is to set up support/discussion groups for teachers to share their concerns, feelings, and awareness about their jobs. We have found in our work in the inner city that teachers have a lot more strength and resources than they are aware of, and that they discover them when they can talk with their colleagues. Bull sessions are not particularly helpful, and neither are gossip sessions. The discussion should involve teachers exchanging ideas and taking responsibility for their own feelings.

Drug Abuse

A good program to curb illegal use of drugs involves two main parts: prevention and action. The prevention part should involve a variety of regularly scheduled stress reduction activities for students and activities that are fun. Fantasy and imagination should be a part of every class in one way or another. As the school administrator, you can legitimize this kind of program. Students who are turned off, bored, or stressed should be given individual attention before a problem with drugs is created. Special attention for the gifted, bright, and creative should be a regular part of the school programming.

When you set up a drug information program, be sure to emphasize that drugs are a part of society and avoid the scare tactics that often push kids towards drugs. Be rational and informative. Acknowledge the truth about drugs. Bring in ex-drug users to talk about their experiences. Ex-users have more credibility with youngsters than the police, doctors, or pharmacists.

When students are found to be drug users, set limits on their behavior. You cannot condone drug use, but you cannot stop it either—especially if they take drugs at home, or off school grounds. You can and should limit the way students should act in school. If drugs are causing behavior problems, set limits and implement consequences based on the misbehavior. Above all, don't accept excuses or empty promises as a way of avoiding consequences.

We recommend that you speak with the local law enforcement in your community and find out what your legal responsibilities and restrictions are in relation to drug use. Inform your faculty of this information. Then use the information as a base to set up a school-wide policy about students who are caught with drugs.

You can also set up a class or discussion group for parents, informing them of the symptoms of drug use and what they can do to be helpful to their children. Emphasize ways to prevent drug use and to help the child who has already started to experiment with drugs.

References

1. See Gordon, Thomas, *Teacher Effectiveness Training*, New York: Wyden, 1974, for more information.

2. Mendler, A., "The Effects of a Combined Behavior Skills/Anxiety Management Program Upon Teacher Stress and Disruptive Student Behavior," Unpublished doctoral dissertation, 1981.

3. "New York State United Teachers Stress Survey Information Bulletin," New York State United Teachers Research and Educational Services, 1979.

4. Hawkes, T. H., and Koff, R. H., "Differences in Anxiety of Private School and Inner-City Public Elementary School Children," *Psychology in the Schools*, 7, 1970, pp. 250–259.

5. Hawkes, T. H., and Furst, N. F., "Research Note: Race, S.E.S, Achievement, I.Q. and Teachers' Ratings of Behavior as Factors Relating to Anxiety in Upper Elementary School Children," *Sociology of Education*, *44(3)*, 1971, pp. 333–350.

6. Hawkes, T. H., and Furst, N. F., "An Investigation of the (mis) Conceptions of Pre and In-Service Teachers as to the Manifestations of Anxiety in Upper Elementary School Children From Different Racial-socioeconomic Backgrounds," *Psychology In the Schools*, *10(1)*, 1973, pp. 23–32.

7. Baysner, Elizabeth C., "New Parental Push Against Marijuana," *New York Times Sunday Magazine*, August 1981.

8. Birdwhistell, R. L., *Introduction to Kinesics*, Louisville: University of Louisville Press, 1952.

9. Griffiths, R., *Imagination In Early Childhood*, London: Kegan Paul, 1935.

10. Klinger, E., *Structure and Functions of Fantasy*, New York: Wiley-Interscience, 1971.

11. Morris, J., "Meditation In the Classroom," *Learning*, *5(4)*, 1976, pp. 22–25.

12. Aronson, E.; Blaney, N.; Stephan, C.; Sikes, J.; and Snapp, M., *The Jigsaw Classroom*, Beverly Hills: Sage Publications Inc., 1978.

NINE

Discipline and the Process of Teaching

*M*otivated students cause fewer discipline problems because they care about what they are learning. Enthusiastic teachers who present their material in stimulating, meaningful ways motivate students. When students are actively learning content that has personal meaning for them, they have neither the time nor the energy to create discipline problems. Conversely, when students feel that they are passive receptacles for irrelevant knowledge, they become bored, turned off, and find gratification in acting out.

In other chapters of this book, we focused upon how to establish a classroom management system that includes student involvement, student decision making, and, most importantly, student responsibility. In this chapter, we will explore how to teach so that students are motivated to learn, not to misbehave. We will emphasize the factors within the teaching-learning process that prevent discipline problems. As such, our focus becomes how you can have a classroom which encourages healthy competition; how to adapt your style of teaching to fit a variety of students' learning styles; how to vary your style of presentation so as to minimize the possibility of students becoming bored; how to maintain energy and aliveness for yourself and for those you teach. Let us begin by examining some of the characteristics of a healthy classroom environment that are conducive to students' being motivated to learn.

Characteristics of a Healthy Classroom

1. Trust is established. The learner trusts his abilities and his environment (including those who are helping him learn). Fear is minimized.

2. The learner perceives the benefits of changing his behavior. Learning is a change in behavior; if the need for change is not perceived by the learner, then there is no reason for him to change.

3. The learner is aware of the different choices and options to him and is able to make a growth choice. This choice cannot be made for the learner. Education is structured to help the learner see different alternatives and to provide the opportunity to make choices that are real, meaningful, and significant.

4. The evaluation of learning actively engages the learner. Evaluation by others is effective when it is perceived by the learner as important to him. Both teacher and student share the responsibility for defining what is to be learned and how well it was learned. Mutual evaluation helps maintain the trusting environment. Because the goals of learning are personal, only the learner is truly capable of analyzing how well the goals are being met. The teacher lends his expertise in helping to define a level of outcome needed to ensure competence.

5. Learning facts and concepts are important but incomplete goals for the learner. These two levels are not the final results of education. Personal meanings, uses, and understandings are the ends for which the first two levels are means.

6. Learning is conceived as meaningful. Even in structured situations where the activities might be planned and the outcomes are left open for the learner to discover (uncover), effective learning takes place.

7. Learning is growth producing, actualizing, and therefore enjoyable. This does not mean that it is necessarily frivolous or light. It provides the true joy that comes from knowing and being more complete than previous to the learning. True learning is not merely tension reduction nor is it drudgery. It is genuinely pleasurable.

8. Learning is process- and people-oriented rather than product- and subject-oriented. True education helps students learn a

process for successful living that applies to any situation. Product orientations are too limited and self-defeating to have any permanent useful effect.

9. Learning includes more than just the cognitive or affective domains. The separation of these two is artificial and unnatural. Feelings and thoughts are both incorporated for learning to have personal and lasting usefulness. One or the other exclusively is incomplete.

These characteristics of healthy classrooms are often difficult to translate into action. Lack of resources, rigid curriculum requirements of the state or school, and pressure from parents and administrators for high test scores all leave even the most enthusiastic teacher unable to teach creatively and manage students. Yet by setting up a preventive behavior program and changing the structure of the content in gradual, but significant ways, teachers can incorporate many of these characteristics into an everyday part of their teaching. One of the biggest mistakes that the educational revolutionaries of the sixties made when they tried to free up the education system in the United States was to assume that total freedom was not only possible but desirable. "Free" schools, which opened up their classes allowing students to do whatever they wanted, were doomed to failure because the students did not have the skills to handle what was asked of them, nor were they developmentally ready for that much freedom without responsibility. On the other hand, it is impossible for students to learn to be responsible unless they are free to make both good and bad choices. George Brown describes the main goal of his Ford Foundation Project:

> A goal we were striving for in our work was to help students become both *more free* and *more responsible*. We believed this could be done by increasing the student's sense of his own power to take responsibility for his behavior. Further, by providing experiences that made available ways to become free, followed by the actual experience of increasing freedom, we could help the student attain the personal satisfaction that is unique to feeling free.[1]

One way to provide opportunity for freedom and responsibility as part of the teaching process is to structure lessons in a way that not only delivers the content, but also provides students the opportunity to learn about themselves and their environment.

The following educational model is designed to show you how this goal can be accomplished. It divides learning into two parts: the process (what students do in order to learn) and the outcome (what they have learned at the end of the lesson). The process can be open or closed. If it is closed, it is selected for students by the teacher. This is a closed system because the students have no choice of how they will learn. For example, a closed system is one in which a teacher assigns a specific book to be read, specific pages in a workbook to be completed, or a paragraph to be written about a specific theme. An open system is one in which the students can choose whatever activity they want to learn about a given subject. (A limited open system might offer a limited number of choices.) An example of an open system is a teacher who says, ''Your responsibility is to learn about American Indians. You each have one week to design a project and complete it. I will help you with the design, research, and development stages of your project.''

The outcomes (what students will learn from a lesson) can also be open or closed. If students are told what they must be able to do or know at the end of a lesson, the outcomes are closed. Examples are a teacher who tells his students that they must be able to spell all the words on their list, or a teacher who assigns five types of math problems that the students must be able to solve. Open outcomes are those lessons in which the student might learn any number of things. The outcomes are not predetermined by the teacher, all outcomes are acceptable. Some examples are:

- a science experiment that has no preconceived outcome
- a self-awareness activity in which the student learns something about himself
- a writing assignment of personal expression, the topic chosen by the student

The following figure illustrates these four possible structures.

Using this model as a guide we can see that the kind of freedom advocated during the sixties was open process and open outcomes. In this system, students are allowed to learn whatever they want by whatever means they want. No wonder students had trouble handling a system such as this. Few adults could learn under these conditions. On the other hand, classrooms that are totally closed process and closed outcomes are just as difficult to learn in. Most schools in the ''Back to Basics'' era fit this schema. When the teacher tells the student what will be learned and how it will be learned, students may resort to acting out as a way to feel some sense of identity and control. Many students who are fearful of such a rigid approach might not act

FIGURE ONE[2]   **Structure of Open and Closed Systems of Curriculum**

OUTCOMES

Open	_Closed_
Outcomes are determined by learner. Goals and results are not predetermined.	Outcomes are determined for learner. Goals are predetermined.

PROCESS

Open	_Closed_
Process is determined by learner. The process and activities are unstructured.	Process is determined for learner. The process and activities are structured.

Learning can be:

Process	Outcomes
C	C
C	O
O	C
O	O

out publicly but do so in their own quiet way, by not paying attention, by forgetting what was learned immediately after the test, and by other passive/aggressive means.

The best learning environments are those combining all four learning structures at various times based upon the needs of the students and the goals of the lesson. Notice the following examples.

Open Process/Closed Outcome   Students can select from an unlimited number of choices to learn a skill or gain an awareness that was chosen by the teacher.

1. "I don't care how you learn your multiplication table (open process), but by Friday you must know it (closed outcome)."

2. "Your job is to be able to describe the causes of the Second World War (closed outcome). You can read about it in the library, you can interview the people on this list, you can watch the upcoming television documentary, you can read newspaper accounts, which I have collected and I will loan out. The choice is yours (open process)."

Closed Process/Open Outcomes   The teacher provides a structure for all students to follow, but what is learned by experiencing the structure is determined by the student.

1. "I want you to take a nature walk on the blue trail (closed process) and record what you see, and make any observation (open outcome) about the relationship between animal and plant life in the forest."
2. "I want you to examine your room tonight (closed process) and see what are your most prized possessions (open outcome). Make a statement about what you value as a result of this experiment."

Open Process/Open Outcome   The student provides his own structure and defines the outcome.

1. "You can choose any activities (open process) that you want to do in the learning centers. After each activity, write down what you learned and any questions that you have (open outcome)."
2. "You can do any of the 15 science experiments in the science corner (open process). When you have finished, I will meet with you to discuss what you learned, how the experiment turned out, and to answer any questions you might have (open process)."

Closed Process/Closed Outcome   The teacher determines what is to be learned and how it is to be learned.

1. "You are to learn your times tables by Friday (closed outcome), and we will spend ½ hour each day memorizing them (closed process."
2. "You are to do a book report on the life of Edgar Allan Poe (closed outcome) by first reading three of his poems (specified) (closed process)."

Learning Styles

Effective teaching means varying one's style of presentation. Because students have different learning styles, their level of motivation is dependent upon your ability to address these varying styles. Students who are disorganized and unable to define their own structure tend to benefit from a closed system, as long as the system contains content that they feel is relevant and meaningful. By contrast, there are students who have good organizational skills and who can define their own method(s) by which they learn most effectively. Open systems are more appropriate for these students.

It is important for you to pay close attention to your style of teaching. If you are teaching with only one system and you are having problems with "unmotivated" students, it may well be that your fixed style of presentation is contributing to unruly student behavior. Experiment with different process and outcome styles.

It probably seems apparent that instruction with only one curriculum for everybody with the same set of academic demands placed upon all is a closed process and closed outcome system. Because open process or open outcomes often allow for more than one "right" answer, these processes are often excluded in classrooms which emphasize traditional "one right answer" outcomes. Science and mathematics teachers find it especially difficult to create learning options because of such an emphasis. Varying one's style of teaching seems easier for subjects like English, History, and Psychology because these subjects lend themselves to questions of feelings and inference in which more than one correct answer is often possible. Despite these additional difficulties faced by math and science teachers, it is certainly possible to vary one's style of teaching in even these subject areas. We have included three sample units (two science and one math) to illustrate a mixture between open and closed process and content. These units were designed for third through sixth grade students and are adaptable for students at all grade levels.

Science Activity 1: Crush the Can [3]

Focus

When air is removed from a can and a vacuum is created, the can is crushed by the forces surrounding it. Often, metaphorically, we are crushed by the forces surrounding us. This activity teaches students the concept of pressure and its effects as both a scientific phenomenon and a human experience.

Materials

A one-gallon metal can with screw-on cap, water, hot plate or similar heating source.

Procedure

The students are to observe a metal can collapsing from air pressure and make observations regarding it. Then, they are to apply what they have learned to human situations.

Directions

1. Ask the students to watch the procedure carefully.
2. Fill the one-gallon can one-eighth full of water.
3. Boil the water.
4. Shut off heat.
5. Put the lid on the can very tightly.
6. Watch the can collapse.

Questions for Discussion

1. What was the initial state of the can and its contents?
2. What happened next?
3. Did anything leave the can? What, if anything?
4. What is left of the can? Why?
5. How did it happen?
6. Do you ever feel crushed?
7. What do you feel like when you are crushed?
8. What do you lose when you are crushed?
9. How can you be restored? Can the can be restored?

Science Activity 2: Observation and Inference[4]

Focus

This activity gives the students a chance to recognize the differences in both natural and human phenomena.

Materials

Part of an engine, such as a crankshaft, a bobbin, the top of a toaster an old potato masher, an Allen wrench, a nail set, a cotter pin, styrofoam packing material, a glass cutter, and an old style collar fastener. (This is only a sample set of materials—any collection of unfamiliar items will do.)

Procedure

Students will examine a series of unfamiliar objects; they will determine their functions by making observations and then inferences about the observations. They will then try the same procedure as they observe unfamiliar human behavior to determine what the behavior means.

Directions

1. Arrange the class in a semicircle with a table at the open end.

2. Place one of the unfamiliar objects on the table. If a student knows what the object is used for, he should disqualify himself.

3. As a group, have the students determine the purpose of the object, using the following procedure:

    A student says, "I see. . . ." and makes one observation about the object to the class. If the observation is accurate, let him continue. If it's not, don't let him proceed. If he can go on he says, "And I imagine. . . ." For example, bobbin—"I see that it is round." "I imagine that it turns like a wheel." He finishes his observation with a guess as to what the object is used for, using his original observation as a clue. Tell the class whether or not his assumption is true, then it can be used as an observable fact and another person can make an assumption from it. Explain that students must listen very carefully to what other class members have said. This will aid them in their guesses.

4. This procedure is followed until the use of the object is discovered. It is important that you give no clues and continue until the class finds the correct answer.

5. The activity may be repeated, about once a week, with different objects until students develop skill in making observations and drawing inferences about the observations.

6. Try the same procedure with a human interaction problem and give the students a chance to use what they have learned. The following are possible situations you may use. The task is for the students who are observers to discover what the students who are actors have done.

    a. Have two students stare intently at each other for two or three minutes, pretending they are blind and listening for sounds. They should pretend to be unaware that they are looking for each other. Have the class use the "I see. . . . I imagine. . . ." formula to discover what they are actually doing.

    b. Unnoticed by the rest of the class, give a student a watch. Have him sit in the front of the class, reading or thumbing through a magazine, constantly twitching the arm wearing the watch in a very nervous fashion. The class probably will assume that he is nervous or afraid. Actually, he has a self-winding watch that he is trying to wind as he waits. Have the class use the "I see. . . . I imagine. . . ." formula to discover what he is really doing.

Questions for Discussion

1. What is harder to make observations about, objects or people?
2. Which is harder to make inferences about, objects or people?
3. What happens when you are wrong in your observation about an object?
4. What happens when you are wrong in your inference about an object?
5. What happens when you are wrong about your observation about a person?
6. What happens when you are wrong about your inference about a person?
7. How can you make more accurate observations?
8. How can you make sure your inferences are true?
9. How can you make sure you are not confusing an inference with an observation?

Footnote   It is essential for students to learn that inferences often appear as observations and that it is dangerous to confuse the two. This activity will clearly demonstrate the differences. As other examples occur spontaneously in class, be sure to point them out to students.

Math Activity: Value Word Problems[5]

Focus

We often present students with word problems to give mathematical computations contextual meaning and to make computations realistic and interesting. You can invent problems that develop mathematic skills while giving students a chance to consider value questions that actually apply to life. This activity suggests problems that have proven to be both meaningful and challenging to students.

Materials

Samples of work problems (see below).

Procedure

Present word problems to the class as you would any math word problem. Discussion of answers can follow. Here are four examples of different value word problems.

1. You get one dollar a week for doing chores that take ten hours a week of your time, and your younger brother gets 50 cents a week for doing one hour's worth of chores. How much do you get an hour? How much does your brother get an hour? Is your rate of pay fair? How do you feel about the fact that your younger brother gets a different rate of pay? How much allowance do you think you should get for ten hours of work? How much is that per hour?

2. You have a job calling people on the phone and telling them about a special sale at a nearby store. You get paid five cents a call but cannot receive more than five dollars. There is no way that the owner of the store can check on the number of calls you make. If you actually make 75 calls, how much do you earn? If you cheated and said you earned all of the five dollars, how many calls must you claim? How many calls will you actually claim? Why? How much more can you get by lying? Is it worth it to you?

3. Your mother bought you a fifty dollar tricycle when you were four-years old. You are now eight-years old and you want a new bicycle. The trike is being used by your younger sister. Your father says that he will pay for half of a new bike, which costs eighty dollars, but you must pay the other half. How much of your own money will you need? The bike store will take your trike in trade; the owner will take off ten dollars from the original price for the first year of age and three dollars for every year after that. How much will he give you for your old tricycle? Do you think it is a fair price? If you sell the trike to the store, your sister will have no trike and your mother will have to buy her one. Your mother says the decision is yours. Will you sell it? If you sell it, how much more will you still have to earn? What ways can you earn that much money? How long will it take you to get the amount you need? Do you think it's right for you to sell a bike that was a gift to you, knowing that the person who bought the gift will have to spend more money because of what you're now doing?

4. Every day after school you have three hours before supper; this time is yours to do with as you please. You can play ball, have a

paper route, join a school club, or take part in any one of several activities. If you play ball, it will take up the entire time. If you have a paper route, it will take two hours and your other hour will be free. The school club takes one hour. You can collect for the community fund for one to two hours. You can do homework for one and a half hours and be able to watch TV after supper for one and a half hours. You can play with a friend who can only spend one hour with you. How will you spend your time? What percent of your time would be spent on each activity?

Footnote   You can convert any word problem into a life process problem by combining the calculations and mathematical procedures with questions concerning why a student needs to learn math and what he might use it for in his life. Remember, all process questions must have the word "you" for the subject.

Teaching and Learning Styles

Much research has been conducted in the last five years on styles of learning. There have been a large number of models developed that are purported to delineate several styles of learning, and a number of tests have been designed to measure several variables that can determine what type of learner each student is. The most important development that has emerged from all of this activity is the notion that students who have a particular learning style have difficulty with teaching and instructional styles that are incompatible. The better the match between instruction, teacher, and student learning style, the better the student will learn. When students are mismatched, they may become frustrated, confused, anxious, and likely candidates to act out in class.

It is beyond the scope of this book to review all of the literature on learning styles, but the following figure serves as a useful summary. It divides learning and teaching styles into three basic categories: dependent, collaborative, and independent. Notice Figure two, which states what is needed by the student, what teacher role is needed, and what teacher behavior is associated with each particular learning style.

FIGURE TWO

Learner Style	Need	Teacher Role	Teacher Behavior
Dependent (closed systems suggested)	information approval reinforcement esteem from authority	expert authority	lectures directions assignments criticism rewards
Collaborative (mixed systems suggested)	social acceptance peer exchange varied ideas esteem from peers	co-leader environment setter feedback giver	discussion leader resource provider sharer
Independent (open systems suggested)	ego needs self-esteem	facilitator	resource

While it is true that many people have a characteristic learning style, it is also true that learning styles vary for different topics. For example, Bill is a dependent learner when it comes to learning how to tune a car engine. He wants specific instructions from his teacher, who he wants to act as an authority. He also wants direct criticisms and specific assignments broken down into very small clear steps. When it comes to photography, Bill is more comfortable in a collaborative style. He likes taking pictures with his friends, comparing them, and learning from each other.

Bill is also an avid reader of science fiction. For this activity he prefers to learn alone, independently, reading his books and mulling over his new ideas, occasionally discussing them with others. He uses other people to suggest new books for him to read.

Dependent learners often are agitated and confused when put into a collaborative or independent situation. School-age children will act out if they are given more responsibility than they can handle. Students who are asked to be dependent when they are more natural in a collaborative or independent state either become easily bored or turned off to the structure. Thus, the most effective teachers are those who have a variety of activities that allow for differences in learning styles, so that students can learn in the mode most comfortable for them.

Dependent learners often need more closed structure (as described above) than collaborative or independent learners, who need more open structures. By developing activities that are both open and closed and by matching or allowing your students to match themselves to the most appropriate styles, you will reach them more completely and eliminate many of the classroom based causes for misbehavior in your class.

Locus of Control

One of the significant research findings related to learning styles explores a construct termed "locus of control." Simply stated, locus of control describes how much control each student feels about his own learning and behavior. There are two ways of perceiving locus of control which are quite different from one another. *Externals* are those students who feel that control is outside of them. They usually see the world as made up of forces beyond their influence that make them behave in certain ways. They tend to feel that they have little to do with what happens to them. When an external fails a test, he might feel that the teacher didn't like him or that the test was unfair.

Internals feel that they are responsible for everything that happens to them. They believe that they can influence their environment and that they behave the way they choose. An internal who fails a test might attribute the failure to a lack of sufficient time spent studying.

Studies with students of all ages have consistently shown that *internals* need less structure. They flourish in open-ended classroom environments that allow them to make decisions on how they will learn. When internals are given rigid structure, their scores decrease and they begin to act in disruptive ways.

On the other hand, *externals* learn less when they receive less structure, and they tend to demand more attention from the teacher to make up for the lack of structure.

We define structure as providing clear, specific directions, summaries of information in brief intervals, continuous feedback, outlines, exact specifications for success, and instructional objectives.

By recognizing that many of your behavior problems might be due to a mismatch between locus of control and instructional style, you can begin to modify your lessons to accommodate each student's style. For those students who act out or demand your constant attention, who are always asking what seems like stupid questions, and who need to have directions repeated over and over again, you can provide a much more highly structured lesson. The more structure you give them, the less they will act out.

On the other hand, for those students who continually demonstrate that they want more responsibility, give them less structure. Let them design their own learning. Use either open process or open content situations with them much of the time. This will lessen their need to demonstrate their power to you in mostly negative ways.

How to Teach

We have found in our own teaching and in observing hundreds of classrooms that the attention span of students is a key ingredient in determining the extent of discipline problems that exist. Teachers who easily flow from one method of teaching to another are better able to maintain a student's attention than teachers who do not. Many teachers unknowingly encourage many minor classroom irritations such as out-of-seat behavior, foot stomping, pencil tapping, and talking by not varying the way that information is presented in the classroom. Most frequently, the teacher is the focal point in the classroom because he stands in front of the classroom and presents information to the students who are all seated facing him.

We forget how difficult it was for many of us to sit through a fifty-minute lecture in college, looking for ways to distract ourselves from our aching behinds and the drone of the professor's voice. Most of us sat politely still because it was more important to get a good grade and the college credit rather than to voice our dissatisfaction.

Students who are unmotivated by the good grade and who have little value for the importance of education are not so polite. Being referred to the principal for classroom misbehavior can be more rewarding than being bored by the teacher. When teachers shift from one mode of presentation to another, they are better able to maintain student interest than when instruction occurs in one fixed mode. More specifically, if you spend more than ten minutes (elementary age children) or fifteen minutes (junior high and high school students) in any one mode, you can count on a significant number of students becoming inattentive. The following represents teacher modes of instruction that, when varied, lead to a rich learning experience for students and less hassle with discipline.

1. *Lecture*   This mode is most familiar to teachers. The teacher dispenses information to students and is the focal point of the lesson. All questions and student responses are teacher directed.

2. *Large Group Discussion*   The teacher and all students mutually participate in a discussion related to a topic. The topic may be defined by the teacher, but all students are invited to share their thoughts and ideas concerning the subject. Effective large group discussion is directed towards soliciting opinions from the students by asking them to become immersed in the subject itself and to comment on its personal relevance.

3. *Small Group Discussion*   Groups of two to six students are formed and are given a task to do or a topic to discuss. One student from each group may be selected to report a summary of its' discussion to the total class.

4. *Independent Seat Work*   Following a teacher-directed or group discussion, each student is assigned a project to consider or work to be completed that has a relationship to that which preceded it.

5. *Student Support Teams*   All students are assigned to teams. Teams are heterogeneously grouped so that each team contains dependent, collaborative, and independent learners. Groups include four to six learners. The teacher may assign either a group project or individual seatwork. If it is a group project, then all students are evaluated according to their group's performance. If it is an individual assignment, then students who are having trouble with their work must first solicit the help of team members before they can ask the teacher for assistance. It is only when a child cannot understand what to do after he has solicited such help that he may approach the teacher for such help. Marilyn Burns, a leading educator and classroom teacher, has reported extremely good results in using a method similar to this. She claims that she has more time to work with small instructional groups because she is interrupted far less frequently by students who don't know what to do.[6]

By varying your mode of presentation, you are far more likely to adequately address your students' different learning styles. When you are planning your lessons, consider how you can flow from one mode to another so that your instructional objectives are met.

Excitement and Enthusiasm

There can be little dispute that some students misbehave because of a mismatch between course content and individual learning needs. However, how the teacher presents his material is more important than the content itself. It is not the teacher's job to entertain his students vis-a-vis Abe Kotter or Big Bird, but it is essential to both feel and exude positive energy for what the teacher does. If a teacher is bored with his subject, then he will do little more than go through the motions of presenting it. Bored teachers most typically speak in a monotone, use few non-verbal hand and body gestures, and smile infrequently. They are often resistant towards self-reflection and refuse to consider that their boring way of being may be influential in generating disinterested learners. Perhaps saddest of all, they come to view the fringe benefits of teaching as the main reason for continuing in the classroom and feel little interest in pursuing professional growth experiences.

Solutions to the problem of teacher boredom are beyond the scope of this book. But there is a relationship between student boredom and teacher boredom. Boredom, like enthusiasm, is contagious! An alive teacher who smiles, loves his subject area, and who can communicate his excitement to students creates a stimulating environment in which acting out because of boredom becomes unnecessary.

There are many reasons why our classrooms lack excitement. Art Combs lists ten characteristics of the modern classroom that hinder learning:

1. preoccupations with order, categorization, and classifying
2. overvaluing authority, support, evidence, and the "scientific method"—all the good answers are someone else's
3. exclusive emphasis upon the historical view, implying that all the good things have been discovered already
4. cookbook approaches, filling blanks, etc.
5. solitary learning, with its discouragement of communication
6. the elimination of self from the classroom—only what the book says is important, not what I think
7. emphasis upon force, threat, or coercion; what diminishes the self-diminishes creativity
8. the idea that mistakes are sinful

9. the idea that students are not to be trusted

10. lock-step organization[7]

Students who are processed through a school like the one described above come to school with basic needs, such as identity, power, connectedness, and achievement. When students begin to see how their needs are subservient to the daily curriculum, the seeds for trouble have been sown.

Evaluation and Grading

Evaluation is a critical link between behavior and learning. Evaluation gives students information that can be used for self-understanding. We know that children who receive poor evaluations often become poor learners. Students who have had a history of failure in the public school will often prefer to drop out either physically or mentally and find other ways to be successful. One way students can turn failure into success is to succeed at becoming a behavior problem and to win approval through failing grades.

Mr. Andrews taught a seventh grade class of emotionally disturbed students. These students never received a higher grade than a C and their averages were closer to F + . As an experiment for the first quarter, the teacher gave every student either an A or B in every subject regardless of "what they earned." Actually there was no way of knowing what they "earned" because of the nature of the curriculum and more importantly, the problems of the students. Once report cards went home, many parents called to see whether it was their child or the teacher who was "sick." The teacher began the second quarter by telling the students that they could all maintain their A's by working just a little harder. This message was repeated the two next quarters, but the work required increased each time. Most students tried hard to keep the A's, a prize they had never known before.

This experiment highlights the need for students to receive positive feedback. Students who never receive good grades do not try for them because they know they are beyond reach. It is much more rewarding to be a nuisance than to try for an unattainable goal. On the other hand, once they felt that a good grade was not only achieveable, but within their grasp, they had a lot more energy to maintain the good grades, even if it meant more work. A system of evaluation that either forces students to compete with each other or maintains the same criteria for all students despite intellectual and academic differences is destined to produce winners and losers. The losers, more often than not, are tomorrow's discipline problems. They have learned that if they work hard, are well motivated, and do their best, then they are rewarded with a C or D that illuminates their mediocrity. Few of us can sustain "doing our best" for very long with such minimal validation. How many of us continue to paint pictures beyond our elementary school years after we have discovered the limited talent we have?

Discipline problems can be prevented by making it genuinely possible for all students in your class to receive grades of "A". If you teach eighth grade math and have students who are functioning at the fourth grade level then you can prevent discipline problems in two ways. You can try to have the child removed to a lower functioning classroom. If, however, the student is to remain in your class, then you must secure the necessary curricula and staff resources to provide instruction at his level. And evaluation for him should be based upon effort and performance at *that* level. If you fail to provide instruction for students at their academic level, then they cannot be faulted for aggressing against a system that won't accept them as they are.

It is a good practice to have conferences periodically with children in which you provide each with statements concerning their assets and areas needing improvement. You might also consider asking them to describe how they feel about being in the class.

Performance contracting, which is similar to a self-contract, is an evaluation strategy especially useful with older students. A performance contract should specify what the teacher wants from the student, what the student wants to learn for himself, and how the final evaluation will be determined. Like a social contract, a performance contract may have a flag component, what the teacher must have for the contract to be valid; and a negotiable component, what the teacher and student can mutually agree to. Like a social contract, an effective performance contract should be re-evaluated every two–three weeks to see that it is working and still appropriate. Many good performance contracts do not work because teachers and students think that once they are signed, they cannot be re-evaluated. Flexibility is an important part of all phases of evaluation.

Performance contracting is not the only method of incorporating student input into your evaluation system. You can elicit test questions from students; you can incorporate student ideas as to what information should be on the test; you can have students test each other, write test questions for themselves, evaluate their own and each others' tests, use group projects as well as tests, and a host of other evaluative methods. (See bibliography for resources to help provide options.) The key to any evaluation method that will help minimize classroom discipline problems is that it provides as much responsibility for the student as possible, and that all students have a reasonable chance for success.

Competition

Related to evaluation is the issue of competition in the classroom. Some competitions are more healthy than others.

The teacher can change a negative competitive classroom into a positive one. The first step is to identify different areas of competition that exist in individual classrooms. Each classroom has its own unique competitive characteristics. The teacher can then examine each competition, determine its nature, and assess its relative effects on the students involved. With the help of students and colleagues (including administrators), a teacher can then determine ways to derive maximum benefits from the competitions.

It is predominantly up to the teacher to ensure that competitions are positive experiences for students. By choosing competitive structures that are voluntary and focus on process rather than outcomes, the teacher can, in effect, reap many of the rewards of competition while avoiding most of the pitfalls.

Students who are forced into negative competitive situations, characterized by the lack of choice to compete and which stress winning more than playing, are likely candidates for behavior problems. By selecting competitive situations that are chosen by the student and which are means (process) emphasized, you will be encouraging responsibility on the part of the student and minimizing the need your students will have for breaking your social contract.

Summary

In this chapter we have explored the process of teaching and learning. We know that boredom, lack of responsibility, lack of involvement, unfair evaluation practices, and unenthusiastic teachers can alienate students from school. By organizing the way you teach and the way you evaluate student learning so that you are teaching students first and your subject matter second, you will actively capture the attention of your students so that they will not want to busy themselves by breaking rules.

For the Administrator

You can be a valuable resource to teachers by sensitively offering your wisdom and experience, your knowledge of curriculum, and your broad view of your school's educational program. Most teachers feel more trapped by the demands of the curriculum than they need be. With your encouragement for experimentation and innovation and your support for curriculum modifications that meet student needs, your teachers will not only minimize discipline problems, but improve all aspects of their teaching. You can provide the leadership necessary for curriculum reform.

While it is critical for teachers to feel administrative support before innovation can occur, support alone is not sufficient. Teachers need examples of what can be done in concrete terms. They need release time to develop their ideas, and, most importantly, they need to feel safe so that they can learn from their failures as well as from their successes without penalty. Like many problem students, teachers often unnecessarily feel threatened by the administration. Provide more than lip service that alternative teaching styles are acceptable and desirable.

Because boredom is a major cause of classroom disruption, we suggest that you establish a task force to examine your curriculum. Update it so that it is relevant and focuses attention on more than facts. Encourage the task force members to actually take quizzes and tests, to participate in classroom activities, and to try workbook problems. If the curriculum is boring to adults it will most likely be boring to students. The goal of the task force should be to positively interact with teachers to minimize student boredom. Specific recommendations in the form of a report or summary at a faculty meeting can be most helpful.

You can also examine your evaluation systems and consider alternate ways of reporting student progress. Try to use methods that describe strengths and areas for improvement without judging them. All students should be able to achieve success in your school. Do your best to minimize competition in your school that pits student against student, and find as many ways as possible to encourage cooperation. When competition does exist, see that it is voluntary and focuses more on the process of learning than on winning. There should be at least some form of competition that every student can both participate in and win.

Have as one of your goals the development of teacher support groups. Teacher boredom can be minimized when a vital group of teachers learns to trust each other and to share methods, ideas, and lessons with each other. Help them learn how to observe each other non-judgmentally so that they may look to each other for inspirational support before the going gets rough.

Emphasize the importance to teachers of how varying one's process of teaching and methods of instruction can positively affect discipline problems in the classroom.

References

1. Brown, G. I., *Human Teaching For Human Learning*, New York: Viking Press, 1971, p. 228.
2. Curwin, R. *Values Clarification Approach to Teaching Secondary English Methods.* Unpublished Doctoral Dissertation, Univ. of Massachusetts, 1972, p. 120.
3. Curwin, R., and Curwin, G., *Developing Individual Values in the Classroom*, Palo Alto: Learning Handbooks, 1974, pp. 66–68.
4. Ibid, pp. 66–68.
5. Ibid, pp. 70–71.
6. Burns, M. *Groups of Four: Solving the Management Problem*, Learning 10(2), pp. 46–51.
7. Combs, A., *The Professional Education of Teachers*, Boston: Allyn and Bacon, 1965, p. 36.

TEN

Twenty Questions

*I*n our monthly column in *Instructor Magazine* (Sept. 1980–May 1982), titled ''Readers Ask,'' we answered questions from teachers about discipline and other related topics. In this chapter we have included the twenty questions and answers from our column which we felt were the most representative of the needs and concerns of most teachers who ask us questions. All of the answers are related to *Three Dimensional Discipline* and are related to the information, strategies, and ideas presented in this book.

To help organize the questions into a meaningful pattern, we have divided them into three categories, each representing one of the three dimensions: Prevention, Action, and Resolution.

I Prevention

1. Question: There have been a number of thefts in my classroom. During the last few months, books, supplies, and games have been taken. I'm pretty sure I know who is responsible, but I have no actual proof. How can I handle this question?

• **Answer:**   You are not an investigative detective, and if you are like most teachers, you probably won't enjoy playing policeman. Begin by having an open-ended class discussion in which you inform the class that various books, games, and other supplies are missing. Tell them that it makes you feel sad and upset when people take things that belong to you or to the students in the class. Ask the class if anyone has ever had anything of value taken from them. Allow enough time for a thorough discussion. It is wise to end the discussion by saying, ''In this classroom, people have a right to their own belongings, and nobody may take what belongs to somebody else unless they have asked for and received permission.'' Make eye contact and be in close physical proximity to the child that you suspect as you set this limit.

It is important to realize that stealing is engaged in at one time or another by virtually every child for a number of reasons. The child may have a need or desire to hoard or a desire for objects or money of which he feels he has been deprived; he may steal to demonstrate his generosity or courage by giving away the booty to others; or he may want revenge against perceived wrongdoings by peers or adults. Whatever the reasons, the child's reputation and integrity are crucial, and setting limits must be balanced with preserving his self-concept.

Stealing can be combatted by setting up opportunities in class in which the child can be responsible. Such possibilities include making him the line leader, custodial helper, or class monitor. If you suspect that this is a deprived child, you might actually give him some paper or crayons that he can take home and own. You might also wish to encourage the class to make gifts to one another as a way of showing their caring and generosity. If the stealing persists following these actions, then it would be wise for you to refer the child to either a child guidance clinic or to the appropriate school mental health personnel for further evaluation.

2. Question: I recently read in a Dear Abby column that group punishment is an effective weapon for dealing with class problems. I don't like punishing the whole class for the violations of others, but I can't think of an alternative when I don't know who was the rule breaker. Can you help?

• Answer: Dear Abby is wrong! Group punishments are almost always ineffective. They generate resentment in the innocent students who learn to think that they might as well break the rules because they will be punished anyway, and they teach the rule violators that they will not have to take responsibility for their actions.

We first suggest that you rid yourself of the idea that punishment and retribution will improve the behavior of rule violators. Focus on teaching correct behavior through natural and logical consequences. Define your rules clearly and specifically before misbehavior occurs. Present your rules to your class and suggest various privileges that the class can earn for each day that the rules are followed. You might even encourage them to brainstorm high-interest, rewarding activities that can be offered when the class behaves itself. Encourage students, and permit yourself, to be as creative as possible in inventing ideas. Offering privileges will increase desirable behavior much more effectively than will group punishments. You might also try brainstorming with your class possible consequences when someone breaks a rule and you don't know who did it. Offer the two choices, ignoring it and punishing the whole class, and see what other alternatives you and your class can create. Use some consequences from this list when this situation occurs again. These strategies give your students some ownership and responsibility for the problem and provide you with far more flexible and creative options than group punishment.

3. Question: I am appalled at how little support I get from the principal and vice principal. I often feel put on the spot to justify a disciplinary referral and more often than not, I feel like I'm made out to be the "bad guy." To make matters worse, I see little improvement in students after they have returned from a meeting with the administrator.

• **Answer:**   Most administrators feel heavily burdened with the number of students referred. In many schools, the criteria for disciplinary referral is unclear. Insubordination, belligerence, and defiance are often mentioned as school rules that require some form of disciplinary action, but neither the specific rules nor the consequences for violation are made clear. Because the rules and consequences lack specificity, it is expected that the teacher will use his or her discretion in defining when a student's behavior warrants a referral. The problem is that what may constitute "insubordination" to you is viewed as little more than "normal" behavior by the teacher next door or the administrator in your building. The result of unclear guidelines is often an overwhelming number of referrals for infractions ranging from refusal to pick up a piece of paper to physical assault. The administrator must then make judgments about which referrals are most worthy of his time.

Before you are faced with the next difficult situation, jot down which rule violations you believe to be worthy of administrative referral. Set up a time to meet with your administrator for a full discussion of your guidelines. If you have established a social contract with your class, then you can indicate which of your rules has a consequence of administrative referral that was agreed to by your class(es). It is also useful to share the totality of the social contract so that the administrators can have a complete picture of all classroom rules and consequences. Make sure you and your administration know exactly when you will use the referral, and what you have tried prior to using it. Agree on your plan by compromising when necessary. The important point is to reach agreement prior to an incident when raging feelings make problem-solving difficult. Then follow your plan. If it doesn't work, discuss any modifications before changing the agreement on your own.

We suggest that you use a referral as your last line of defense. Follow-up the referral by contacting the administrator and asking what he decided to do with the referred student. Some students, even rascals, can be very convincing in pinning the blame on you and may elicit the sympathies of the administrator. To guard against this, try wherever possible to attend the meeting (between administrator and student) so that you will know what happened and may actually have some input into what will happen. If you find that a number of your colleagues feel as you do, then raise the issue of needing a clearer set of guidelines around disciplinary referrals as a small group. You may do this at a faculty meeting, in your yearly targets, or in another way that is relatively comfortable for you.

4. Question: There is another teacher in my school who teaches the same grade as I do. Her rules are much more liberal than mine, and when both our students discuss their classes, I come out looking more rigid and strict. When I discipline my students I always hear, ''Mrs. Smith lets her class do it, why can't we?'' This is driving me crazy.

• **Answer:**   First, check with Mrs. Smith and make sure that your students are accurate in their statements. It might help to prepare a list of questions in advance of your meeting with her. If you find that her rules and consequences are very different from yours and that she allows for more freedom and privileges in her class, it might be helpful to discuss your differences in a non-threatening way. See if you can find some points of agreement to generate some consistency between your two classrooms. But remember, you do not have to be like Mrs. Smith and she doesn't have to be like you. Consistency can help, but you both must feel comfortable within your own style of teaching.

After your discussion with Mrs. Smith, set aside some time to discuss this matter with your class. Tell them that Mrs. Smith teaches her way and you teach yours. Not all classes are alike just as not all homes are alike. Tell the class that you are willing to hear their suggestions for improving things in your class, but you are not Mrs. Smith and prefer not to be compared with her. Concern yourself with the validity of their gripes, listen to what they have to say, and act according to what you professionally believe.

5. Question: I recently read your first book, *The Discipline Book*, and while there seemed to be several good suggestions around how to set up a preventive classroom environment, it seems to require too much time. I'm not sure that I will have enough problems to warrant doing so much work in advance of problems actually happening. Can you explain why you feel so much time is needed prior to discipline events?

• **Answer:** The book offers suggestions, not prescriptions, for preventing problems before they begin. If you do not have the kinds of problems that warrant following all of the suggestions, choose only the ones that make sense to you and your personal needs.

We believe that prevention is necessary because most problems are much harder to solve after they have already occurred. A power struggle, for example, is almost never adequately resolved without countless hours of work, worry, and luck. Yet, by practicing a few relatively simple procedures, many power struggles can be avoided. The prevention activities were designed with the joint goals of preventing misbehavior and setting a tone for a positive classroom atmosphere conducive to the business of learning. Perhaps more importantly, resolving conflicts with misbehaving students is less likely to generate hostility and resentment when done in an environment that has emphasized prevention.

Another point to remember is that many of the preventive steps suggested become easier each time you do them, so that by the third time you go through the process, they will not require as much time as the first time through.

The final decision is yours. Do what feels right for you! If your style tells you that you prefer to deal with problems after they occur, then by all means handle discipline in that way.

6. Question: The biggest single problem that I have is lack of parent cooperation. Phone calls home are seldom returned, and some parents who want to be of help often have more problems controlling their child than I do. Any suggestions?

• **Answer:** First of all, you have a perfect right to both want and expect cooperation from parents. There are several ways to go about getting it. Be certain that each child's parents receive a copy of your classroom rules and consequences before a disruption occurs. We suggest that at least one alternative consequence for each rule includes a phone call home. By doing this, you are setting the stage for parents to know that they will be called if their child's behavior warrants such an action. If you have consequences that allow for retaining the child after school, let the parents know in advance that *they* will be responsible for providing after school transportation. If you receive no response in the mail, then try phoning the parents at home or call them at work. When a problem occurs—don't wait!! Make contact with the parent as soon as you suspect the youngster's problem. Too often, parental complaints of teachers rightly or wrongly center around their view that the teacher waited too long or never made them aware of the problem. Avoid this pitfall by letting them know early and by documenting your efforts at involvement in writing. It is also a sound and effective practice to send home "positive" notes when youngsters do as expected—praising their accomplishments, good behavior, or both. Setting a positive tone provides good modeling to be emulated by parents. If parents confide difficulty in managing their youngster's behavior, be prepared to suggest alternatives such as the school guidance counselor, psychologist, or child guidance clinic for assistance.

7. Question: I teach a gym class, and I have a few students who are physically awkward. These students are reluctant to try class activities, and what's worse, the other students are constantly making fun of them when they do try. Can you offer any suggestions?

• **Answer:** We all vaguely remember how awkward it is to grow up, wondering whether or not our bodies will mature and whether or not others will find us attractive. To young students, these questions are important. There is no greater fear for a growing youngster than to look foolish in front of his peers, and unfortunately, physical education classes show a student's clumsiness more overtly than English or math. However, there are some things that you can do to help improve the situation. First, examine your curriculum and see how competitive it is. Second, look to see how many choices are offered to your students. We believe that competitive activities should only be for those participants who choose them. Develop a number of non-competitive activities for those not wishing to compete. These can include group activities, such as frisbee, body spelling, people puzzles, dance, and the like. Encourage all students to choose the best activities for them.

It is important that you allow awkward students to choose activities that they are good at and then slowly allow them a chance to try new, more risky activities. If you don't have enough options, then use a class period to brainstorm with the students as many new activities, both competitive and non-competitive as they can think of; then use the list as options for the awkward students and any others who wish to participate in them.

One other point to consider is adapting a rule that forbids put-downs in class, with the consequence of doing one nice thing for the victim if a student violates the rule. You can introduce this new rule as a safety rule, in the same way that you forbid unsupervised activity on the parallel bars, running on the courts, and playing games without the proper equipment. Mental and emotional safety must be learned in the same way that you teach physical safety, and by making that connection clear to your students, you will help them learn a valuable lesson for life.

II Action

8. Question: Amy and Gary are two students in my fourth grade class who pick on each other constantly. It seems that five minutes can't go by without a flair up between these two. Sometimes the most simple comment can create fireworks. I have tried having them negotiate between themselves and tried separating them from each other, but nothing works. They seem to gravitate toward each other, and then fight.

• **Answer:** It sounds like the gravity pulling Amy and Gary towards each other is "love." Students at that age have few acceptable outlets for showing affection. Fourth graders usually frown upon "love" relationships. It might help to have another talk. But this time let them know that you are aware that they are fond of each other (in spite of their denials), and that they can work together on various projects providing they no longer disturb the class. You might offer them ways that they can interact that are more fun and less disturbing than fighting. In any case, encourage them to be aware of their feelings and to share them in ways that are more direct than fighting. Sharing feelings can be and is a wonderful skill for students of all ages to learn.

9. Question: I have a student in my second grade class who believes that as long as she tries, regardless of the results, her efforts will be rewarded. When I ask to see her work, she always has an excuse such as, "I can't do it," or "I did my best," or "I really tried hard but I didn't know how to do it." I think that she is being manipulative, but I don't know how to respond to her. Any suggestions?

• **Answer:** Stop accepting her excuses. "Just try to do your best" is a message that persists with popularity, and some children misinterpret this to mean that as long as they tell somebody that they tried, all will go well for them. Children who become adept at trying and not doing have often found an effective manipulative method that usually results in "trying the nerves" of people around them.

Assuming that your student is developmentally capable of doing the assigned work, you can put an end to her manipulative excuse making by refusing to accept her "trying" as an end product. Tell her that you want to see exactly how she tried and what she accomplished. Let her know that you will accept no more excuses and that if she doesn't understand how to do something, she is to ask for help. If she does not ask for help and if the assignment remains tried and not done, then tell her that she will have to miss recess or remain after school to show you exactly how hard she tries. Dreikurs has pointed out that some students seek attention through displays of inadequacy. You can teach your student how to feel adequate by rewarding her real effort, by actively refusing to accept her excuses, and by confronting her displays of inadequacy.

10. Question: When students misbehave in my class, I usually make them publicly apologize to either me or when appropriate, to another student. This consequence seems to have little effect on their behavior. Do you think that public apologies are useful consequences?

• **Answer:** Most public apologies embarrass students. Students who must apologize see themselves as the object of ridicule much in the same way the nineteenth century felons did when they were in the public stockade. We have seen students who apologize to teachers while at the same time making obscene gestures behind their backs. Generally, except for very few students, public apologies will evoke either embarrassment or anger, neither of which will help the student learn a new, more acceptable behavior.

We suspect that you have chosen apologies as a consequence to show students that misbehavior can hurt and that they should feel sorry for hurting others. Private apologies can serve the same purpose, and they are less likely to evoke negative reactions. Other consequences are usually more effective than apologies, such as asking the student (in private) to role play the misbehavior and then role play the victim. Discuss his feelings in each role. Brainstorm possible alternative behaviors with the victimizer and then role play a more positive one from the last. This kind of consequence takes more time, but (1) it does not anger or embarrass, (2) it teaches how people feel, (3) it offers some positive options, and (4) it opens the door for futher communication.

11. Question: What do you do with the child who habitually tattles?

• **Answer:** Parents and teachers may unwittingly encourage and reinforce such behavior. "If Joey pushes you or Sally hits you or Freddy does mean things, then tell me," are examples of messages that are frequently communicated to children as alternatives to taking retaliatory actions when others say or do something that upsets the child. What we really want is for the child to tell us when he has observed something that is potentially dangerous and at the same time to learn how to be responsible for solving minor interpersonal hassles without telling the teacher.

Habitual tattlers have often failed to learn the distinction between dangerous events that warrant teacher attention from those that do not. They have also learned to seek attention and approval from adults because they do not feel accepted by peers. It is almost certain that the tattler feels unnoticed and unappreciated and believes that the only way to stand out is at the expense of others. Treat the problem as symptomatic of the child's underlying feeling of detachment from and rejection by his peers. It is useful, as with all forms of disruptive behavior, to appreciate the child when they are engaged in behavior that is incompatible with tattling. "Susie, I really like the way you are playing with Denise." "Billy (privately), today I didn't hear you complain about any of the kids and that makes me feel really good" are a few examples of how this can be done. Other possibilities include classroom role playing in which one child is instructed to tattle on another followed by a class discussion, listing examples of tattling on the blackboard (with students contributing), and then the teacher discussing those that warrant telling (the teacher) from those that don't; giving a satisfactory acknowledgment to the tattler such as "Thanks, when I see that happen I'll have a chat and now you can go back to your seat"; providing classroom activities that promote positive peer interaction. "Tattlers" may be really asking for some order and safety from continually being hassled by the disruptive children—and in a way trying to put the responsibility for the chaos and disorder where it belongs—on the kids doing it and the teachers. If there is an abundance of tattling in your class it may well be a message that you need to provide more safety and security for the kids.

12. Question: In some classes, there is a large percentage of disruptive children. When they set the general tone for the class, how can you change the personality of the group (and do it without constantly lecturing to them about poor behavior)?

• **Answer:** Because group problems are more complex than those with only one student, effective resolution calls for considerable flexibility on your part. You may need to temporarily abandon your lesson plans to deal directly with the class. It is important for you to begin by specifically defining, first for yourself and then with your students, what you mean by "disruptive behavior." Encourage your students, either verbally or in writing, to let you know what they need in order to improve their behavior. Some of the more vocal students may register complaints about your style of teaching or personal attributes. It is important that you learn to "active listen" non-defensively to these complaints and to consider instructional or behavioral modification as a result. If you feel that you cannot or will not change your style, then explain your position. An open exchange of differences in which teacher and students experience no negative consequences for self-expression is sometimes sufficient to curb negative behaviors. Other possibilities include the following.

a. Meet with the ringleaders to acknowledge their leadership. You might say something like, "Most days, I have a very hard time teaching the class because of interruptions, fights, name-calling, etc. I'm tired of lecturing, yelling, and threatening, and I am hoping that maybe you guys (gals) can give me some advice as to how to stop this stuff."

b. Consider developing a social contract with your class in which both students and teacher develop a set of rules and consequences regarding classroom behavior. For a complete discussion, see Chapter 4.

c. Allow students to develop a "reward cookbook" of activities and privileges that they enjoy. Keep a daily or weekly record of classroom disruption and tell the students that each day (or week) that improvement is noted (be sure to define the success criteria in advance), they will be able to choose one of the activities during a designated time.

d. Send a letter home to each child's parents letting them know of the disruptive classroom atmosphere. Be specific without personalizing, and request that they thoroughly discuss your concerns with their child.

e. Set up a "gripe box" in your classroom. Explain to your students that their misbehavior is telling you that they have gripes and complaints about you or the classroom or each other. Let them know that from now on the gripe box is the place to register all such complaints, and that at a designated time you will read all gripes aloud. When you do this, be sure to involve your students in problem solving the complaint through brainstorming.

13. Question: Sometimes I find it necessary to let the rest of the class know how a particular problem was resolved with one particular student so the class understands that the student didn't get away with anything. Is it best to share with the rest of the class or just keep the incident between the student and myself?

• **Answer:** By informing the entire class of the result of your incident with this student, you may let them know you "won," but you will also be telling them that you will use them as examples should the need arise and that they cannot trust you to keep your transactions with them private. These learnings will make it difficult for the class to feel safe with you and to interact normally with you. They will tend to keep their guard up.

    We feel it is better for you to keep all interactions with individual students private and not to show publicly that you have won with a difficult student. It is better for your students to learn that you are in charge by seeing the improved behavior of the disruptive student. If the student's behavior hasn't changed as a result of your intervention, then you haven't "won" anyway.

III Resolution

14. Question: Sam is in my fourth grade class and is constantly being a nuisance. Slamming his arm on the desk, dropping pencils, making noises in class, "accidentally" brushing up against others are but a few of his many behaviors that make me wish for his absence. Naturally, he has a perfect attendance record. When I correct him either by telling him to stop or sending him to the principal's office, he becomes verbally abusive and puts me on the defensive. I don't know what else to do!

• **Answer:** Sam sounds like a classic "uproar" player. He is determined to bug you until you finally blow up at him. If you simply ignore him, then he'll continue to goad you until you lose control, and when you do, he'll complain to his friends, parents, principal, and anybody else who listens that you are unfair and out to get him. "All I did was tap my desk while I was looking for my book and she screamed at me" is a predictable outcry. Students like Sam have a way of choosing to forget the fifty or more incidents that preceded the blow-up by focusing on the minor event that in and of itself was relatively innocuous. His payoff is the perceived recognition and status that he achieves from his peers (although in reality they view him as a stupid schlemiel) for warring with the teacher.

You must develop a calm, firm, and consistent manner in dealing with Sam. This is necessary but difficult to do because of his desire to get under your skin. After class, tell Sam exactly what he does that irritates you. Don't hesitate to show him as well. Let him know that from now on, the first time during any forty-five minute interval (vary the time interval in accordance with Sam, your schedule, etc.) he will receive a reminder. The next time any disruptive behavior occurs will mean a visit to the principal for at least fifteen minutes. When he returns, the reminder to principal sequence of consequences will again take effect for the next forty-five minutes. In any day, if he chooses to visit the principal on two or more occasions, then a phone call home will occur. At your discretion, you may wish to put a tape recorder on "record" so that his parents and principal will know exactly what he is doing that is of concern. As you will need the cooperation of the principal and hopefully his parents, let them know of your plan.

Since Sam has strong needs for attention, be sure to catch him being good and to acknowledge any improvement in his behavior. Visiting him at a setting outside the classroom such as on the playground after school, taking him for an ice cream after a good day, and sending positive notes home are strategies that are likely to pay big dividends.

15. Question: I have a third grade boy who continually wets his pants. Ronald's mother claims this never happens at home. We have tried putting him in the kindergarten as a helper to make him feel special. We have tried everything from embarrassing him to rewarding him with praise when he used the toilet. He does not seem bothered when he tells me that his pants are wet again, in fact, he seems rather proud. What can I do?

• **Answer:** Stop trying so hard! You and his mother are unwittingly contributing to this problem because of all the special attention that he receives. Handle the matter in a low-key manner. Although it is unlikely that Ronald's problem is organically based (especially if confined to the school situation), be sure to have him checked by the school physician just in case.

Have a private meeting with Ronald and tell him that you want him to bring two pairs of clean underwear and two pairs of pants to school. Arrange for a place in which he can store these clothes and can retrieve them by himself. Tell him that from now on, when he wets himself, he is to go directly to the prearranged place in which his clothes are stored. He is to retrieve a pair of clean underwear and a pair of clean pants. Should he wet himself more than twice in any day, then he will simply have to spend the remainder of the day in wet clothes. Before the end of the day, check Ronald's clothes supply. If he has fewer than two pairs of clothes for changing, then remind him to take home the dirty laundry and bring clean laundry the next day. Set aside a few minutes before day's end to ask Ronald how he did during the day. During your private chat, tell him that it is no longer necessary for him to tell you when he wets, but to simply take a supply of clean clothes and change. If he persists in telling you then either ignore him or casually remind him that he knows what to do.

It is important that Ron's wetting does not become the centerpiece of your relationship with him. Be certain to provide a variety of positive reinforcers for appropriate classroom behavior. You might wish to explore with Ronald what he likes and does not like about school and to arrange things so that he may be doing more of what he likes.

As his mother is likely to be feeling quite anxious and embarrassed with her son's wetting, you would be well-advised to inform her of your plan in a casual, low-key manner.

16. Question: I'm having a bad time with one of my kids. Eric is hostile and resentful in class with a very low tolerance for frustration. He disrupts the other students and seems to use his outbursts to manipulate me. I suspect his hostility stems from a rocky home life. How can I reach this child?

• **Answer:** Eric's hostility must not be allowed to interfere with your ability to teach and the other children to learn. As it is unlikely that Eric will easily give up his resentments, it is suggested that you meet with him when you and he are alone to balance your understanding of his problems with a strong and clear statement of limits. During this meeting it is important to provide more acceptable alternatives in which he can express his hostility. For example, ''Eric, I will no longer tolerate your pushing or fighting (or whatever other specific behaviors it is that you wish to eliminate). When you feel angry in class you may write your angry thoughts on a piece of paper and rip it up, or you may go to the time-out area until you cool down, or you may leave the classroom until you feel better.'' You might also want to check out any other options that Eric can think of. When you observe him expressing his resentments more acceptably, be sure to let him know that you appreciate his effort. Children with a low frustration tolerance can often be helped by giving them tasks in which success is practically guaranteed; by making them a teacher's helper, and by giving them the responsibility to work with younger students in a helper's role. As for the rocky home life you suspect, it might well be worth your effort to check this out during a parent conference and/or in consultation with colleagues or resource personnel. But remember, many teachers render themselves helpless to classroom disruption by attributing blame to an unsettled home. Effective action, with or without home support (preferably with), can and often does stop misbehavior dead in its tracks.

17. Question: I have a nine-year-old boy in my class who does virtually no work, almost never turns in his homework, and spends most of his time daydreaming. I have cajoled him, threatened him, and had two parent conferences, all to no avail. He likes candy, and recently I offered him a candy bar for each day in which he completed two assignments and had his homework done. Result: he got even worse! What do I do now!

• **Answer:** Refuse to give him any homework assignments and do *not* give him any books, papers, or other materials for classwork. The next time you give a class homework assignment, tell him privately that he has a special assignment. He is to make sure that he comes in with NO homework the following day. When you check the children's homework, ask him if he did his assignment. If he did his special assignment, then tell him matter-of-factly how glad you are that he remembered to do as told. Similarly, announce to him privately that from now on he may not use any books or papers in class. He may daydream all day if he would like! If he should decide that he would like to be treated like the rest of the children, then he must ask you for work. Emphasize that he still must follow all of the rules for behavior.

Your student sounds like a passive/aggressive child who may be expressing his anger through refusal to do as expected. The more that you threaten or praise him, the worse he will get. It is therefore wise for you to encourage him to continue to behave as he has been. If he does as told (nothing) then he has followed the rule. If he does his work to defy you (or his parents), then he has behaved in a socially acceptable way. Either way, you win!!

It is also a good idea to refer him to your child study team for an intellectual and personality assessment. He may need more than you can offer him.

18. Question: Joey is in my sixth grade class and throws things around, fights with other students, and does not work. Whenever I discipline him, he grins, laughs, and refuses to obey my directive.

Frankly, I'm afraid that he might turn on me and physically injure me. Any advice?

- **Answer:** We suggest proceeding in the following way:

  a. Be very clear and firm with Joey and tell him that you will no longer tolerate his fighting and throwing things.

  b. Tell Joey exactly what you will do should this unacceptable behavior continue.

  c. Let Joey know how he will be rewarded for each day (you might reduce this to a half-day or each hour) that passes without an incident.

  d. Write his parent(s) a letter that specifically details (1) Joey's misbehavior, (2) what you will do if this continues, and (3) how Joey will be rewarded if he decides to behave more acceptably. Follow this letter with a phone call and arrange for periodic conferences.

  e. Catch Joey being good. If you realize that fifteen minutes or a half-hour have passed and you haven't been aware of him, take time to notice and respond to him in a positive way.

  f. Send home daily or weekly reports that specify Joey's progress. At first, daily reports are preferable, and you may later wish to move towards weekly reports. See if his parent(s) are willing to institute a home-based reward system that is contingent upon positive reports from school.

  g. If no improvement is noted, approach a colleague or the principal and ask for help. It is advisable at this stage to find someone with an intimidating presence who is not beyond the use of tough talk. You want somebody who has no problem in firmly imposing his thoughts and values upon this youngster.

  h. When you have gone through steps (a) through (g) on three or four occasions and still no change in behavior has occurred, then refer Joey to resource specialists for an evaluation to determine what kind of help he needs. Be certain to document your efforts so that others will have a complete picture of Joey's classroom disturbance with corrective steps taken.

19. Question: Billy is a handicapped student in my fifth grade class who is being mainstreamed for the first time. He desperately wants friends but doesn't know how to go about it. He is often boisterous and seems to unknowingly invite a negative reaction from his peers.

He complains that nobody likes him. What can I do to help him feel more positively involved with the class?

• **Answer:**   It sounds like your student needs some straight feedback, and don't be afraid to give it to him. Begin by focusing on his theme of "nobody likes me," with reflective or active listening skills. (For a thorough overview of this method we suggest Thomas Gordon's *Teacher Effectiveness Training*.) After he's had an opportunity to share his feelings, ask him if he is aware of anything that he says or does that might cause others to dislike him. If he is, then this may lead to a good discussion with some new ways for him to act or behave with his peers. If he says, "I don't know," then offer him your feedback. Tell him directly, "Billy, I sometimes notice that you talk very loudly and the other students are not used to this. Although I'm not positive, I think that this might be one reason why they aren't more friendly to you. Would you be willing for the next few days to speak more softly and see if their reaction to you changes?" You might then choose to do some role playing or modeling with him so that you are sure that he understands what you mean. This may also be a good time to let him know that for many students, he is their first encounter with somebody with a handicap, and they may be unsure of how to react to him.

Allow yourself to become acquainted with any special needs and problems that the student experiences in your classroom. Most handicapped individuals prefer to be treated the same as all other students providing that their unique disability is accounted for. After you have talked with this child, we suggest you meet with the class when Billy is not present—perhaps you can arrange a special activity for that student. In your class meeting allow an open discussion of feelings, by allowing and encouraging all feelings to be shared. One technique we have used in situations like this works as follows: have each student write on a paper, with no names, an ending to the following sentence. "Billy makes me feel _____ because _____ _____." Collect the papers and read all of them to the class. Once these feelings have been shared, brainstorm ways for the class to be more receptive to the student and activities in which the class and Billy can get to know each other better.

Later, include your handicapped student in a follow-up discussion. Give him an opportunity to share his feelings about being in your class and feelings about his fellow students. This must be done with sensitivity so that he won't feel singled out. It would be better if it was part of a general class discussion in which all students shared their feelings, not just Billy.

And in Summary

20. Question: My mother is a junior high school teacher who bitches all the time about how bad students are today. I hope that you print my letter so that teachers might realize that most of us kids care about school, and so that they can understand what it's like to be a kid. In most of my classes, the teacher gives us an endless amount of worksheets to keep us busy and they expect us to care about such boring assignments. Nobody ever asks us what we want to do or what is important to us. We're just supposed to sit in our hard seats all day and pay attention to what the teacher says. Us kids don't want to be compared to our brothers and sisters, we don't want to be made fun of when we don't know an answer, we don't want to be embarrassed by being yelled at in front of our friends and we don't want teachers to call us names. We also don't like it when teachers play favorites.

Maybe if the teachers treated us with more respect then we would do the same and there would be less discipline problems. Maybe if teachers spent some time listening to our problems we wouldn't need to create problems in their class.

The few teachers I have liked treated us as people. They let us get to know them. They told us when they were having a bad day. They talked about their own ideas and feelings and listened to ours. They let us get to know them not only as teachers but also as people. They were tough when we acted up but didn't keep grudges. They enjoyed what they were doing and we enjoyed being with them. I wish that more teachers understood that school is a tense place for a lot of students. Maybe if they did, I wouldn't be thinking of dropping out!

• **Answer:** Thank you for taking the time to share your thoughts. Perhaps your sensitive recollections will help teachers to understand the enormous influence that they have upon their students. Good luck with what we are sure is a very difficult decision for you.

ELEVEN

Conclusion

*I*n this book we have presented to you what we feel is a flexible, yet structured, plan for taking charge in your classroom. It is our hope that you will no longer see DISCIPLINE as a problem but rather as an opportunity for you to learn and grow as a professional and as a person. We hope you will use the activities, suggestions, and strategies in this book to help you express your values in the classroom, to establish a clearly defined structure that creates cohesion rather than chaos and that helps you to be responsible for yourself and to let your students be responsible for themselves.

It is time for you to expect acceptable behavior in the classroom regardless of the outside influences that impinge upon your students. It is time for you to recognize how your style of teaching and the content of what you teach often contribute to school and classroom discipline problems. It is time for you to use your creativity to go beyond what you have already done when confronted with "out-of-control" students and "chronic rule breakers." Finally, it is time to stop burning out and rusting out, and to start feeling alive again to one of the most difficult and rewarding professions on earth: educating children.

It is our hope that this book will contribute much to the lives of our readers. The principles and practices stated in this book are designed to create effective communication because we feel strongly that the hallmark of good teaching is effective communication. To help us communicate with you beyond the boundaries of this book, we encourage our readers to write us and tell us how you have put the principles into action. We would love to hear equally the gains and the setbacks, the joys and the frustrations of facing the challenge of disciplining children. Please contact us by writing to:

DISCIPLINE ASSOCIATES
P. O. Box 9931
Rochester, New York 14467

or

DISCIPLINE ASSOCIATES WEST
330 Mississippi St.
San Francisco, CA. 94107

Bibliography

Abidin, Richard. *Parenting Skills: Trainer's Manual*, New York: Human Science Press, 1976.

Alschuler, Alfred; Tabor, Diane; and McIntyre, James. *Teaching Achievement Motivation*, Middletown, Conn.: Education Ventures, Inc., 1971.

Andersen, M. S., and Savary, L. M. *Passages: A Guide For Pilgrims of the Mind*, New York: Harper and Row, 1972.

Aronson, E.; Blaney, N.; Stephan, C.; Sikes, J.; and Snapp, M. *The Jigsaw Classroom*, Beverly Hills: Sage Publications Inc., 1978.

Bandura, Albert, and Walters, R. H. *Social Learning and Personality Development*, New York: Holt, Rinehart and Winston, 1963.

Baysner, Elizabeth C. "New Parental Push Against Marijuana," *New York Times Sunday Magazine*, August 1981.

Becker, Wesley C. *Parents Are Teachers*, Champaign, Ill.: Research Press, 1971.

Benson, H. *The Relaxation Response*, New York: Avon, 1976.

Berne, Eric. *Games People Play*, New York: Grove Press, 1964.

Bessell, Harold. *Methods in Human Development*, San Diego: Human Development Training Institute, 1970.

Birdwhistell, R. L. *Introduction to Kinesics*, Louisville: University of Louisville Press, 1952.

Bloch, A. M. "Combat Neurosis in Inner-City Schools," *American Journal of Psychiatry*, 135(10), 1978, pp. 1189–1192.

Borton, Terry. *Reach, Touch, and Teach: Student Concerns and Process Education*, New York: McGraw-Hill, 1970.

Brown, George. *Human Teaching for Human Learning: An Introduction to Confluent Education*, New York: Random House, 1971.

Brutten, Milton; Richardson, Sylvia O.; and Mangel, Charles. *Something's Wrong with My Child*, New York: Harcourt Brace Jovanovich, Inc., 1973.

Burns, M. *Group of Four: Solving the Management Problem*, 1981, Learning 10(2), pp. 46–51.

Buscaglia, Leo. *Love*, New York: Fawcett Crest, 1972.

"Can Public Learn from Private," *Time*, *117*, April 20, 1981.

Canfield, Jack, and Wells, John. *100 Ways to Enhance Self-Concept in the Classroom*, Englewood Cliffs, N.J.: Prentice-Hall, 1976.

Carrington, Patricia. *Freedom in Meditation*, Garden City, N.Y.: Anchor Books, 1978.

Cichon, D. J., and Kloff, R. H., *The Teaching Events Stress Inventory*, Paper presented at the meeting of the American Educational Research Association Conference, Toronto, Ontario, March 1978 (Eric Document Reproduction Service, No. 160 662).

Combs, Arthur W.; Avila, Donald L.; and Purkey, William W. *Helping Relationships: Basic Concepts for the Helping Professions*, Boston: Allyn & Bacon, 1971.

Combs, A. *The Professional Education of Teachers*, Boston: Allyn & Bacon, 1965.

Cowen, Emory L., et al. *New Ways in School Mental Health*, New York: Human Sciences Press, 1975.

Curwin, Richard L., and Curwin, Geri. *Developing Individual Values in the Classroom*, Palo Alto, Calif.: Learning Handbooks, 1974.

Curwin, G.; Curwin, R.; Kramer, R.; Simmons, M.; and Walsh, K. *Search for Values*, Dayton, Ohio: Pflaum/Standard, 1972.

Curwin, Richard L., and Fuhrmann, Barbara. *Discovering Your Teaching Self: Humanistic Approaches to Effective Teaching*, Englewood Cliffs, N.J.: Prentice-Hall, 1975.

Curwin, Richard L., and Fuhrmann, Barbara. "Mirror, Mirror on the Wall—Developing Teacher Congruency," *The Humanist Educator*, Vol. 17, No. 1, Sept. 1978.

Curwin, Richard L., and Mendler, Allen. "Three-Dimensional Discipline: A New Approach to an Old Problem," *American Middle School Education*, Univ. of Georgia, Athens, Ga., Vol. 1. No. 4, 1979.

Curwin, Richard, and Mendler, Allen. "Discipline: Three Dimensions" in *Partnership–A Journal for Leaders in Education*, Journal of the Center for Educational Leadership and Evaluation, University of Delaware, (Newark, Delaware, Vol. 6, Fall 1981).

Curwin, Richard, and Mendler, Allen. *The Discipline Book: A Complete*

Guide to School and Classroom Management, Reston, Va.: Reston Publishing Co., 1980.

Curwin, Richard. "Are Your Students Addicted to Praise?," *Instructor*, October 1980.

Curwin, R.; Mendler, A.; and Culhane, B. "Kids and Teachers Discipline One Another," *Learning Magazine*, Vol. 8, No. 6, February 1980, pp. 96–100.

Dillon, E. A. "Did We All Let Barry Die?", *Journal of Teacher Education*, *29(5)*, 1978.

Dodson, Fitzhugh. *How to Parent*, New York: New American Library, 1971.

Dodson, Fitzhugh. *How to Discipline With Love*, New York: Rawson Associates, 1977.

Dreikurs, Rudolf. *Children: The Challenge*, New York: Hawthorn Books, Inc., 1964.

Epstein, Charlotte, *Classroom Management and Teaching*, Reston, Va.: Reston Publishing Co., 1979.

Ernst, Ken. *Games Students Play*, Millbrae, Calif.: Celestial Arts, 1972.

Fantini, Mario D., and Weinstein, Gerald. *Making Urban Schools Work: Social Realities and the Urban School*, New York: Holt, Rinehart and Winston, 1968.

Frankl, V. E. *Man's Search For Meaning: An Introduction to Logotherapy*, New York: Pocket books, 1963.

Gailbraith, Ronald E., and Jones, Thomas M. *Moral Reasoning: A Teaching Handbook for Adapting Kohlberg to the Classroom*, Minneapolis, Minn.: Greenhaven Press Inc., 1976.

Ginott, Haim. *Teacher and Child*, New York: Macmillan, 1972.

Glasser, William. *The Identity Society*, New York: Harper and Row, 1972.

Glasser, William. *Reality Therapy*, New York: Harper and Row, 1965.

Glasser, William. *Schools Without Failure*, New York: Harper and Row, 1969.

Goldhammer, Robert. *Clinical Supervision: Special Methods for the Supervision of Teachers*, New York: Holt, Rinehart and Winston, 1969.

Gordon, Thomas. *Teacher Effectiveness Training*, New York: Peter H. Wyden, 1974.

Griffiths, R. *Imagination in Early Childhood*, London: Kegan Paul, 1935.

Harris, Thomas. *I'm OK—You're OK*, New York: Harper and Row, 1967.

Hawkes, T. H., and Koff, R. H. "Differences in Anxiety of Private School and Inner-City Public Elementary School Children," *Psychology in the Schools*, 7, 1970.

Hawkes, T. H., and Furst, N. F. "Research Note: Race, S.E.S., Achievement, I.Q. and Teachers' Ratings of Behavior as Factors Relating to Anxiety in Upper Elementary School Children," *Sociology of Education*, *44(3)*, 1971.

Hawkes, T. H., and Furst, N. F. "An Investigation of the (mis) Conceptions of Pre and In-Service Teachers as to the Manifestations of Anxiety in Upper Elementary School Children from Different Racial-Socioeconomic Backgrounds," *Psychology In the Schools, 10(1),* 1973.

Heisner, J. "The Ugly Side of the Urban Coin," *Instructor, 90(10),* 1981.

Hendrickson, B. "Teacher Burnout: How to Recognize It, What To Do About It," *Learning,* 7(5), 1979, pp. 36–38.

Hendricks, Gay, and Roberts, Thomas B. *The Second Centering Book,* Englewood Cliffs, N.J.: Prentice-Hall, 1977.

Holmes, Monica; Holmes, Douglas; and Field, Judith. *The Therapeutic Classroom,* New York: Jason Aronson, 1974.

House, E., Lapan, S. *Survival In the Classroom,* (abridged ed.). Boston: Allyn & Bacon, 1979.

Howard, Carey in Brown, B. *Stress and the Art of Biofeedback,* New York: Bantam Books, 1977.

Key, Wilson Bryant. *Subliminal Seduction,* New Jersey: Prentice-Hall, 1973.

Key, Wilson Bryant. *Media Sexploitation,* New Jersey: Prentice-Hall, 1976.

Kirschenbaum, H.; Simon, S.; and Napier, P. *Wadjaget, The Grading Game in American Education,* New York: Hart, 1971.

Klinger, E. *Structure and Functions of Fantasy,* New York: Wiley-Interscience, 1971.

Kyriacou, C., and Sutcliffe, J. "Teacher Stress: Prevalence, Sources and Symptoms," *British Journal of Educational Psychology,* 48(2), 1978, pp. 159–167.

Lazarus, R. S. *Patterns of Adjustment,* New York: McGraw-Hill, 1976.

Lerlech, Johanna. *Classroom Management,* New York: Harper and Row, 1979.

Marquis, John N.; Morgan, Wesley G.; and Piaget, Gerald W. *A Guidebook for Systematic Desensitization,* Palo Alto, Calif.: Veteran's Workshop, 1971.

Maslow, Abraham H. *Toward a Psychology of Being* (2nd ed.), New York: Van Nostrand Reinhold, 1968.

Maslow, Abraham H. *Motivation and Personality* (2nd ed.), New York: Harper and Row, 1970.

Masters R., and Houston, J. *Mind Games.* New York: Dell Publishing Co., 1972.

Mendler, A. "The Effect of a Combined Behavior Skills/Anxiety Management Program upon Teacher Stress and Disruptive Student Behavior," Unpublished doctoral dissertation, 1981.

Morris, J. "Meditation in the Classroom," *Learning, 5(4),* 1976.

Moscowitz, E., and Hayman, J. L. "Interaction Patterns of First Year, Typical and 'Best' Teachers in Inner-City Schools," *Journal of Educational Research, 67(5),* 1974.

Neill, A. S. *Summerhill: A Radical Approach to Child Rearing*, New York: Hart, 1960.

Nevin, E.; Nevin, S.; and Danzig, E. *Blocks to Creativity: Guide to Program*, Cleveland: Danzig-Nevin International, Inc., 1970.

"New York State United Teachers Stress Survey Information Bulletin," New York State United Teachers Research and Educational Services, 1979.

"Our Nations' Schools, A Report Card," report of the Subcommittee to Investigate Juvenile Delinquency to the Committee on the Judiciary of the U.S. Senate, Washington, D.C.: U.S. Government Printing Office, 1975.

Postman, Neil, and Weingartner, Charles. *Teaching as a Subversive Activity*, New York: Delacorte, 1969.

Poteet, James. *Behavior Modification: A Practical Guide for Teachers*, Minneapolis: Burgess, 1973.

Raths, Louis E.; Harmin, Merrill; and Simon, Sidney B. *Values and Teaching: Working with Values in the Classroom*, Columbus, Ohio: Charles E. Merrill, 1966.

"Report of Stress Conditions Within the Tacoma Public Schools," Tacoma Association of Classroom Teachers (Prepared by Irene Mazer), May 1979.

Rubin, Jeffrey. "The Psychology of Entrapment," *Psychology Today*, March 1981.

Rutter, M.; Maughan, B.; Mortimore, P.; Ouston, J.; with Smith, A. *Fifteen Thousand Hours*, Cambridge, Mass.: Harvard University Press, 1979.

Schein, Edgar. *Process Consultation: Its Role in Organizational Development*, Reading, Mass.: Addison-Wesley, 1969.

Schrag, Peter, and Divoky, Diane. *The Myth of the Hyperactive Child*, New York: Pantheon Books, 1975.

Selye, H. *Stress Without Distress*, New York: The New American Library Inc., 1974.

Silberman, Charles E. *Crisis in the Classroom*, New York: Random House, 1970.

Simon, Sidney B.; Howe, Leland W.; and Kirschenbaum, Howard. *Values Clarification: A Handbook of Practical Strategies for Teachers and Students*, New York: Hart, 1972.

Simon, S., and Bellanca, J., eds. *Degrading the Grading Myths: A Primer of Alternatives to Grades and Marks*, Washington, D.C.: ASCD, 1976.

Sloane, Howard N. *Classroom Management: Remediation and Prevention*, New York: John Wiley and Sons, 1976.

Snygg, D., and Combs, A. W. *Individual Behavior*, New York: Harper, 1949.

Stevens, John O. *Awareness: Exploring, Experimenting, Experiencing*, New York: Bantam Books, 1973.

Thoresen, C. E.; Alper, T.; Hannum, J. W.; Barrick, J.; and Jacks, R. N. "Effects of Systematic Desensitization and Behavior Training with Elementary Teachers," Unpublished paper, Stanford University, 1973.

270   Bibliography

Tyrell, Ronald; Johns, Frank; and McCarthy, Frederick. *Growing Pains in the Classroom: A Guide for Teachers of Adolescents*, Reston, Va.: Reston Publishing Co., 1977.

United States Department of Health, Education and Welfare, "Violent Schools—Safe Schools. The Safe School Study Report to the Congress, 1978," (Eric Document Reproduction Service No. Ed 149 464.).

Weinstein, Gerald; Hardin, Joy; and Weinstein, Matt. *Education of the Self*, Amherst, Mass.: Mandala, 1976.

Weinstein, Gerald, and Mario D. Fantini, eds. *Toward Humanistic Education: A Curriculum of Affect*, New York: Praeger, 1970.

White, R., and Lippitt, R. "Leader Behavior and Member Reaction in Three 'Social Climates'". In Cartwright, D., and Zander, A., eds. *Group Dynamics in Researched Theory* (2nd ed.), New York: Harper and Row, 1960.

Wolfgang, C., and Glickman, C. *Solving Discipline Problems*, Boston: Allyn and Bacon, 1980.

Wolpe, Joseph, and Lazarus, A. *Behavior Therapy Techniques*, Oxford: Pergamon Press, 1966.

Index